WHAT'D YOU EXPECT? FOREVER IS A LONG TIME...

Contents

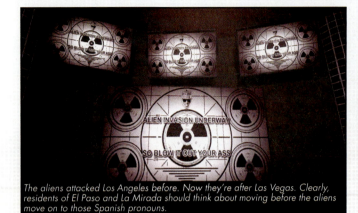

The aliens attacked Los Angeles before. Now they're after Las Vegas. Clearly, residents of El Paso and La Mirada should think about moving before the aliens move on to those Spanish pronouns.

Duke Nukem Forever is full of, and to a great extent predicated on, pop culture references spanning far and wide. From film to TV to music, and even other games of the last several decades, nothing is safe from tongue-in-cheek ribbing or sly homage.

ABOUT THIS GUIDE

Duke Nukem Forever has distinct single player and multiplayer components. So too does this guide. In the single-player chapters, there are breakdowns of gameplay, weapons, and enemies, along with a full walkthrough and maps of the single-player campaign. The multiplayer chapters include a rundown of multiplayer progression, different weapon parameters, unlockable items for your "Digs," and maps and strategy for each multiplayer area and mode. Lastly, this book has a Trophy, Achievement, and Ego Boost appendix in which those global unlockables are compiled.

THERE AND BACK AGAIN: A DUKE'S TALE

Duke Nukem released in 1991, followed by Duke Nukem II in 1993. Both of these games were Commander Keen-style side-scrolling PC platformers. Duke Nukem 3D, released in 1996, was more a re-envisioning than a second sequel. The groundbreaking Build engine was used to take advantage of increasingly powerful PC processors, pushing Duke boldly into the 3D era. Duke Nukem 3D opened as Duke returned to Earth directly following the events of Duke Nukem II. Aliens staging an invasion shot down Duke's shuttle over Los Angeles, robbing him of any kind of breather. Duke's revenge for the aliens is to thwart their invasion, kill their ruler (and punt his eye between the uprights!) in the process. Payback's a bitch, eh?

Duke Nukem 3D was wildly successful—and with good reason. Underneath the broad pop culture satire and tongue-in-cheek chauvinism, Duke Nukem 3D remains one of the most varied, frenetic, fun, and influential ac-

tion games to date. The presence of novel weapons (like Holodukes, Pipe Bombs, Trip Mines, Jet Packs, Shrink Rays, and Freeze Rays) resulted in an array of possible combat scenarios and decisions besides "which weapon do I shoot the enemies with?"

Meanwhile, other shooters really were just shooters. Interaction with the environment was rudimentary at best and the breadth of potential combat situations didn't expand beyond "shoot until it dies." Further, technology was still a limiting factor. Early standout FPS efforts like Apogee's Wolfenstein 3D and Rise of the Triad could not have rooms on top of rooms, walls could only meet at right angles, and there was no variability to the height of floors and ceilings. In eliminating or disguising some of these problems, and essentially inventing online competitive play, id Software's DOOM became the first FPS game to truly break through and achieve lasting, deeply

Version 1.3d of Duke Nukem 3D (Retail) is shipped to game retailers worldwide. Duke Nukem 3D is a massive success that for many defined an entire generation of gaming. Conceptualization and discussion of a sequel immediately begins inside 3D Realms headquarters near Dallas, Texas.

MAY 1996

GT Interactive acquires the publishing rights for Duke Nukem Forever in a licensing agreement with 3D Realms.

JUNE 1996

Duke Nukem Forever is officially announced by 3D Realms with the intention to release in 1998. Likewise, 3D Realms also officially announces that DNF will be created with the Quake 2 Engine.

APRIL 1997

JUNE 1996

Duke Nukem 4Ever, a 2D side scrolling game produced by Keith Schuler, has development suspended in favor of prioritizing a Duke Nukem 3D add-on pack and a sequel.

DECEMBER 1996

The Quake 1 engine is licensed by 3D Realms for Duke Nukem Forever, permanently replacing the Build engine. Most of the Duke Nukem 3D team, led by original Duke Nukem developers Todd Replogle and Allen H. Blum III, begins research and development with the technology for game.

MAY 1997

Randy Pitchford and Brian Martel, founders of Gearbox Software, leave 3D Realms to help form Rebel Boat Rocker and then later Gearbox Software.

influential success. Yet *DOOM* still did not allow for truly three-dimensional geometry—you still could not make a building with a room directly on top of another room.

Interaction and level design were where shooters were lacking despite the technological and gameplay breakthroughs. We expect more variety now in no small part thanks to *Duke Nukem 3D* itself. The Build engine that powered *Duke Nukem 3D* allowed true 3D geometry with rooms on top of rooms. Perhaps that doesn't sound like a huge deal now, but try to imagine designing 3D architecture with the caveat that nothing can be above or below anything else! The levels in *Duke Nukem 3D* were large and intricate and were designed to replicate real places. For example, there was a projection booth in a movie theatre and shady video booths in a smut shop. What's more, the environment was not a monolithic, static object. Levels could change, paths could open up, walls could be destroyed. Again, this might not sound like much now, but this was definitely the case once upon a time in the infancy of 3D gaming.

At the beginning of *Duke Nukem Forever* (releasing some 15 years after *Duke Nukem 3D!*), it has been 12 years since Duke repelled the alien invasion of Los Angeles. (This pegs the original invasion around 1999, which works out, since *Duke Nukem* and *Duke Nukem II* are set in the then-near-future of 1997 and 1998.) Saving Earth made Duke an instant overnight superstar. It also made the aliens fairly mad. Now here they are again, parking their enormous mothership in the air over Las Vegas, Duke's new home city. Coincidence? The aliens are not yet engaging in any hostile activity and diplomatic talks are apparently underway between the government and the Cycloid Emperor, ruler of the aliens. But come on... Duke knows better than that.

Nothing bad is going to happen.

It's now been quite some time since there was a "main" title in the Duke franchise. Sure, there have been a couple spin-off titles and numerous versions of *Duke Nukem 3D* (even on cell phones!), but no new Duke flagship title. Surely such a successful franchise would have plans for a sequel at some point? Why would the developers rest on their laurels for so long?

The short answer is: they weren't resting. *Duke Nukem Forever* was announced in April 1997, with plans to release in 1998! Of course, that didn't happen. *Duke Nukem Forever* had a gestation period unmatched in gaming history.

Duke Nukem 3D released on PC during the era of the Sega Saturn and Sony PlayStation. Nintendo's N64 was available not long after the release of *Duke Nukem 3D* and Nintendo bucked trends of what people assumed the family-friendly gaming giant would allow by hosting multiple Duke titles on the console. Since the announcement of *Duke Nukem Forever* in 1997, the hardware scene has changed just a teeny, tiny bit.

THE DUKE NUKEM "GAMEOGRAPHY"

GAME	YEAR RELEASED
Duke Nukem (PC)	1991
Duke Nukem II (PC)	1993
Duke Nukem 3D (Various)	1996
Duke Nukem 64 (N64)	1997
Duke Nukem: Time to Kill (PS1)	1998
Duke Nukem: Zero Hour (N64)	1999
Duke Nukem (Game Boy Color)	1999
Duke Nukem: Land of the Babes (PS1)	2000
Duke Nukem Advance (Game Boy Advance)	2002
Duke Nukem: Manhattan Project (PC)	2002
Duke Nukem Forever (Various)	2011

GAME SYSTEMS RELEASED BETWEEN THE ANNOUNCEMENT AND RELEASE OF DUKE NUKEM FOREVER

GAMING SYSTEM	RELEASE YEAR
Nintendo Game Boy Color	1998
Sega Dreamcast	1998
Sony PlayStation 2	2000
Nintendo Game Boy Advance	2001
Microsoft Xbox	2001
Nintendo Gamecube	2001
Nintendo DS	2004
Sony PlayStation Portable	2005
Microsoft Xbox 360	2005
Sony PlayStation 3	2006
Nintendo Wii	2006
Nintendo 3DS	2011

Duke Nukem Forever appears on the cover of PC Gamer magazine. Inside are the first screenshots ever released for the game.

NOVEMBER 1997

3D Realms announces a change to the Unreal Engine for Duke Nukem Forever.

JUNE 1998

PC Gamer's infamous 'Miss Me?' cover story, featuring Duke Nukem Forever, hits newsstands. Inside are a large number of new screenshots for Duke Nukem Forever that expose how the game looks with a new engine.

NOVEMBER 1999

MAY 1998

The first reveal trailer for Duke Nukem Forever is released to the public during the Electronic Entertainment Expo.

MARCH 1999

3D Realms announces that Megadeth is to cover and record the theme song for Duke Nukem Forever.

DECEMBER 1999

GT Interactive, then publisher of Duke Nukem games, is purchased by Infogrames. Publishing rights for Duke Nukem Forever are transferred.

MAY 2000
Gathering of Developers, a publisher comprised entirely of developer members (including 3D Realms), is purchased by Take-Two Interactive.

MAY 2001
At E3 2001, the highly regarded Duke Nukem Forever 10th anniversary trailer is released. It is arguably considered to be one of the best video game trailers of all time.

AUGUST 2006
Shacknews reports and confirms a rumor that a large contingent of employees had left 3D Realms. Most of them have relocated to Gearbox Software which is also based in the Dallas area.

DECEMBER 2007
Shacknews breaks the first video teaser for Duke Nukem Forever in over 6 years. Included were small snippets of in-game footage.

DECEMBER 2000
Gathering of Developers announces that the company has acquired the PC publishing rights for the highly anticipated Duke Nukem Forever. Take-Two Interactive also acquires the publishing rights for the complete catalog of previously-released Duke Nukem products, including rights to certain future products.

SEPTEMBER 2004
3D Realms announces that a new in-game physics system, Meqon Game Dynamics, has been chosen for Duke Nukem Forever.

JULY 2007
The famous "Ventrilo Harassment" video using the voice of Duke Nukem to torment on-line game players was uploaded to YouTube and has been viewed more than 6 million times.

The same technological leaps that worked in the favor of *Duke Nukem 3D* would harm the development of *Duke Nukem Forever*. Then, as now, technology evolved so quickly that a studio might be outdated at release simply by following the normal demands of a standard year or two game development cycle. *Duke Nukem 3D's* Build engine was cutting edge during the year-and-a-half or so *Duke Nukem 3D* required for development. But in the next several years, superior engines released from companies making their own games and competing for engine licensing revenue. id Software released first *Quake*, then *Quake II* as follow-ups to their seminal *DOOM* franchise. Rather than build another engine from scratch, it was deemed easier to license the *Quake* engine from id Software. The development of *Duke Nukem Forever* commenced on the *Quake* engine in late 1996; in the next year, development was officially announced and had by then moved on to the *Quake II* engine. Epic MegaGames would release their own *Unreal* engine, which leapfrogged the *Quake II* engine in quality. The development of *Duke Nukem Forever* would switch engines yet again to *Unreal* in 1998—just after having shown the first public footage using the *Quake II* engine!

Three engines in three years… If you're keeping score at home, that's not a normal process. Moving to a different engine, depending on the game, can be just like starting over. Perhaps some art assets and concepts can port successfully, but the actual guts of how the game world works must be rebuilt and reimplemented—that's basically what a game engine is, after all. Entire gameplay features may be scrapped entirely or introduced from scratch in the move to a new engine. And any proprietary customization done to the old engine becomes totally lost work.

All this means that, although 1999 rolled around with *Duke Nukem Forever* already in development for over two years (as mentioned previously, footage of the game was even shown publicly in 1998 at E3, just before the *Unreal* engine switch), the end was not coming into view. This was partially due to the engine switches, somewhat due to the growing pains of making games in the increasingly-complex 3D gaming era, and moderately due to unfocused ambition. New features and ideas were added continually without an end goal for the whole game coming into clearer focus.

While 3D Realms developed *Duke Nukem Forever*, the publishing rights for the title changed hands several times. They were initially held by GT Interactive, publisher of *Duke Nukem 3D* (and other successful titles, like *DOOM II: Hell on Earth,* and *Unreal*). GT Interactive was purchased by Infogrames, who then acquired the publishing rights to *Duke Nukem Forever*. Not long after, the rights were transferred again to Gathering of Developers (a publisher made up of developers, including 3D Realms) and Take-Two Interactive.

Work continued. To assure the world that the game did exist, an impressive gameplay trailer was assembled for E3 in 2001 and it actually did accomplish the goal of blowing convention attendees away. Building up public anticipation increased morale for the development team, but work on the same game now approached half a decade and the perennial release date, continually pushed back and pushed back before, had become the mantra "when it's done". Disregarding the gaming public and the gaming media, even some 3D Realms developers were growing restless.

BONUS CONTENT

Complete *Duke Nukem Forever* on any difficulty setting to unlock access to lots of special content. This includes concept art, screenshots taken throughout development, and the gameplay trailers referenced here!

The development of *Duke Nukem Forever* was primarily privately funded by George Broussard and Scott Miller, co-owners of Apogee and 3D Realms. This meant that while publishing companies were continually attached to *Duke Nukem Forever* for when there was a product to ship, those publishing companies were, for the most part, not subsidizing game development. By 2003 the team working on *Duke Nukem Forever* had shrunk to fewer than 20 people and 2004 saw rumors and announcements of yet more game engine changes. Yet 2004 also saw seemingly contradictory rumors that the game would be done in late 2004 or early 2005. Of course, there had been similar rumblings before…

AUGUST 2009
Duke Nukem Forever's narrative script is written at Triptych and approved by 3D Realms. Triptych gets to surprise Jon St. John – the famous English language voice actor who originally played Duke Nukem – with a phone call: 'Hell has finally frozen over.'

DECEMBER 2009
Gearbox and 2K Games begin renegotiation of the publishing agreement for Duke Nukem Forever. The business agreement is finalized and executed approximately six months later with 2K Games and Take-Two Interactive, securing long-term publishing rights to Duke Nukem.

FEBRUARY 2010
Triptych relocates to Gearbox's offices in the Plano, Texas Bank of America Tower and resumes work alongside Gearbox and Piranha to help port Duke Nukem Forever to consoles, add multiplayer, and polish features within the game.

SEPTEMBER 2010
Gearbox Software publicly announces that it has acquired the Duke Nukem brand.
Gearbox Software and 2K Games surprise the public by showing off the first playable build of Duke Nukem Forever at PAX 2010.

NOVEMBER 2009
Single-player work on Duke Nukem Forever content is complete.

JANUARY 2010
Triptych Games locks down their single-player version of the game and begins negotiations with Gearbox Software.

MAY 2010
Take-Two and 3D Realms settle all differences regarding legal complaints from the previous year.

SEPTEMBER 2008
Users discover Duke Nukem Forever unlockable screenshots in the re-release of Duke Nukem 3D.

MAY 2009
Take-Two Interactive and 3D Realms submit legal arguments regarding the business arrangement for developing and publishing of the game.

JUNE 2009
Triptych Games is formed from several ex-3D Realms employees and a couple of new individuals.

JULY 2009
Triptych Games signs paperwork with 3D Realms to complete the Duke Nukem Forever single-player campaign.

DECEMBER 2008
The last official Duke Nukem Forever screenshot from 3D Realms is released to the community.

MAY 2009
The story that 3D Realms has laid off the Duke Nukem Forever development team breaks and tops gaming news websites around the world.

JUNE 2009
Gearbox and 3D Realms begin negotiation of an asset purchase agreement for Duke Nukem franchise and Duke Nukem Forever. The business agreement is finalized and executed approximately six months later and ownership of the game and brand is transferred to Gearbox Software.

Work chugged ever onward, as always, and (unbeknownst to the world at large) the game was actually starting to come together in a form recognizable compared to the finished version you now own. But by the end of 2006 even more 3D Realms employees left, leaving an even smaller staff for a modern blockbuster. However, there was a glimpse of hope on the horizon, as despite setbacks the title was starting to take shape. Hiring took place to double the size of the team to prepare for a final push to get the game out the door in another two years. As if to affirm the new commitment to complete the project, the first public trailer in over half a decade was released at the end of 2007.

Production finally seemed to be on the right track to the finish line, except for one problem—the deep pockets of 3D Realms, born of the huge success of Duke Nukem 3D and the Build engine, were finally running dry. Take-Two and 3D Realms could not come to agreement regarding funding the game through to the end. In May of 2009, the development staff of Duke Nukem Forever was laid off by 3D Realms and development suspended.

But that would not be the end...

For over a year, it seemed to the gaming public and media that Duke Nukem Forever had simply been allowed to perish. Over a decade of development time—and for what? Not until September of 2010 did the world at large get a good look at Duke Nukem again during PAX (the Penny Arcade Expo). And oh, what a look it was. The Duke Nukem Forever booth was one of the dominant features of the show's sizeable expo hall. The official presence of Duke alone would cause a stir at a huge gaming convention, but the game was actually playable! For real! After waiting in line for hours! This was a far cry from vaporware. How did this happen?

Like anything good in life, it was some hard work and good fortune. While the creative team was laid off by 3D Realms, the developer also contacted Gearbox Software to see if there was interest in seeing Duke through to the end. Gearbox Software began talks with 3D Realms to purchase the rights to the Duke Nukem franchise. Meanwhile, several recent ex-employees of 3D Realms formed a new independent game development studio, Triptych Games, with the intention of finishing Duke Nukem Forever under agreement with 3D Realms. Over the course of the next year, a number of pieces locked into place. Most importantly, the single-player content was finally finished! Gearbox Software became the owners of the Duke Nukem franchise, assuming responsibility for Duke Nukem Forever. Gearbox then contracted Triptych Games and moved them into the Gearbox offices to polish the console ports. Piranha Games was also brought on to work on multiplayer modes and console ports.

3D Realms and Take-Two resolved the legal differences from their previous publishing agreement and 2K Games became the new publisher. What, among other things, helped compel Gearbox Software and 2K Games to see Duke Nukem Forever to release?

Flashback to 1997... Two employees of 3D Realms, Randy Pitchford and Brian Martel, left the Duke Nukem team to first start Rebel Boat Rocker, then later Gearbox Software. Duke Nukem 3D was the first game Mr. Pitchford worked on. And now? He's President and CEO of Gearbox. Even Duke gets by with a little help from his friends!

DECEMBER 2010
Duke Nukem Forever reappears on the holiday issue of PC Gamer with the same headline as his cover 11 years prior –'Miss Me?'

FEBRUARY 2011
Duke Nukem, with the help of Borderlands' Claptrap, opens the Academy of Interactive Arts and Sciences 2011 Interactive Achievement Awards in Las Vegas. The show, hosted by comedian Jay Mohr, is streamed live over the Internet and broadcast on television via G4 TV.

MAY 2011
Gearbox Software and 2K Games announce Duke Nukem Forever consumer demo will be available to First Access Club members on June 3, 2011.

OCTOBER 2010
2K Games and Gearbox Software announce the Duke Nukem Forever First Access Club to be included in every copy of the Borderlands Game of the Year Edition, allowing participating customers first access to the Duke Nukem Forever consumer demo.

JANUARY 2011
The first gameplay trailer for Duke Nukem Forever since 2001 is released by Gearbox Software and 2K Games.

JUNE 2011
Gearbox Software, alongside Triptych Games, Piranha Games and 3D Realms, release the approved gold masters for Duke Nukem Forever. After 15 years since work first began on a Duke Nukem 3D sequel, 2K Games launches and ships Duke Nukem Forever video games worldwide to an eager and patient audience.

With Duke's public recognition and great wealth, he's connected all the way up to the top of the U.S. government.

CHARACTERS

The titular hero is back! Twelve years have passed since Duke's victory over the aliens in Los Angeles. The world's population naturally extends gratitude for Duke's accomplishment and awe at his general prowess. He has leveraged this goodwill into considerable success in a variety of ventures. Duke's flagship Duke Burger restaurant stands as the highest point in Las Vegas, overlooking his own popular casino, the Lady Killer. Why, the nation's top late-night program films from a studio on the ground floor of the Lady Killer and it just so happens that Duke has an interview on the show.

DUKE NUKEM

Every king needs his throne.

The Duke Burger spire soars into the stratosphere above the strip.

The pop star twins are also Duke's live-in goddesses. The talented duo resides with Duke in the spacious penthouse of the Lady Killer, which sports an incredible view overlooking the Las Vegas strip. Although they're entrenched deep within Duke's inner circle, the twins are obviously still quite star struck, making them especially eager to please.

Whose haircut do you prefer?

MARY AND KATE HOLSOM

STRIPPERS

CENSORED!

CENSORED!

CENSORED!

Shake it, baby!

These lovely ladies put in a hard day's work at classy places like Duke Nukem's Titty City, arousing onlookers with their seductive moves.

GENERAL GRAVES

The General is the current allied military commander. Naturally, he's known Duke for quite a while and admires him. Of course he would—Graves is a patriotic pragmatist who favors a common sense, getting-it-done attitude over fretting about the bureaucratic and diplomatic consequences.

Officially, the General is compelled to follow the orders of the President. Unofficially, he will try his damndest to do what's right.

THE PRESIDENT

The sitting P.O.T.U.S. is the leader of the free world—and a serious drag. The President holds a deep grudge against Duke Nukem for the collateral destruction caused by Duke's heroic stand against the first alien invasion attempt—Los Angeles is still recovering economically—and regrets that a diplomatic solution could not be reached. The President may even be just a little resentful at how brightly Duke's star shines and how much Duke basks in that bright light. With an apparent second opportunity to score a major political coup by entering into partnership with the aliens, the President is not eager to see Duke mess up his bid to become the broker between aliens and humanity.

The President is crystal clear in his disdain for Duke Nukem.

Sometimes a real soldier is needed on the battlefield—
someone to show all the pansies how it's done.
Oftentimes, that someone is Duke. But it can sometimes be
Captain Dylan. The captain is a rough and rugged officer
in the EDF. His job is to kick ass and chew bubblegum…
OK, his job is basically the same as Duke's.

CAPTAIN DYLAN

They don't come much tougher than Dylan. They don't cuss more, either.

EDF SOLDIERS

The Earth Defense Force (or EDF) was formed after the previous alien invasion attempt. The EDF exists to provide some measure of security against another alien threat beyond "Hope Duke Nukem saves the earth by himself." Wouldn't you know, it just might end up that way again anyway? Nevertheless, these brave souls lay down their lives for human freedom, that is when they're not busy getting mutated into mindless Pigcops by alien Assault Commanders.

EDF soldiers will fight alongside Duke Nukem during some segments of the single-player campaign.

GAME BASICS

"WHAT'D YOU EXPECT? FOREVER'S A LONG TIME."

We won't judge too harshly if you need some time to get readjusted to the controls and world of Duke Nukem. It's been a while, after all, and there are plenty of new wrinkles to the game's mechanics.

DIFFICULTY SETTINGS & UNLOCKABLES

During your first playthrough of the game, there are only three difficulty settings. The hardest difficulty, "Damn, I'm Good," is unlocked by first completing the game on another setting. The difference between the difficulties lies in how much damage Duke deals and how much he receives. On the hardest difficulty, Duke deals half his normal amount of damage, while taking twice as much!

DIFFICULTY	DAMAGE DEALT	DAMAGE SUSTAINED
Piece of Cake (Easy/Novice)	125%	75%
Let's Rock (Normal/Default)	100%	100%
Come Get Some (Hard)	75%	150%
Damn, I'm Good* (Insane)	50%	200%

*Unlocked after clearing every chapter on any other difficulty.

In addition to unlocking a new difficulty setting, defeating the game also reveals other bonuses. You can check out galleries of concept art, development screenshots, pre-release trailers, and photos of Triptych's cushy office. There's a thorough development timeline, a Duke sound board, and a menu full of new game settings to toggle. Those settings include the following:

- Invincibility
- Infinite Ammo
- Instagib (enemies always splatter gruesomely)
- Mirror Mode
- Grayscale Mode
- Game Speed (PC only)
- Head Scale
- Duke 3D Freeze Ray (Freeze Ray fires bouncing projectiles rather than a short-range beam)

HANDLING THE DUKE

PC CONTROLS

The PC is where the Duke Nukem franchise and the first-person shooter genre started. From the beginning, the controls were intended for keyboard and mouse. Consoles have come a long way since the first grudging attempts at a real FPS experience on a console. Controllers are now robust enough that FPS titles can be played with no problem. But there is still an undeniable "snappiness" to mouse and keyboard control that cannot be completely replicated on game controllers.

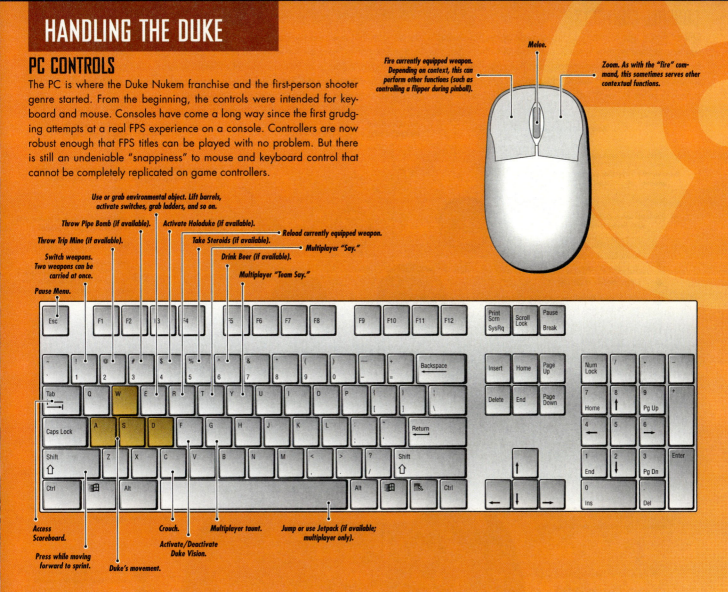

Fire currently equipped weapon. Depending on context, this can perform other functions (such as controlling a flipper during pinball).

Melee.

Zoom. As with the "fire" command, this sometimes serves other contextual functions.

Use or grab environmental object. Lift barrels, activate switches, grab ladders, and so on.

Throw Pipe Bomb (if available).

Activate Holoduke (if available).

Throw Trip Mine (if available).

Take Steroids (if available).

Reload currently equipped weapon.

Switch weapons. Two weapons can be carried at once.

Drink Beer (if available).

Multiplayer "Say."

Multiplayer "Team Say."

Pause Menu.

Access Scoreboard.

Crouch.

Multiplayer taunt.

Jump or use Jetpack (if available; multiplayer only).

Press while moving forward to sprint.

Activate/Deactivate Duke Vision.

Duke's movement.

WASD ALTERNATIVES & PC CONFIGURATION PERSONALIZATION

Console players have four control schemes from which to choose. In contrast, PC gamers have a dizzying array of customization options. Apart from the endless number of key bindings on a keyboard and mouse, there are also myriad varieties of both devices with all sorts of hardware features and button arrangements specific to each one.

All said, the consensus was arrived at long ago that WASD was the sacrosanct building block of PC control schemes for FPS titles. There's nothing wrong with this control scheme, but it does require that you frequently move your middle finger back and forth from W to S whenever you want to change from moving backward to forward, or vice-versa. Although it may not sound like much, but over the course of the campaign, or several heated multiplayer matches, this will amount to thousands of small movements. With just minor modifications to the control scheme, you can create a setup that requires less finger movement and thus less strain and fatigue.

You'll even end up changing direction slightly faster—a difference of a few milliseconds might not sound like much, but hey, every little bit helps.

A: Move backward; **S:** Left strafe; **D:** Move forward, **F:** Right strafe.

The basic idea is that instead of having "move forward" directly above "move backward," you simply array all four movement commands in a line. Your pinky will then always be ready to move Duke backward, while your middle finger is always ready to move Duke forward. Meanwhile, your ring and pointer fingers cover both strafe directions. No key travel is required to cover every movement direction! Depending on your particular hands and fingers, you may find it more comfortable to assign "move backward" to the Z key rather than the A key, but the idea remains the same. Of course, you'll still need to move your pinky to press the shift key to sprint, but that is a given regardless.

Along the same lines, if you have a mouse with extra buttons, it's wise to consider mapping the Trip Mine and Pipe Bomb commands to the mouse. To throw one of these explosives on the PC version, you must take a finger completely off the movement keys to press either the 2 or 3 key. Especially if you're trying to stick a Trip Mine directly to a moving target, having your own forward or lateral movement hampered while you prepare to throw is a terrible disadvantage. But meanwhile, the thumb on your mouse hand was doing basically nothing. Instead, use it to press the side mouse buttons so you can retain full movement control of Duke.

Of course, PC configuration is largely personal preference and born of experience and habit. Perhaps you have the default schemes too ingrained to worry about a change. But regardless, it's worth scrutinizing the default control scheme for just a minute to see whether you can streamline your performance and make your hands, and the gameplay itself, more to your liking.

CONSOLE CONTROLS

Duke Nukem has a history of fun console ports. For example, the version that released for PlayStation 1 (The "Total Meltdown" edition) had an extra episode added with individual levels themed after other PlayStation franchises, such as Resident Evil and Wipeout. *Duke Nukem Forever* marks the first time Duke Nukem arrives on consoles concurrently with the PC version. Apart from obvious control differences, and extra customization options for graphics and sound on PC, the versions are almost identical. The only differences are minor ones: two Achievements on Xbox 360 have different names than on PC or PlayStation 3, and the European PlayStation 3 version does not allow rats to be microwaved.

Throw Trip Mine (if available).

Zoom. Level of zoom depends on the currently equipped weapon. For example, the Railgun zooms in considerably further than the pistol. Like the "fire command," this sometimes does different things.

Access Scoreboard (multiplayer only).

Access Pause Menu.

Throw Pipe Bomb (if available). Active Pipe Bombs are detonated by pulling the right trigger.

Well, this is the important one, isn't it? This fires Duke's current weapon. You knew that, didn't you? Contextually, this sometimes does other things.

Duke's movement. Push in the left stick while moving forward to sprint.

D-PAD	RESULT
↑	Activate Duke Vision in single-player; Taunt in multiplayer
↓	Activate Holoduke (if available)
←	Take Steroids (if available, don't try this at home, kids)
→	Drink beer (if available)

Reload current weapon, or interact with environmental object (if available).

Swap weapons.

Jump or use Jetpack (if available, multiplayer only). When swimming, holding down the jump button makes Duke ascend in the water.

Melee.

The d-pad controls Duke's equipment. No, not that equipment…

Aim. Push in the right stick to crouch. While swimming, holding down the right stick button makes Duke descend in the water.

Throw Trip Mine (if available).

Zoom. Level of zoom depends on the currently equipped weapon. For example, the Railgun zooms in considerably further than the pistol. Like the "fire command," this sometimes does different things.

Access Scoreboard (multiplayer only).

Access Pause Menu.

Throw Pipe Bomb (if available). Active Pipe Bombs are detonated by pulling the right trigger.

This fires Duke's current weapon. Contextually, this sometimes does other things.

The d-pad controls Duke's equipment.

D-PAD	RESULT
↑	Activate Duke Vision in single-player; Taunt in multiplayer
↓	Activate Holoduke (if available)
←	Take Steroids (if available, don't try this at home, kids)
→	Drink beer (if available)

Reload current weapon, or interact with environmental object (if available).

Swap weapons.

Jump or use Jetpack (if available, multiplayer only). When swimming, holding down the jump button makes Duke ascend in the water.

Melee.

Duke's movement. Push in the left stick while moving forward to sprint.

Aim. Push in the right stick to crouch. While swimming, holding down the right stick button makes Duke descend in the water.

In addition to the default control scheme, there are three alternate arrangements. These configurations mimic the controls of some other shooters that you may have heard about, while you stayed faithful to Duke and waited patiently for his return. You stayed faithful to Duke, didn't you?

DISPLAY

In *Duke Nukem 3D*, all health and ammo information was displayed in a readout across the bottom of the screen. Nowadays, most games eschew using too much screen real estate for display elements when that space is better served to showcase the game and *Duke Nukem Forever* follows this trend. The heads-up display will appear only when it's needed, like in the middle of firefights with enemies or whenever you press the "reload" command. The rest of the time, the display will fade away, leaving an unobstructed view of the world of Duke Nukem.

Duke's Ego and health. Enemy boss health, when appropriate, is displayed underneath Duke's Ego meter. Note that this can be disabled in the game's options if you prefer.

Quest items for single-player campaign progression.

Available equipment. Shows availability of Beer, Steroids, Duke Vision, and Holodukes.

Remaining ammo for current weapon, along with reserve stock of Trip Mines and Pipe Bombs.

O2 gauge. Only relevant when underwater. Shows the amount of oxygen remaining before Duke starts to drown.

EGO

Duke's health is protected by his formidable Ego. While other first-person heroes need impact shields or body armor to protect themselves from damage, Duke needs only his unequaled machismo. As he sustains damage, his Ego gets depleted. Avoid damage for a few seconds and Duke's Ego will regenerate. If his Ego gets completely depleted, Duke can only withstand a little direct damage before he dies. Once Duke's Ego is utterly drained and the screen begins to turn red, find a place to hide and recover quickly before it's too late!

Duke's Ego is represented as a bar in the top-left corner of the screen. The maximum numeric value of Duke's Ego starts at 40, although this is not expressed overtly in the game. Max Ego can be increased by defeating bosses and by interacting with the environment in certain ways. Many actions in the environment, such as using a microwave or requesting a special dance from a stripper, result in a permanent, one-time boost to maximum Ego the first time they are performed. By finding every opportunity to boost max Ego in each chapter, you'll ensure that Duke is tougher for all encounters going forward. If you find every Ego-boosting action in the game, Duke's maximum Ego will be 100—over twice the max starting value! (You will also unlock an **Achievement/Trophy** for snagging every Ego boost.) Ego progress is retained if you use Chapter Select to swap to a different chapter, but Ego is reset if you start a totally new single-player campaign.

A full list of Ego boosts is located in the Trophies, Achievements, and Ego Boosts chapter.

MULTIPLAYER EGO

In multiplayer modes, Ego is set to 100 for all players. Weapons have different properties in multiplayer than in single player, so refer to the multiplayer chapters for more specifics regarding those modes.

GUNS & AMMO

The fire button discharges the currently-held firearms. Duke can carry two different guns at a time and each weapon has a maximum amount of ammo. Some weapons also have a finite magazine size; expend all the rounds of ammunition in a magazine and Duke will reload the weapon to continue firing. Some weapons, like the RPG or Devastator, do not have magazines; instead, they simply deplete ammo from Duke's overall stock. The max ammo for a given weapon includes whatever is in the current magazine. Duke does not have separate totals for reserve ammo and loaded ammo, only one overarching value for all of it.

Execution: Bring an enemy close to death and he may start swooning in a groggy fashion. Approach and press the "use" command to perform an execution, a down-and-dirty takedown of the target that fully refills Duke's Ego!

Contextual cues will appear on-screen when you get close enough to a new weapon to pick it up. If you only have one gun, picking up another one will mean that you have two. With two guns in hand, picking up another weapon replaces whichever weapon was last held with the new one, while dropping the old one to the ground. Passing over a spare weapon of a model you already carry will add ammunition to that weapon's tally, if there is room to spare. This will also remove the weapon from the world, so don't carelessly walk over ammo replacements when you're only missing a few rounds off the max. Pick up weapons when needed to maximize available ammo.

You'll find more weapons inside breakable item crates and more ammo in bottomless Ammo Crates and Ammo Piles.

MOVEMENT

Duke Nukem Forever is the direct sequel to one of the granddaddies of all first-person shooters, *Duke Nukem 3D*. The basic vocabulary of control hasn't changed too much in the intervening decade or so. Duke's locomotion is still handled by walking forward or backward and strafing, while his orientation is changed by using either the mouse or the right analog stick.

STRAFING

In case you've been living under a rock since before *Wolfenstein 3D*, then *DOOM*, then *Duke Nukem 3D* changed video gaming forever, it's important to note how important strafing is. Strafing is simply walking sideways. On the console, this is accomplished by moving the left analog stick either left or right, while on PC this is done by pressing either the A or D keys (depending on your keyboard setup). Let's say a Pigcop Captain fires an RPG grenade, or an Octabrain hurls a psychic blast or object your way. It's probably a good idea to sidestep the incoming projectile by strafing. Sure, Duke's Ego can absorb a serious pounding if you'd just like Duke to catch the object with his face, but this is an approach that will only go so far. It will take you as far as seeing the loading screen—again and again... It's important to learn how to strafe left and right while keeping your gun trained on your target.

Some enemies will attack Duke by leaping or firing objects directly at him. Against these foes, given enough space, you can strafe in one direction while continually aiming at the enemy. In effect, you'll be dancing a circle around the foe while peppering the beast with pain. You might not be surprised to learn that gamers call this "circle strafing."

Some enemies, such as the Octabrains, will "lead" Duke with their projectiles if you're strafing while they're firing. For these baddies, circle strafing won't suffice. Don't change direction and you'll just eat whatever they feed you. Instead, you'll want to "juke" rather than strafe continually in one direction. Move to one side until the enemy releases a projectile, then immediately strafe in the opposite direction.

SPRINTING

When you need Duke to hoof it a little faster, press the appropriate sprint button while moving forward. You don't have to hold down the sprint command—you just have to input it while moving forward. Keep moving forward and Duke will keep sprinting. A physical specimen like Duke can haul ass with the best of 'em, but no one can sprint indefinitely, so keep that in mind. A well-rested Duke can sprint for about eight consecutive seconds.

MULTIPLAYER SPRINTING

In multiplayer modes, players can sprint indefinitely!

Forward movement of any kind allows Duke to sprint, so you can move forward but also strafe to one side when you start sprinting, and he will move faster at a wider angle. You can't sprint directly sideways with just strafing, though. Sometimes you may want to move laterally around an enemy or object faster than strafing alone allows. For example, you'll fight some bosses that are accompanied by lesser enemies. You may have all your attention trained on strafing around the boss, only to realize you're surrounded in closer proximity by their underlings. Well, you gotta get the hell out of there for the sake of Duke's Ego! In this case, you'll want to break your line of sight with the boss and sprint laterally around the whole mess of monsters. Once you've created some separation, you can re-orient to all the enemies and resume strafing normally.

JUMPING

True to classic form, *Duke Nukem Forever* requires a ton of legwork out of our hero, in addition to liberal exercise of his trigger finger. Luckily, Duke has prepared with plenty of squats and can leap with the best of 'em. It's a good thing, as several sections of the game are platforming-heavy. Our hero's hamstrings are up to the task, but is your thumb? In general, if you have any trouble making jumps in difficult sections, remember that you can probably leap later. Look down and you'll see Duke's handsome legs—this can help serve as a guideline, if you're having trouble.

The key assigned to jumping is also used in a few situational cases, like when Duke grapples with a Pigcop or Pregnator. An on-screen prompt will direct you to input the key or button assigned to the jump command to break free. This kind of thing also happens occasionally when trying to pry open a stubborn door or gate. In these cases, you'll want to mash on the jump button over and over until success is achieved.

Jumps can be a matter of life and death.

You'll have to make some jumps in a couple vehicles, too.

Berserk Pigcops and Pregnators can both leap on Duke and force a strength tap challenge. Mash the jump button quickly to survive.

ENVIRONMENTAL INTERACTION

There's plenty to do in the game besides blasting aliens and ogling hot chicks. Your curious inquisitions into the world of Duke Nukem will be rewarded in various ways. These interactions are handled by the key or button assigned to the "use" command. Note that while the PC version assigns "use" and "reload" to different keys, the console versions consolidate these functions.

In some cases, the use command simply allows Duke to observe an object, such as admiring himself in the mirror or ogling his babes in the multiplayer "My Digs" mode. In other cases, the interaction is more complex. For example, Duke can open a microwave, then pick up something that is right at home in a microwave, such as a bag of microwaveable popcorn, then place said object inside the microwave. Then, the microwave can be closed and turned on.

Usable items in the environment that have a critical function will emit a glow, as long as tips are "on" in the options!

Many items can be picked up and tossed. Jump right before tossing an object to add power and distance to the throw.

Some objects blocking your path are breakable, like wooden boxes, or padlocks.

Some objects can be picked up and held with the use command. Once in hand, depending on the object, you can set the object down again by facing a nearby flat surface and inputting the fire command, or you can toss the object by facing something that's further away and pressing the fire button. Another option or two may present itself, depending on what Duke holds. In any case, on-screen prompts will indicate when an action is available.

WEAPONS & EQUIPMENT

"THIS IS TAKING FOREVER!"

There are a lot of aliens that need killing and, luckily, weapons are in abundance throughout the single-player campaign. Weapon specifics are a little different in multiplayer modes compared to the main story mode, so refer to the multiplayer chapters for details about online play. Some pieces of equipment also aid in the quest to liberate Earth. Much of Duke's arsenal will be familiar to long-time fans of the King, but there are a few new weapons and gear to keep things interesting.

Pipe Bombs and Trip Mines, which create splashy, explosive firepower, allow Duke to set traps and fight out of harm's way. Objects from the environment can help, too. Explosive barrels will kill anything nearby when they go off; heavy barrels and objects can be tossed into foes; fire extinguishers can be destroyed to put out nearby blazes; and vehicles of various types allow for expanded travel and alien-crushing options.

WHISKEY & JETPACKS

The Jetpack is back—just not during the single-player campaign. It is, however, available in multiplayer modes. Whiskey, which grants invincibility, is also an item unique to multiplayer. Just like in real life, the best thing to drink while operating a Jetpack is hard liquor.

Each piece of equipment has its own parameters and purpose, which are detailed in this chapter. Although some weapons are clearly better than others during certain circumstances, a skilled player can utilize just about any weapon in any situation. The exception occurs during boss fights and vehicle combat. Huge, heavily-armored targets can only be damaged by explosive weapons and turrets.

EDF Ammo Crates and Ammo Piles provide unlimited ammo and explosive replenishment. Take advantage whenever these resources are nearby during a battle.

Weapons are frequently found near deceased EDF soldiers, aliens, and Pigcops or inside item crates or webbed corpses.

Explosive items can turn into remote weapons, as they will explode after being punctured. They can also be tossed directly at enemies.

DIFFICULTY	DAMAGE DEALT	DAMAGE SUSTAINED
Piece of Cake (Easy/Novice)	125%	75%
Let's Rock (Normal/Default)	100%	100%
Come Get Some (Hard)	75%	150%
Damn, I'm Good* (Insane)	50%	200%

DIFFICULTY SETTINGS

The weapon damage referenced in this chapter is based upon the default difficulty of "Let's Rock." On the lowest difficulty, Duke deals 125% of normal damage, while on harder difficulties, he inflicts much less. On "Damn, I'm Good" Duke deals half the normal damage! Essentially, it requires twice the ammunition to kill each foe.

The heavier damage taken from enemies on harder difficulties also places a precious premium on effective use of equipment. Beer, Holodukes, and Steroids can all be lifesavers in some situations, allowing Duke to make chicken salad out of chicken snot. Using Pipe Bombs and Trip Mines as effective, efficient supplements to primary weapons also becomes invaluable.

THE DUKE NUKEM ARSENAL

WEAPON	DAMAGE PER ROUND	RATE OF FIRE	ROUNDS PER MAGAZINE	DAMAGE PER MAGAZINE	MAX AMMO COUNT	MAX DMG PER FULLY LOADED WEAPON	AMMO PICKUP	RELOAD SPEED	MELEE SPEED	FIRE FASTER WITH MANUAL BUTTON PRESSES?
Fists	40	.833 seconds	N/A	N/A	N/A	N/A	N/A	N/A	.833 seconds	No
 Pistol	20	.37 seconds	8	160	64	1280	40~64	2.17 seconds	.625 seconds	Yes
 Shotgun	Close Range: 15 per pellet, for 15~150 total; Long Range: 10 per pellet, for 10~100 total	1.0 seconds	7	Close Range: 105~1050; Long Range: 70~700	28	4200	19~28	.83 seconds for first shell, .5 for subsequent	.8 seconds	No
 Ripper	9	.1 second for first round, .067 for subsequent	50	450	200	1800	140~200	3 seconds	.8 seconds	No
 Railgun	135	1.33 seconds	3	405	12	1620	8~12	2.33 seonds	.8 seconds	No
 RPG	125 (with large splash damage radius)	1.33 seconds	N/A	N/A	5	625	3~5	N/A	.933 seconds	No
 Devastator	20 (with small splash damage radius)	.33 seconds	N/A	N/A	69	1380	69	N/A	.833 seconds	No
 Shrink Ray	N/A (simply shrinks target; very small "splash shrink" radius)	.5 seconds	N/A	N/A	10	N/A	7~10	N/A	.933 seconds	No
 Freeze Ray	120 "ice" damage per second	30 rounds per second	N/A	N/A	200	800 "ice" damage	150~200	Recharges slowly over time (roughly 6.7 rounds per second, or full recharge in 30 seconds)	.833 seconds	No
 AT Laser	20 (60 per 3-round burst)	1.33 seconds (3-round burst)	N/A	N/A	60	1200	42~60	N/A	.933 seconds	No
 AT Captain Laser	20	1 second for first round, .5 for subsequent	N/A	N/A	80	1600	56~80	N/A	.933 seconds	No
 Enforcer Gun	55 (165 per 3-round burst; medium splash damage radius)	1.33 seconds (3-round burst)	N/A	N/A	15	825	10~15	N/A	.933 seconds	No
 Trip Mine	125	N/A	N/A	N/A	4	500	1	N/A	N/A	No
 Pipe Bomb	125	N/A	N/A	N/A	4	500	1	N/A	.833 seconds	No

FISTS & MELEE

PUNCH/MELEE VITALS

Damage Per Punch/Melee Swing	40 (128 with Steroids)
Melee Speed	.833 seconds

Melee strikes have a lot of practical uses. Up close, they are quite powerful compared to individual rounds from many weapons. In a pinch, you can usually punch a berserk Pigcop or two to death with no problem. Melee attacks are also great for eliminating weaker enemies like Pregnators and Octababies. Of course, you'll also be bashing boxes apart, crushing egg pods, and knocking around webbed corpse piñatas. Melee strikes also work like a charm against frozen enemies, or reeling foes ready for execution. If you don't need the instant Ego refill that an execution kill provides, just bash the enemy to death with a quick melee attack.

MELEE SPEED	WEAPON
.625 seconds	Pistol
.8 seconds	Shotgun, Ripper, Railgun
.833 seconds	Bare-handed, Devastator, Freeze Ray, Pipe Bomb
.933 seconds	RPG, Shrink Ray, AT Laser, AT Captain Laser

The speed of a melee attack differs very slightly depending on the weapon in hand. Power doesn't differ, however; every melee attack deals 40 points of damage, or twice the damage of a Pistol shot. Drugs provide an exception, though. While under the influence of Steroids, Duke's punching power rockets from 40 to 128! Steroids briefly put punches on par with RPG rockets and Railgun rounds!

Melee attacks can destroy certain environmental objects.

Hands and feet are used in execution attacks.

PISTOL

PISTOL VITALS	
Damage Per Round	20
Rate of Fire	.37 seconds
Rounds Per Magazine	8
Maximum Ammo Count	64
Ammo Pickup	40–64
Reload Speed	2.17 seconds
Melee Speed	.625 seconds

The semi-automatic M1911 Pistol is the preferred sidearm of Duke Nukem. This is notably the only weapon in the game that fires faster if you manually press the fire button repeatedly, rather than just hold it down. The Pistol is also the only weapon that allows for a faster melee attack than normal!

Don't let the diminutive size of this weapon compared to Duke's other weapons fool you. With some finesse and trigger discipline, the Pistol is a formidable weapon even on the game's hardest difficulty, "Damn, I'm Good." (On the hardest difficulty, Duke's damage output is diminished sufficiently that the Pistol finally underwhelms compared to heavier choices.) Go for headshots and opt for controlled, aimed shots over frantic bullet spam and the Pistol should serve you well. Remember to take advantage of the extra-fast melee swing against enemies that get too close.

The reticle turns red when the weapon is pointed directly at a hostile target. The Pistol has terrific range.

The normal Pistol and Duke's golden Pistol both perform identically. The golden Pistol just looks way cooler and serves as the basis of a big Trophy/Achievement.

Score headshots to greatly increase the power of the Pistol.

THE GOLDEN GUNSLINGER

There's no mistaking Duke's custom, gold-plated M1911 Pistol. You'll first acquire this gleaming weapon from the Duke Cave early in the campaign. Finish every subsequent chapter with the golden Pistol on Duke to unlock one of the game's most valuable Achievements/Trophies.

SHOTGUN

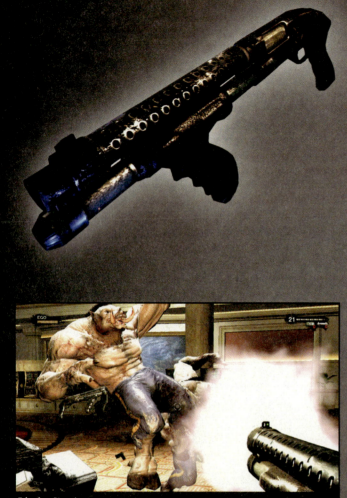

PUNCH/MELEE VITALS

Damage Per Pellet, Close Range	15 (10 pellets per shot, 15~150 total)
Damage Per Pellet, Long Range	10 (10 pellets per shot, 10~100 total)
Rate of Fire	1.0 seconds
Rounds Per Magazine	7
Maximum Ammo Count	28
Ammo Pickup	19~28
Reload Speed	.83 seconds for first shell, .5 seconds for subsequent
Melee Speed	.8 seconds

What would a respectable first-person shooter be without a dominant Shotgun? *Duke Nukem 3D* laid down the ground rules years ago—Shotguns have been anointed by the gaming gods as the perfect weapon. *Duke Nukem Forever* is not exempt from these unwritten rules. The Shotgun is, pound for pound, buckshot for buckshot, the best weapon in the game. If you aim carefully and put every Shotgun shell center-mass on a target, no other weapon even comes close in terms of damage on a per-full-weapon basis. This makes the Shotgun even more valuable on higher difficulty settings, where ammo can become an endangered resource.

Take that, Pigcop!

There are a few caveats to the Shotgun's superiority, though. Although it inflicts ferocious damage up close and diminished (but still great) damage at mid range, it is ineffective at long distances. The Shotgun also has by far the longest reload time of any weapon—Duke has to individually chamber each shell during a reload. The Shotgun is also ineffective against bosses and vehicles, but then that's true of all non-explosive weapons.

FRONT LOADING DAMAGE

The Shotgun fires 10 pellets per trigger squeeze and each pellet deals its damage instantly. Weapons like the Pistol or Ripper deal damage over time, one projectile at a time. This means the Shotgun shines over those weapons at close to mid range, especially against foes who will die from one well-placed Shotgun blast.

Even though the Ripper fires with alarming speed, putting one Shotgun shell dead center into a Pigcop is still faster (and easier) than nailing the first 11 or so Ripper rounds without missing a single one (or, similarly, getting 3~5 Pistol rounds on target without a miss).

This also means that the Shotgun is capable of more kills per magazine than a Ripper or Pistol. Seven rounds per Shotgun magazine can end up scoring seven kills against Assault Trooper Captains and Pigcops, while the most you can hope to squeeze from a Ripper per reload is about four kills. The Ripper is also a much larger headache to deploy against Assault Trooper Captains, who will teleport repeatedly before dying due to the slower buildup of damage. With a good hit from the Shotgun, there is no "buildup" of damage; the Assault Trooper Captain is just toast, with no time to deploy pesky teleport.

Only enemies equal to or tougher than a Pigcop Captain can survive a full Shotgun blast, and only Enforcers or tougher foes can survive more than two.

RIPPER

RIPPER VITALS

Damage Per Round	9
Rate of Fire	.1 seconds for first round, .067 for subsequent
Rounds Per Magazine	50
Maximum Ammo Count	200
Ammo Pickup	140~200
Reload Speed	3 seconds
Melee Speed	.8 seconds

The Ripper is Duke's machine gun. It boasts an incredible rate of fire and, with a 50-round reservoir, the deepest magazine of any non-explosive terrestrial weapon (the Devastator holds 69 mini-rockets, but it cannot be reloaded). The flat, multi-barrel arrangement gives the Ripper a firing rate comparable to a chaingun! The Ripper fires so fast that it empties a magazine almost as fast as Duke can reload.

The Ripper chews through enemies very quickly. Multiple hits also result in many opportunities to cause enemies to flinch, interrupting their actions.

The Ripper is a versatile weapon that can be found throughout most of the game. Like Pistols and Shotguns, Pigcops frequently tote a Ripper, so even if spare Rippers aren't lying around or hidden in item crates, you'll still usually find them on slaughtered swine.

The Ripper makes a fine anti-Pigcop weapon since it's effective at any range in any situation.

Against especially stout enemies like shielded Enforcers, try dumping a full magazine into them, then tossing a Pipe Bomb as a fatal one-two punch.

Like the Pistol, the Ripper is more desirable on lower difficulty settings, while it falls behind a bit on the hardest difficulty. It can take half of a magazine to put down a single Pigcop on "Damn, I'm Good." So you may only get eight kills out of all four magazines of a full Ripper and that's assuming you don't miss any shots!

When compared to the Shotgun as a long-range weapon, the Ripper naturally wins. At mid range, the Ripper would eventually win against the Shotgun if it didn't drain all four magazines so quickly. If the means are available to keep the Ripper restocked (like from EDF Ammo Crates or ammo pickups), the Ripper is the better choice over the Shotgun at mid range. But just as the Ripper wins at long range, the Shotgun dominates at close-range damage.

RAILGUN VITALS

Damage Per Round	135
Rate of Fire	1.33 seconds
Rounds Per Magazine	3
Maximum Ammo Count	12
Ammo Pickup	8~12
Reload Speed	2.33 seconds
Melee Speed	.8 seconds

Railguns are made possible by modern technology that utilizes electromagnets to charge and hurl projectiles at incredible velocities. Remember that the next time you're checking your pockets for metal objects before an MRI exam. The Railgun projectile travels in a straight, precise path and passes through solid objects with an operational range that is functionally infinite.

Outfitted with a scope, the Railgun makes a natural sniper rifle.

At long range and with precise aim, the Ripper outpaces the Railgun. However, it's probably a taller order to land 45 out of 50 shots on target with the Ripper's recoil and lessened zoom versus landing 3 out of 3 heavily-zoomed, deliberately spaced shots with the Railgun. Additionally, Ripper bullets are absorbed by their targets, while Railgun rounds aren't stopped by anything. Railgun projectiles will pierce multiple targets, if they're lined up, and will even pass through solid cover!

The Railgun is powerful in its versatility. While its enormous range and scope make it ideal for long-range altercations, it works just fine as a close-range weapon against one or two foes. On difficulty set-

The Railgun is a non-explosive weapon with strong individual shots and much more ammo in comparison to the RPG or Enforcer Gun.

tings below "Damn, I'm Good," this firearm works just like a Shotgun up close—one shot, one kill against Assault Trooper Captains and Pigcops.

The only thing holding it back as a primary weapon for any situation is its diminutive magazine. So if you get jumped by several pigs or aliens, you should swap to a better phone booth weapon, like the Ripper or Shotgun, perhaps after killing two or three enemies with a magazine of Railgun rounds. If you can manage to line up close-range enemies with Railgun blasts to cut through them all, then even better.

The Railgun becomes much more potent when you're near an EDF Ammo Crate. This allows you to be much more cavalier with Railgun use without having to save it for long-range targets.

Railgun headshots have unique death animations.

RPG

RPG VITALS	
Damage Per Round	125
Splash Damage Radius	Large
Rate of Fire	1.33 seconds
Maximum Ammo Count	5
Ammo Pickup	3–5
Melee Speed	.933 seconds

The RPG (rocket-propelled grenade) is Duke's rocket launcher. This weapon can be dumb-fired without a lock-on, which results in the rocket traveling straight down the path it was aimed. Hold the reticle over a target for a second, however, and the RPG will establish a lock-on. Fire with a lock-on active and the rocket is virtually guaranteed to hit the target.

SPLASH DAMAGE

RPG rockets not only inflict damage to their direct target, but also in a large area around the impact zone. This makes RPG rockets great for clearing out clustered groups of most any types (Assault Troopers, Pigcops, even Pregnators and Octababies). Just don't fire RPG rockets at Octabrains—mature Octabrains will "catch" incoming rockets, then hurl them right back at Duke with deadly accuracy.

Pigcop Captains (an infrequent, higher-ranking version of a regular Pigcop) are always equipped with RPGs. On their own, they're not too bad—just strafe around their rockets and make sure a wall isn't right behind Duke to avoid any potential splash damage. Pigcops will sometimes attack in groups, though, or with other enemies. Be especially mindful of any Octabrains, as they will make the rocket problem much worse. Octabrains hurl rockets faster than they travel when launched!

Thanks to lock-on, the effective range of the RPG is almost unlimited.

The RPG is one of the best weapons against bosses and it will usually be available in those situations.

As the explosive weapon in most available supply, the RPG will serve as a main option during most boss fights. Bosses are immune to non-explosive damage, which means you'll need to rely on RPGs, Devastators, Pipe Bombs, Trip Mines, and Enforcer Guns. Of those, RPGs are usually both the most practical and plentiful available armament.

DEVASTATOR

DEVASTATOR VITALS

Damage Per Round	20
Splash Damage Radius	Small
Rate of Fire	.33 seconds
Maximum Ammo Count	69
Ammo Pickup	69
Melee Speed	.833 seconds

The Devastator is Duke's signature heavy weapon. This cannon's symmetrical design features dual rocket launcher barrels and requires Duke to use both arms to carry it. The barrels alternate firing rockets so that a constant stream is kept on the target. The Devastator has a deep supply of rockets (69 to be precise), but it cannot be reloaded. You can only find another Devastator or refill at an EDF Ammo Crate. On the plus side, Octabrains have a hard time catching Devastator rockets like they can RPG rockets, Pipe Bombs, and Enforcer Gun missiles.

The Shotgun was heralded as the game's best weapon mainly for its ubiquity and efficiency. It's damage is spread out over time in big chunks with lulls in between. The Devastator, on the other hand, outputs tremendous damage at any range with splash damage to boot! Whenever you can use a Devastator, you'll definitely want to—especially if an EDF Ammo Crate is around.

The splash damage radius of Devastator rockets is very prominent, but still small compared to the RPG or Enforcer Gun. Still, be careful when firing the Devastator at nearby targets. Last, because Devastator rockets cause little damage, this should not be your weapon of choice when playing as a shrunken Duke.

The answer to "What is the Devastator good at damaging?" is "Everything!"

Perhaps the happiest sight in the game.

SHRINK RAY

SHRINK RAY VITALS

Shrink Splash Radius	Very small
Rate of Fire	.5 seconds
Maximum Ammo Count	10
Ammo Pickup	7–10
Melee Speed	.933 seconds

The Shrink Ray fires a shining projectile that induces spontaneous shrinkage in targets at the point of impact. The Shrink Ray's projectiles actually have a small splash radius, so it's possible to shrink more than one enemy at a time with one shot.

The Shrink Ray turns earth-shaking foes into rodent-sized runts.

Enemies will remain shrunk for several seconds, during which time they are more or less defenseless. Although they can still fire their weapons, the effect is much less than normal. You can easily kill shrunken targets by either running over them while looking downward at them, hitting them with a melee attack, or shooting them with any weapon.

Assault Commanders can be very tough...unless you just shrink them.

Far and away the most valuable target for the Shrink Ray is the Assault Commander. These hovering heavies have about three times the resiliency of the next-toughest alien, the Enforcer, which is about three times as tough as a run-of-the-mill Pigcop. Shrinking and then squishing an Assault Commander can save a lot of time and ammo. Otherwise, you may end up dumping about half the ammo of any terrestrial weapon, plus all the ammo of any explosive weapon, trying to fell the flier (assuming normal difficulty; on "Come Get Some" and "Damn, I'm Good" Assault Commanders are even more obnoxiously sturdy).

HIPPY STOMPER

The "Hippy Stomper" Achievement/Trophy is unlocked by squishing 12 tiny foes. They don't have to be shrunken by the Shrink Ray, though, as stepping on rats or Octababies counts toward that total, too.

FREEZE RAY

FREEZE RAY VITALS

Damage Per Round	120 "ice" damage per second
Rate of Fire	30 "ice" rounds per second
Maximum Ammo Count	200
Ammo Pickup	150–200
Recharge Speed	6.7 rounds per second (full recharge in roughly 30 seconds)
Melee Speed	.833 seconds

The Freeze Ray is capable of freezing any organic material to a brittle, rock-solid finish in a matter of seconds. Unlike other weapons, the Freeze Ray does not use ammo. Instead, it recharges its ice potential over time. To reload the weapon, you simply don't fire it. After complete depletion, the Freeze Ray will be fully loaded again in about 30 seconds.

Frozen targets can be easily shattered.

The range of the Freeze Ray is by no means infinite; instead, its projections of icy energy extend to about the edge of mid range. This serves as a useful marker, actually, as the maximum range the Freeze Ray can hit an enemy from roughly the same point at which the Shotgun stops loses its effectiveness. Past that range, the Freeze Ray will fail to connect while the Shotgun may still deal damage, but with greatly diminished power.

Smaller frozen creatures, like Pregnators, can only be shattered, not executed.

As the Freeze Ray is discharged, ice energy will rapidly deplete over time. If the beam is positioned over a target, it will receive ice damage. Most targets will freeze solid less than a second after contact! Try to get comfortable firing just enough ice energy to freeze a target, rather than continuing to fire needlessly while they're freezing solid anyway. Once a full-sized target (like a Pigcop) is frozen, you can either execute it for a full Ego refill, or simply melee bash it for the kill. The melee bash is a lot faster if you don't need the Ego refill.

Don't worry about smashing an Octabrain after freezing it—they'll shatter when they hit the floor!

Its range and overall nature make the Freeze Ray a unique substitute for the Shotgun. Although their function (close-range dominance) is identical, the means differ.

AT LASER

AT LASER VITALS

Damage Per Round	20 (3 rounds per trigger pull)
Rate of Fire	1.33 seconds (3-round bursts)
Maximum Ammo Count	60
Ammo Pickup	42~60
Melee Speed	.933 seconds

The AT Laser is the weapon used by lowly Assault Troopers, and thus it's one of the first weapons you'll pick up during Duke Nukem Forever. This alien weapon is powered by an irreplaceable fuel cell, meaning it cannot be reloaded. Just like the Devastator or RPG, you must just pick up a new weapon to replenish ammo.

When fired, the AT Laser unleashes a burst of three blue energy projectiles. These projectiles deal excellent damage. The disadvantage of the alien's energy weapons versus terrestrial, kinetic ammunition is simply that the projectiles travel slower. Bullets arrive on target more or less instantly, giving enemies no chance to dodge. AT Laser shots, on the other hand, have a transit time, which may make them miss if the target moves drastically. The problem is especially pronounced against extremely mobile enemies like Assault Trooper Captains and Octabrains. The AT Laser isn't a bad weapon, but you'll want to trade up whenever possible.

AT CAPTAIN LASER

AT CAPTAIN LASER VITALS

Damage Per Round	20
Rate of Fire	1 second for first round, .5 for subsequent
Maximum Ammo Count	80
Ammo Pickup	56–80
Melee Speed	.933 seconds

The AT Captain Laser is an upgraded alien sidearm that works a little bit differently. It fires the same basic projectile, but instead of doing so in three-round bursts, the AT Captain Laser spins up a drum mechanism that begins firing a constant stream of the blue bullets. The weapon cannot fire until the drum spins up, which takes a full second.

This makes the AT Captain Laser a poor weapon when you're unsure what's coming—that spin-up time may become an eternity if a berserk Pigcop jumps into your face. On the other hand, it's a terrific weapon when you know you're about to battle several enemies at once. Spin the barrel up in advance and approach your adversaries with energy bullets already flying. The AT Captain Laser is not about conservation of ammo; if you're going to use it, let 'er rip!

Like the AT Laser, the AT Captain Laser's main deficiency is projectile travel time.

*Acting like a laser chaingun, the **AT Captain Laser** is potent against groups of enemy grunts.*

ENFORCER GUN

ENFORCER GUN VITALS

Damage Per Round	55 per missile (3 missiles per trigger pull)
Splash Damage Radius	Medium
Rate of Fire	1.33 seconds (3-round bursts)
Maximum Ammo Count	15
Ammo Pickup	10–15
Melee Speed	.933 seconds

The Enforcer Gun, carried appropriately enough by Enforcers, has more damage potential from a single trigger squeeze than any other weapon. When fired, the Enforcer Gun launches three blue drunk missiles. These missiles will travel in the general direction in which they're fired and search for any enemies along that path. Detected enemies will cause the rockets to detour toward them with almost-unerring accuracy. Most enemies will not survive if two or three of the missiles connect.

Enforcer Gun missiles do not track over an infinite range. If they've traveled about twice the distance of the edge of mid range (as defined by the range of the Freeze Ray), they'll stop homing in to potential targets. This means the Enforcer Gun doesn't work as a total replacement for the RPG in confrontations requiring heavy artillery. Also, Enforcer Gun rockets lose their effectiveness at long range, which makes it less effective during certain battles.

Enforcer Gun missiles come in fire-and-forget bursts of three that will track down enemies through nearly any evasive action.

When you're close enough for the missiles to track properly, the Enforcer Gun makes an even better weapon in boss fights than the RPG.

These drunk missiles don't require much aiming precision to do their job, making the Enforcer Gun a fantastic weapon from behind cover

The Enforcer Gun carries 15 missiles, but at three rounds per burst, that's only five total uses. Like other weapons with limited ammo or availability, the Enforcer Gun shines near an EDF Ammo Crate. In fact, if the enemies are close enough, you can simply sit at the Ammo Crate and spam Enforcer Gun bursts in the near vicinity, using the Crate to rearm as necessary. No enemy can withstand a constant onslaught of incoming homing missiles and you don't even have to bother much with aiming.

TRIP MINE

TRIP MINE VITALS

Damage Per Mine	125
Splash Damage Radius	Large
Maximum Ammo Count	4
Ammo Pickup	1
Melee Speed	.933 seconds

Once armed, Trip Mines are rigged explosives that project a laser of infinite range. If the path of the laser is broken by a moving humanoid (including Duke), the Trip Mine will explode. The explosion doesn't project splash damage along the full range of the beam, but it does deal heavy damage in a large area where the Trip Mine was deployed.

Trip Mines are armed by being thrown. Once thrown, they will stick and arm automatically to the first surface they touch. Depending on how they stick, they laser will orient differently. Throw a Trip Mine low on a wall and enemies may have to jump to avoid it (and they almost certainly won't, except perhaps a berserk Pigcop). Throw a Trip Mine high on the wall and it may be possible to crouch underneath the laser, or even run under cleanly. Toss a Trip Mine onto the floor and the laser will align straight up, which doesn't provide much of a lateral trap, but will be deadly to anything that passes directly on top.

Trip Mines can be set as traps. Place them near Pipe Bombs or existing environmental explosives to create a stronger trap.

There's a Trophy/Achievement to unlock by killing enough enemies with Trip Mines.

OCTOPUS CATCH

Octabrains can be killed with ease when they're close enough by tossing a Trip Mine onto them. Once it is armed, it will destabilize the hovering Octabrain and detonate as it spins out of control! There's an Achievement/Trophy to unlock for placing a Trip Mine on a living enemy.

PIPE BOMB

PIPE BOMB VITALS

Damage Per Pipe	125
Splash Damage Radius	Large
Maximum Ammo Count	4
Ammo Pickup	1
Melee Speed	.833 seconds
Melee Speed	.933 seconds

Pipe Bombs are remotely-detonated explosives that can be used in several ways. Most directly, you can treat them like grenades. Simply toss them at a target, then detonate immediately. They can also be set as active traps by tossing a Pipe Bomb into an enemy's path, then detonating it as the enemy passes nearby. Passive traps are possible, too. Place a Pipe Bomb near an explosive barrel or armed Trip Mine and the exploding barrel or mine will detonate the Pipe Bomb, too.

After Pipe Bombs are thrown, they must be manually detonated.

Pigcops carry Pipe Bombs and will frequently use them. They will often drop spare Pipe Bombs when they die. Between Pipe Bombs from dead Pigcops, smashed item crates, and Ammo Piles, you have no reason to hoard Pipe Bombs. Use them as you see fit, as Pipe Bombs deal great damage in a wide radius.

Pipe Bombs can be thrown off bounce pads, which is crucial to solving some puzzles.

TRIP MINES & PIPE BOMBS—EXPLOSIVE LIMITS

Duke can carry up to four Pipe Bombs and four Trip Mines at a time. Up to 10 of any combination of Pipe Bombs and Trip Mines can be active at a time in the world, though. It doesn't matter the combination, as long as there are 10 or fewer explosives. If you throw another explosive into the world while 10 are deployed, the first explosive will vanish.

HOLODUKE

Another favorite item returning from *Duke Nukem 3D,* the Holoduke provides an almost perfect distraction to all enemy forces once it's deployed. The device accomplishes two things: it generates a convincing hologram copy of Duke and it cloaks the real Duke. This allows you to maneuver and aim without being detected, focusing on the enemies that are harmlessly attacking Duke's post-digital double.

EGO

5   4   4

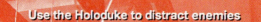

Use the Holoduke to distract enemies

Some stretches of the game are extremely difficult without the use of a Holoduke.

BEER

Beer impairs Duke's vision—the world becomes a vague blur. It also greatly increases Duke's resistance to damage, allowing him to withstand much more Ego bruising than normal. There are Achievements/Trophies to unlock for drinking your first Beer, drinking a Beer and taking Steroids together, and for drinking every Beer in the strip club.

STEROIDS

STEROID VITALS	
Damage Per Punch	128
Melee Speed	.833 seconds

Steriods place Duke's Ego at 75% of maximum and grant him incredible punching strength. No normal enemy can withstand much of Duke's pummeling under the influence of these health supplements. Steroids are best used against large groups of middling aliens and Pigcops.

ENEMIES

"I'M FROM LAS VEGAS, AND I SAY KILL 'EM ALL!"

Duke doesn't have many enemies on Earth. In fact, everyone on Earth just wants his attention; it takes an intergalactic beef to provide Duke with antagonists. With few exceptions, *Duke Nukem Forever* foes are fiends from across the vast sea of space. These Cycloid forces tried to mess with humanity over a decade ago and Duke Nukem thwarted the alien invasion single-handedly in a battle that began in Los Angeles, before spanning to the moon and back. The Cycloid spent the intervening 12 years retooling for a second attempt, so some staple units of their old army have been upgraded or replaced, while previously unknown units have been revealed.

ENEMIES & DIFFICULTY SETTINGS

Changing the game's difficulty setting affects two things: the damage that Duke can deal and the Ego damage that Duke sustains. Keep this in mind when studying the quantitative alien stats presented in this chapter. These stats equate to the "Let's Rock" setting, which can be considered "normal" difficulty.

DIFFICULTY	DAMAGE DEALT	EGO DAMAGE SUSTAINED
Piece of Cake (Easy/Novice)	125%	75%
Let's Rock (Normal/Default)	100%	100%
Come Get Some (Hard)	75%	150%
Damn, I'm Good* (Insane)	50%	200%

*Unlocked after clearing every chapter on any other difficulty.

CATEGORY

VERMIN

RATS

Okay, so these aren't aliens and they're not even close to enemies—they're more like pests. However, some of the action in *Duke Nukem Forever* takes place with our hero shrunk to the size of his own action figures. When a rat is suddenly the size of a bear, it becomes more than just a pest.

RAT SALAD

Rats also occasionally serve a purpose besides threatening a pint-sized Duke. At normal size, Duke can squash rats by walking over them while looking down at the ground, or pick them up. After picking up a rat, it can be thrown or squashed—throwing a rat can actually be useful, say, if you want to set off a Trip Mine from afar. Rats can also be placed in microwaves and nuked, earning an **Ego boost**. (Note, however, that rats cannot be microwaved in PS3 versions of *Duke Nukem Forever* sold in Europe.)

WHINY TALENT

Nobody likes a whiner, especially a pampered one who gets to keep his job saying things that would get anyone else fired. The first order of business for Duke's fists in *Duke Nukem Forever* is taking out the late-night trash. Deck the arrogant actor to unlock the appropriately-titled "Nobody Likes a Whiner" Achievement/Trophy.

CATEGORY
ALIEN TROOPERS

ASSAULT TROOPER

Assault Troopers make a return appearance from Duke Nukem 3D, where they were usually called "Liz Troopers" because of their reptilian appearance.

HEALTH	DESTRUCTIBLE ARMOR	
55	Yes	
MELEE CAPABLE		MELEE DAMAGE
Yes		20
USES COVER & TACTICS	GRAPPLE ATTACK CAPABLE	VULNERABLE TO EXECUTION
Yes	No	Yes

WEAPON	WEAPON DAMAGE	WEAPON DROP
AT Laser	3	AT Laser

Assault Troopers are the entry-level grunts in the Cycloid military force. As standard issue, they are outfitted with Jetpacks and armed with AT Lasers. From afar they will fire three-round bursts from their lasers, but when fighting up close they will go for a lunging melee attack. Their Jetpacks allow them to hover and fly, which means these creatures can attack from any angle. These entry-level foes are easily identified by their green chestplates. Assault Troopers are seen frequently throughout the game, usually in groups, and drop AT Lasers when they die.

Thanks to their Jetpacks, Assault Troopers can attack from the air as well as the ground.

ASSAULT TROOPER CAPTAIN

Assault Trooper Captains also return, bringing their red armor with them.

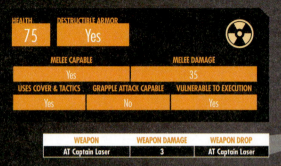

HEALTH	DESTRUCTIBLE ARMOR	
75	Yes	
MELEE CAPABLE		MELEE DAMAGE
Yes		35
USES COVER & TACTICS	GRAPPLE ATTACK CAPABLE	VULNERABLE TO EXECUTION
Yes	No	Yes

WEAPON	WEAPON DAMAGE	WEAPON DROP
AT Captain Laser	3	AT Captain Laser

Assault Trooper Captains exceed their brethren in both rank and power. Bearing red chestplates, they can dish out and take more damage than their subordinate counterparts. They are issued AT Captain Lasers rather than the standard issue three-round burst model, making for more appealing spoils than an AT Laser.

Both the phase-out disappearing phase of a teleport and the phase-in are signaled by an extremely bright flash of light, so stay on the alert.

The biggest difference between Captains and their lesser comrades, however, is the Captains' power of teleportation. Whenever an Assault Trooper Captain is in danger, the beast will teleport, then reappear several seconds later out of harm's way. Because of the teleport, firefights with AT Captains can be drawn out if you fail to utilize sustained damage before they can teleport away. Try to get a one-shot blast from the shotgun, or hit them from afar with the Railgun. If you only have a weapon that deals damage in smaller chunks, be prepared for a longer fight.

ASSAULT COMMANDER

Still serving as leaders in the Cycloid ground force, Assault Commanders return from Duke Nukem 3D.

HEALTH	DESTRUCTIBLE ARMOR	
1000	Yes	
MELEE CAPABLE		MELEE DAMAGE
Yes: Spinning Blade Charge		8 (and causes knockdown)
USES COVER & TACTICS	GRAPPLE ATTACK CAPABLE	VULNERABLE TO EXECUTION
Yes (in air only)	No	No

WEAPON	WEAPON DAMAGE	WEAPON DROP
Rockets, Spinning Blades	40	N/A

Assault Commanders are the highest-ranking members of the Cycloid military's forward assault force. These bulging, slug-like beings travel by hovering in mid-air. They can fire rockets from their rear end and charge forward with a spinning blade attack. The Assault Commanders are responsible for converting Earth Defense Force soldiers and local police forces into Pigcops.

Assault Commanders are susceptible to the Shrink Ray. Shrinking and then crushing them is definitely the fastest way to dispose of these serious threats. Otherwise, you'll be forced to whittle away at their sizable pools of health. Strafe from side to side to avoid their rockets, but be prepared to strafe in a wider arc if they charge with the spinning blade attack. Return fire with the strongest weapon in Duke's arsenal (up close, a Shotgun or Enforcer Gun; from afar, a Railgun or RPG). Hovering Assault Commanders also make easy targets for Pipe Bombs or Trip Mines pointed straight into the air.

After shrinking an Assault Commander, you can squash it with a lone melee hit or a single shot from any weapon.

PIGCOP

Pigcops return from Duke Nukem 3D, but this time with a little more variety in their weapon selection.

HEALTH	DESTRUCTIBLE ARMOR		
100	Yes		☢

MELEE CAPABLE		MELEE DAMAGE	
Yes		30	

USES COVER & TACTICS	GRAPPLE ATTACK CAPABLE	VULNERABLE TO EXECUTION
Yes (only when armed)	Yes (only when berserk)	Yes

WEAPON	WEAPON DAMAGE	WEAPON DROP
Dual Pistols	4	Pistol (Pipe Bomb on occasion)
Ripper	4	Ripper (Pipe Bomb on occasion)
Shotgun	7–80 (10 pellets at 7–8 per pellet, distance pending)	Shotgun (Pipe Bomb on occasion)

These former members of the EDF and local police forces were deformed and enslaved by the technology of Assault Commanders. Nothing can be done for these former allies, sadly—they are now mortal enemies.

Shotgun-wielding Pigcops are actually one of the most threatening enemies. In most versions of Duke Nukem 3D, Pigcops only used shotguns!

Some Pigcops retain enough of their faculties to use firearms. You'll encounter Pigcops with dual-wielding pistols, while others will tote a shotgun or Ripper. They'll also throw Pipe Bombs on occasion. Armed Pigcops will drop their weapons when they die, in addition to the random Pipe Bomb.

Berserk Pigcops will rush straight for Duke, jumping incredible distances with fists flailing.

As they near death, some Pigcops will snort a cloud of blood, drop their weapons, and go berserk.

Some Pigcops are totally berserk and will charge relentlessly. Hell-bent on inflicting pain on Duke, they'll leap from long range. Up close, they'll brutally strike with flailing punches or initiate a grapple sequence. The grapple sequence requires a successful strength tap to avoid a sudden death; on the bright side, mash successfully and the enemy will die.

DUKE NUKEM, PIG HERDER

Strafe laterally around berserk Pigcops to avoid their long-range pounces and close-range swipes. When fighting groups of berserk Pigcops in open spaces, run forward and shoot your way out from the middle of the fray, rather than backing away and firing at advancing foes. By running forward, you can sprint when the opportunity presents itself. Then from further away, you can turn and have several enemies in your sights.

PIGCOP CAPTAIN

A stronger version of the Pigcop variety.

HEALTH	DESTRUCTIBLE ARMOR
150	Yes

MELEE CAPABLE		MELEE DAMAGE	
Yes		30	

USES COVER & TACTICS	GRAPPLE ATTACK CAPABLE	VULNERABLE TO EXECUTION
Yes	No	Yes

WEAPON	WEAPON DAMAGE	WEAPON DROP
RPG, Pipe Bomb	30	RPG (Pipe Bomb on occasion)

Pigcop Captains almost never fight alone.

A few heftier Pigcops are armed with rocket-propelled grenade launchers. These rockets aren't as fast as other types of projectiles, though, so strafing is effective when avoiding incoming fire. Just try to avoid the splash damage from a rocket striking a surface near Duke.

Pigcop Captains will always be accompanied by other types of enemies, making encounters with them more complex. Try to dispose of the Pigcop Captains first to avoid the threat of eating a random rocket while battling some other creature. What's more, removing explosive projectiles from the equation takes on added importance when Octabrains are present. Octabrains will use their psychic powers to telekinetically catch rockets and Pipe Bombs before hurling them at Duke.

ENFORCER

Enforcers have received considerable upgrades since Duke Nukem 3D. They now have stronger armor and a powerful new weapon.

HEALTH	DESTRUCTIBLE ARMOR
300	Sometimes (riot shield)

MELEE CAPABLE		MELEE DAMAGE	
Yes		45	

USES COVER & TACTICS	GRAPPLE ATTACK CAPABLE	VULNERABLE TO EXECUTION
Yes	No	Yes

WEAPON	WEAPON DAMAGE	WEAPON DROP
Enforcer Gun	5 per rocket	Enforcer Gun

Enforcers basically represent the armored division of the alien infantry. These heavily-plated bruisers can take much more punishment than a standard Assault Trooper or Pigcop. Their Enforcer Guns are also one of the best weapons in the game.

Between the speed of a sprinting Enforcer and the strength of its melee attack, it's important to take extreme care when going toe-to-toe with them. The quickest way to deal with them is to use the Shrink Ray to reduce them down to a harmless size, then stomp away. Otherwise, toss some Pipe Bombs and rely on your most powerful weapon. Some Enforcers come equipped with a riot shield. To fight these armored foes, you must first destroy their shields. Afterward, they simply behave like a normal Enforcer.

The Enforcer Gun fires three homing rockets per burst. If possible, strafe in a constant circle around the Enforcer while facing him. This will make most missiles miss.

OCTABRAIN

These brainiacs are back!

HEALTH	DESTRUCTIBLE ARMOR	
175	No	☢

MELEE CAPABLE		MELEE DAMAGE	
Yes		30	
USES COVER & TACTICS	**GRAPPLE ATTACK CAPABLE**	**VULNERABLE TO EXECUTION**	
Yes (in air only)	No	No	

WEAPON	WEAPON DAMAGE	WEAPON DROP
Brain Blasts	30	N/A
Weapon	Weapon Damage	Weapon Drop
Telekinesis	Dependent on object weight and velocity	N/A

Octabrains are alien beings that possess tremendous psychic power. They can manipulate and hurl objects without physically touching them and can project blasts of sheer psychic energy.

Shooting an Octabrain while it charges for a brain blast will briefly interrupt its action. These foes will launch their brain blasts in front of Duke. Strafe in one direction while they charge to mislead them, then reverse course once the projectile is released.

Intelligent and mobile, Octabrains will actively dodge incoming projectiles, especially slow-moving ones. They can catch incoming rockets or Pipe Bombs and use them as projectiles of their own! This means that RPG rounds are largely ineffective against Octabrains, although Pipe Bombs can still be useful since you can manually detonate them when an Octabrain first grabs it.

Don't get careless and fire an RPG rocket at an Octabrain or you'll regret it!

You cannot interrupt an Octabrain's attack when it attempts to throw an object from the environment.

It's possible to attach a Trip Mine onto an Octabrain. The extra weight on the Octabrain's body will cause its psychic flight to destabilize out of control, forcing the foe to spin wildly. Naturally, this triggers the Trip Mine, killing the Octabrain and dealing heavy splash damage to anything else nearby. Incidentally, sticking a Trip Mine directly onto a living enemy snags the "Sticky Bomb Like You" Achievement/Trophy!

Use the Freeze Ray to freeze an Octabrain solid and the ensuing freefall to the ground will shatter the icy foe!

OCTABABY

This nasty, snapping stage of Octabrain development wasn't present during Duke Nukem 3D.

HEALTH	DESTRUCTIBLE ARMOR		
4	No		

	MELEE CAPABLE		MELEE DAMAGE	
	Yes		10	

USES COVER & TACTICS	GRAPPLE ATTACK CAPABLE	VULNERABLE TO EXECUTION
No	No	No

WEAPON	WEAPON DAMAGE	WEAPON DROP
N/A	N/A	N/A

Octabrains are essentially young Octabrains once they've emerged from its human female host. They are vile, leaping annoyances to a full-grown Duke, but a very real threat to a shrunken Duke. A regular-sized Duke can run over an Octababy and stomp it to death, which is extremely convenient.

HIPPY STOMPER

One Achievement/Trophy is unlocked for stomping on 12 small creatures. Stomping is accomplished by running over small foes while looking down at them. Small foes include Octababies, shrunken Pigcops and aliens, and rats. Pregnators are just large enough to avoid the wrath of Duke's mighty foot.

Although it's a straightforward task to stomp a shrunken Pigcop or alien, but it's not quite so simple a task with Octababies because of their leaping ability. Run forward at one that isn't on the ground and you won't be successful. Hang back slightly and bait an Octababy into leaping forward, then run forward to meet the foe with a stomp as it lands.

PREGNATOR

Pregnators hatch from egg pods.

HEALTH	DESTRUCTIBLE ARMOR		
35	No		

	MELEE CAPABLE		MELEE DAMAGE	
	Yes		15	

USES COVER & TACTICS	GRAPPLE ATTACK CAPABLE	VULNERABLE TO EXECUTION
Yes	Yes	No

WEAPON	WEAPON DAMAGE	WEAPON DROP
Goo Bombs	25	N/A

Pregnators are skittering, mobile pests with multiple attack methods. They move quickly around a room when far away, clambering over walls at any angle and leaping great distances to gain positional advantages. They even emit a white goo from afar, which can obscure Duke's vision for a few seconds. When fighting up close, Pregnators will use pounce and melee attacks. The pounce attack initiates a strength tap challenge.

UNPLANNED PARENTHOOD

A peek at Pregnators reveals the alien lifecycle. These bizarre foes actually hatch from egg pods laid by the Alien Queen. Pregnators seek out and latch onto human females, seeking to parasitize them, creating Podgirls. Podgirls go on to gestate Octababies, which then become Octabrains. It's a crazy cycle!

I NEED A TOWEL

Pregnators attack from far away by spraying white goo bombs at their targets. This sticky stuff not only deals damage on contact, but also obscures Duke's vision for a bit! Withstand 10 Pregnator bombs to the face to unlock a Trophy or Achievement.

A leaping Pregnator will initiate a strength tap challenge if it lands on Duke.

PODGIRL

The aliens are still up to no good. There's nothing Duke can do for these beauties.

Babes captured by the aliens are taken to an unknown location to be impregnated by a Pregnator, turning the poor lasses into Podgirls. Like Pigcops, there's nothing you can do for these babes infected with alien parasites. As Duke laments, why do they always take the hot ones? If you feel compelled, though, you can put them out of their misery. If you leave the poor Podgirls to their suffering, they'll eventually die when fresh Pregnators explode from their bodies. You can opt to euthanize Podgirls, or face Octababies later on.

ALIEN TENTACLE CLAW

Tentacles are an occasional environmental hazard. They can be subdued briefly but never destroyed.

HEALTH	DESTRUCTIBLE ARMOR	
N/A	N/A	☢

MELEE CAPABLE		MELEE DAMAGE	
Yes		20	
USES COVER & TACTICS	GRAPPLE ATTACK CAPABLE	VULNERABLE TO EXECUTION	
N/A	N/A	N/A	

WEAPON	WEAPON DAMAGE	WEAPON DROP
N/A	N/A	N/A

Tentacles are an environmental threat present in areas where the bio-organic excretions of the aliens have developed their own extraterrestrial ecosystems. The aliens have planted the tentacles to serve as a sort of organic security system. Tentacles cannot be permanently destroyed; they can only be knocked dormant for a few seconds. While the tentacles are in this dormant state, Duke can pass nearby without any trouble. If Duke gets caught in the tentacles, however, they will deal heavy damage. Just shoot them into submission and proceed forward. Don't accidentally back up or strafe into the tentacles unexpectedly, as doing so will likely result in death!

You can shoot Tentacles individually, or disable a glowing eye to subdue several Tentacles at once.

GASPOD

Like the Bugballs and their sockets, Gaspods are features of the encroaching alien environment that don't attack Duke directly. Unlike Bugballs, however, Gaspods can still inflict damage.

HEALTH	DESTRUCTIBLE ARMOR	
1	No	☢

MELEE CAPABLE		MELEE DAMAGE
Yes: Explosion		35

USES COVER & TACTICS	GRAPPLE ATTACK CAPABLE	VULNERABLE TO EXECUTION
No	No	No

WEAPON	WEAPON DAMAGE	WEAPON DROP
N/A	N/A	N/A

Gaspods are inert at a distance, but will explode into a toxic, explosive cloud when something gets too close. Try to eliminate them from a distance with single shot or a tossed object.

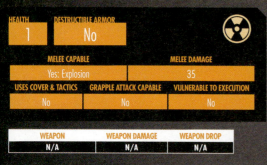

Some platforming challenges are complicated by Gaspods. Scan for these obstacles and dispose of them ahead of time, especially before hopping onto any bounce pads.

Sometimes Gaspods simply make the path impassable until you destroy them.

ALIEN FIGHTER

Alien spacecraft have been present in the series before, but never in such a prominent combat role against Duke.

HEALTH	DESTRUCTIBLE ARMOR	
150	No	☢

USES COVER & TACTICS	GRAPPLE ATTACK CAPABLE	VULNERABLE TO EXECUTION
No	No	No

WEAPON	WEAPON DAMAGE
Fighter Lasers	17
Bombing Laser	50

Alien fighters are the fastest, most agile enemy spacecraft of the entire fleet. Their primary purpose is air-to-air combat in combination with quick, strafing runs at ground targets. In particular, their bombing laser is deadly against stationary targets. When a fighter is incoming with a bombing laser active, the only way to avoid heavy damage or death is to destroy the fighter before it passes overhead.

BARON VON NUKEM

Shoot down 20 alien fighters and you'll unlock a **Trophy** or **Achievement**. You'll have opportunities to gun away at alien fighters during the chapters "Mothership Battle" and "Crash Course."

THE LADY KILLER RETURNS

...AND THE ALIENS DO, TOO.

After a prologue that reprises the events of the end of *Duke Nukem 3D*, the beginning chapters of *Duke Nukem Forever* take place in Duke Nukem's casino, The Lady Killer. This section of the guide details the first five chapters in the game.

DUKE LIVES

EPISODE THREE: SHRAPNEL CITY FINALE (DUKE NUKEM 3D)

OBJECTIVE: Finish the battle for Earth!

STADIUM INTERIOR

05

END

03

02

01

START

04

STADIUM FIELD

07

06

START

ENEMIES

[Cycloid]

WEAPONS AND EQUIPMENT

[Devastator]

TROPHIES & ACHIEVEMENTS

NAME	DESCRIPTION
Turd Burglar	Find and steal a piece of poo.
Drawrings	Doodle something on the whiteboard.
Full Body Tourettes (PS3)/ FBT (360)	Get knocked down 10 times.
Sunday, Black Sunday	Shoot down the blimp above the stadium.
One-Eyed Freak	Defeat the Cycloid.

Before you head downstairs for Duke's interview, take some time to look around. Duke's penthouse is a great place to get acquainted with Duke's Ego. We don't mean his self-image (that's on ample display already), we just mean his health. See, Duke's Ego is so substantial at this point that it has acquired a capital E and become a literal shield against damage. His Ego value, which appears as a bar at the top-left of the screen, starts at 40 and can eventually be increased to 100 by scoring **Ego boosts** throughout the game. Ego boosts are earned by engaging in unique interactions with Duke's surroundings. In this first chapter, a prologue to the larger adventure to follow, there are three Ego boosts to find worth a total of +4 to Duke's Ego.

 Lookin' good, good lookin'. Get Duke to admire himself in the mirror to score your first **Ego boost**. Hail to the king, baby. A few Ego boosts are available in multiple chapters, so if you miss the mirror and toilet here, you can check Duke out and get the same bonus in a few chapters later on. Watch out, though—some Ego boosts only appear in a single chapter.

02 After getting frisky with the twins on the couch, Duke's ready for the restroom, and even manages to avoid the dreaded split stream. Those Holsom twins sure know what they're doing. Notice the phone here in the bathroom. While you're in here, remember that there's an **Achievement** to be had for listening to every phone message in the game. The first phone in the game is right here in Duke's restroom, so don't miss it.

03 Checking your hair in the mirror and using the can are both easy tasks, however, clearing the pool table without scratching the cue ball is a fair bit harder. You can hit the cue ball again even if it hasn't stopped moving, so if you realize it's about to fall into a pocket, try to hit it away before it drops. If it falls in, you have to start all over (also, the twins will taunt Duke about wasting time playing with his balls. Funny, they didn't have much problem with it, themselves). Note that, while the prompt to hit the cue ball only appears if you're close to it, you can target and strike the cue ball from anywhere, as long as you're standing next to the pool table.

04 Join the twins and enjoy the view from the penthouse, but it quickly becomes ominous as an absolutely enormous alien mothership blots out the sky above Vegas, while smaller alien craft flit above the Vegas strip. The news is all over the TV, but Duke may have been a little distracted in the afterglow of playing his game while the twins played theirs. The word from the news is that the aliens seem to be on an ambassadorial mission of peace to meet with world leaders and the president. Duke knows a little better though, doesn't he? They come in peace? Not freakin' likely.

WHO WANTS SOME?

After you're done exploring the penthouse, turn the light switches off to incite a reaction from the twins. It seems they're afraid of the dark without a big, strong hero to hold them.

the ve
mullin
machi
chine
out of

In additi
don't ca

Eat your

After s
"Noms

CHAPTER 1:
DAMN! IT'S LATE...

Backstage, you'll run into Johnny's previous guest berating a late show employee for a perceived slight. Apparently, the employee's background wanderings were a horrific distraction to the pampered pro as he played air hockey with Johnny. Want to get another **Achievement/ Trophy**? Deck the complainer and spare the staffer from the verbal punishment.

"We're done! We're done professionally! You're a nice guy...you're a nice guy...BUT YOU DON'T GET IT!"

 Back in the studio halls, a deep disturbance from either within the casino or from outside on the strip starts causing power fluctuations. It's looking a lot less likely that the aliens are just here to chat up the president and sink their fangs into Duke's burgers.

DAMN... I'M LOOKIN' GOOD!

If you missed the **Ego boosts** for mirror narcissism or bladder relief during the prologue chapter, you can snag them here, in the makeup room and the bathroom.

Some Ego boosts are present in multiple chapters. Any given Ego boost can only be unlocked once, but it doesn't matter when or where you do it.

 To gain entrance to the Duke Cave, you need access to the Observation Room, which requires an elevator ride. Activate the elevator by pushing the buttons.

GOLDEN HINTS

Special objects in the environment that Duke can interact with are indicated by a periodic golden glow. If you ever get stuck, start looking around for objects that flash gold. Or, you can turn off the game hints to make finding these things a little harder.

Look out the elevator's glass window as it ascends and you'll see that the aliens are definitely not interested in Duke Burger. Further disturbances during the ride bring the elevator to a halt; open the emergency hatch, climb out the top, and pry open the powerless doors to access the Observation Room, which contains a museum of Duke memorabilia.

THE MUSEUM OF NATURAL DUKE HISTORY

OBJECTIVE: Use Duke's throne to access the Duke Cave.

THE OBSERVATION ROOM

The Observation Room's huge windows allow for an incredible view of the Vegas strip and the alien mothership. This level also contains the Duke Museum, where all sorts of displays commemorate Duke's victory against the Cycloid some 12 years prior.

01 The roots of Duke Nukem stretch back to 1991. The museum gallery depicts images from *Duke Nukem*, *Duke Nukem II*, and *Duke Nukem 3D*.

It's not necessary to explore the gallery, but it's interesting to remember where Duke came from. The primordial soup that spawned Duke Nukem was the same sludge from which seminal, medium-defining studios and characters emerged, like Apogee and id Software, 3D Realms, Commander Keen, Wolfenstein 3D, and DOOM. Study up, kids. Liking modern video games without knowledge of their roots is like enjoying current action movies without knowing who Sam Peckinpah is.

02 Duke's throne is a major part of the museum tour, and it serves as a photo opportunity for fans and tourists alike. What the masses don't know, however, is that this throne is actually the access point for the Duke Cave—but only when Duke uses it! While most museum goers have started to evacuate by now, one ardent fan hangs around, adamant that he gets his picture taken on the throne.

The kid sitting upon Duke's throne, wearing a t-shirt depicting the answer to life, the universe, and everything.

This photo stand allows you to take the kid's picture so he'll vacate the throne.

CHAPTER 02

THE DUKE CAVE

"I'VE GOT A BAD FEELING ABOUT THIS..."

OBJECTIVE: Find out what the aliens are up to.

UPPER LEVEL

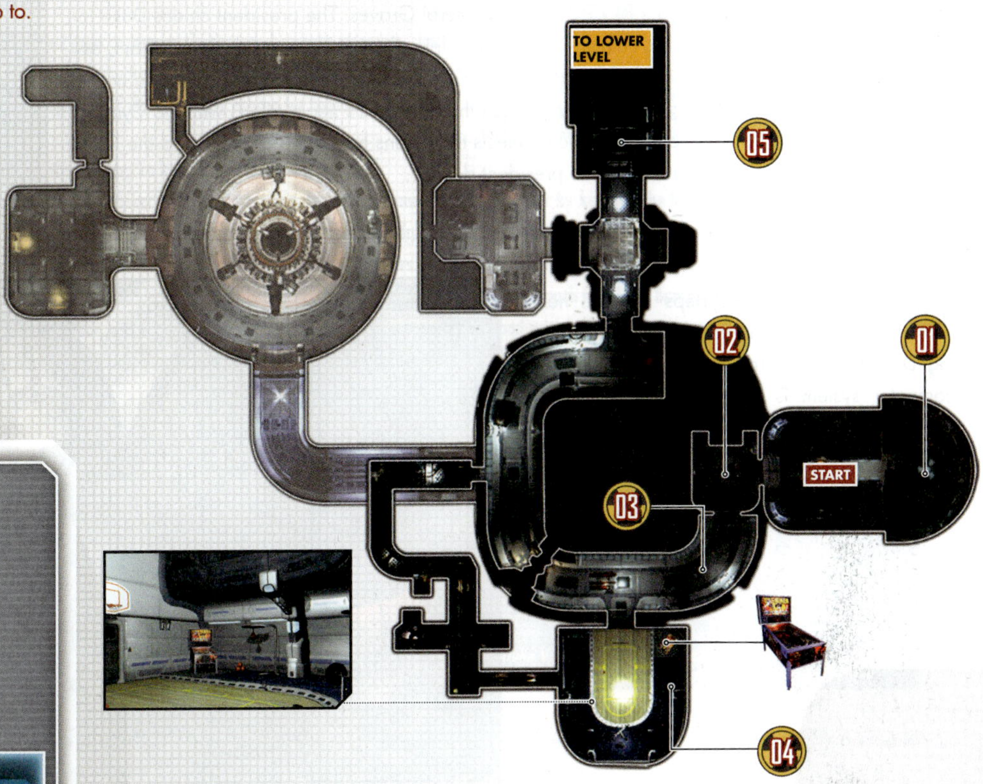

TO LOWER LEVEL

05

02

01

START

03

04

ENEMIES

[Assault Trooper] [Pigcop]

WEAPONS AND EQUIPMENT

[Beer] [AT Laser] [Energy Cell] [Steroids] [Gold Pistol]

EGO BOOSTS

REQUIREMENT	TOTAL EGO BOOST
Curl dumbbell.	+2
Admire self in mirror.	+1
Bench press at least 600 pounds.	+3
Punch speedbag.	+1
Punch punching bag.	+1
Shoot basketball through hoop.	+1
Beat pinball high score (280,897).	+3

TROPHIES & ACHIEVEMENTS

NAME	DESCRIPTION
Tosser in the Literal Sense (PS3)/Downtown Barrel Beatdown (360)	Kill 10 aliens with tossed objects.
Balls of Steel	Earn a 1,000,000 pinball score during the single-player campaign.
Flagon of Chuckles	Drink a beer during the single-player campaign.
Juiced	Take steroids during the single-player campaign.
Duke Angry Duke Smash	Kill 10 aliens with punches while on steroids.

07

SEE-SAW PIPE JUMP

05

LOWER LEVEL

06

08

PICK UP YOUR LAUNDRY

09

END

LOWER LEVEL

07 The storage closet containing the third Energy Cell is locked, but no obstacle is insurmountable for Duke Nukem. Here he'll use his ingenuity and affection for all kinds of gadgets and toys to use a radio-controlled monster truck to push the Energy Cell out of a venting duct on the ground near the frozen door. This RC truck is a small facsimile of Duke's own monster truck, the Mighty Foot!

STEP #1: The Energy Cell is on a shelf on the other side of the glass partition. To push it off the shelf onto the floor, you must navigate the perimeter of the room with the truck starting with this ramp.

STEP #2: Use the truck to push this black block further along the shelf, causing the ramp above to fall. You can simply back the truck up past the ramp again, then drive up to it to reach the next tier.

STEP #3: From the upper tiers, it's just a matter of driving around the edge of the room.

STEP #4: Once the miniature Mighty Foot is at the Energy Cell, just push it off the shelf, then through the hole next to the door.

08 Plugging in the final Energy Cell fully powers up the reactor. It also reveals a secret stash of Duke's Steroids. Just in time, too, as several Assault Troopers will drop in from broken vents above. After quashing this alien attack, the previously sealed southern door will open and release a couple of Pigcops. Take them out with AT Laser bursts or your Steroid-boosted fists before they do too much damage to Duke's Ego.

Steroids enable Duke to run fast and punch with incredible, insta-gibbing force for 21 seconds. Taking Steroids always puts Duke's Ego at 75%.

HERE PIGGY-PIGGY...

This is the first appearance of these mutated former EDF soldiers, but they're no longer Duke's comrades, so take them out with extreme prejudice. Some Pigcops come packing heat, while others prefer to use their fists.

 09 When the Pigcops are no more, you can safely proceed through the southern door. At the end of a corridor, you'll find Duke's golden **M1911 Pistol**, an elegant weapon for a more civilized age.

The final corridor, just past the golden gun, leads to Duke's Super Turret. That's right, our man has a huge cannon embedded into his casino just in case an alien mothership happens to appear. Powering up the reactor core has brought the Super Turret back online, so the last order of business is to make it to the cannon. Several more Assault Troopers swarm these hallways, but between Duke's shiny new golden M1911, the AT Laser, and the explosive red canisters, you should be able to turn these aliens into cooling meat without a problem. Once all the aliens are exterminated, you're ready to bring the Super Turret online.

THE WHOLE GAME?!

Don't worry if it sounds like carrying a pistol the entire game puts you at a disadvantage—it doesn't. The M1911 packs a serious punch at any range and only vehicles and bosses are immune to the pistol. Just watch your ammo—Duke can carry a maximum of 64 rounds of M1911 ammunition.

One of the game's most intensive Achievements/Trophies involves taking this particular pistol all the way through to the end of the game...yes, there are other M1911 Pistols, but this is Duke's personal piece and no other pistol in the game resembles it. You can set the golden pistol down during a given chapter and pick up other weapons, but just make sure you pick the golden gun back up before moving on from a given section. As long as you finish each chapter with the golden gun in tow, you're still on track to unlock the "Gunslinger" Achievement/Trophy.

CHAPTER 03:
MOTHERSHIP BATTLE

THE MOTHERSHIP

OBJECTIVE: Bring down the alien mothership!

WEAPONS AND EQUIPMENT

[Super Turret]

TROPHIES & ACHIEVEMENTS

NAME	DESCRIPTION
Baron von Nukem	Shoot down 20 alien fighters.
Big Guns, Big Ships	Blow up 5 Gunships or Dropships.

ALIEN MOTHERSHIP

The massive mothership hovers in the sky overhead and Duke must bring it down by attacking its weak point—the gigantic, exposed laser cutter weapon. The alien mothership seems unaware of Duke's presence until you start firing. Once the aliens are alerted to Duke and his turret on the roof, the mothership begins using its laser cutters to dice up Duke's casino, along with Vegas at large! You must defeat the mothership while fending off assaults from alien fighters and dropships, all before the Lady Killer is utterly destroyed—and Duke along with it.

Target the laser armature, which is the mothership's only vulnerable part. Pump rounds into it whenever an alien fighter isn't approaching, but keep an eye on the turret's temperature.

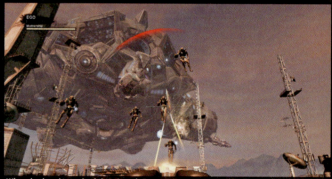

When the dropships unload their Assault Trooper cargo, it means more alien pests to fight. Luckily, the turret chews up fleshy targets without any trouble. Kill them before they have time to exit their dropships to simplify things.

After about 15 laser blasts, the laser cutter will direct its attention at Duke. Unless you're just on the cusp of defeating the mothership, this spells doom for Duke! Try to damage the mothership faster next time.

Alien fighters buzz just over the turret, targeting Duke with laser bombing runs. When three fighters approach in formation, only the lowest fighter will drop its bombs. You really can't afford to let fighters slip through.

The biggest threats to success, apart from the time limit, are the alien fighters. These quick crafts attempt to pass straight over Duke and his turret while firing downward with a bombing laser of sorts. You must shoot down each fighter before it passes overhead and deals damage. Solo fighters can pass overhead, but groups of three fighters will also frequently go on a bombing run. When three fighters approach, just focus on the lowest fighter in formation. On the hardest difficulty, fighters that pass directly overhead can kill Duke with a single shot!

HARDER DIFFICULTIES

On lower difficulty settings, you can essentially take out everything (dropships, Assault Troopers, alien fighters, the works) all while also putting rounds into the alien mothership's beam armature. On harder difficulty settings, though, every enemy target requires more focused fire to take down, but you need to balance this against the constant worry of your turret overheating along with the threat of incoming alien fighters. Therefore, you must be more judicious about what you choose to shoot down and even how often you shoot.

Basically, you can safely ignore the dropships. Oh, sure, kill the Assault Troopers they're dropping off, but don't worry about the actual crafts. Try to destroy alien fighters before they inflict serious damage to Duke, while looking to chip away at the mothership's armature when you're sure an alien fighter isn't incoming. When an alien fighter is approaching, drop everything and focus all your attention on it. Most importantly, watch out for waves of alien fighters back-to-back. Don't relax and turn your attention back to the mothership just because you've taken out one or two fighters, as they'll occasionally sortie in waves of four or five!

Uh-oh…

03 With the fence now open, Duke can access the Particle Expander Pad, which returns him to full size. Also present here, kept safe in a glass case, is the game's first shotgun. As Duke reunites with the Holsom twins, alien dropships crash the party and offload four waves of two Assault Troopers each. Duke's gotta protect his girls, so dust off the would-be alien kidnappers with the shotgun and Duke's golden pistol. Be aware that red-plated Assault Trooper Captains will teleport if they're injured, usually reappearing much closer to Duke or even behind him.

The Holsom twins flank the Particle Expander Pad and an emergency shotgun.

The shotgun is unmatched in brute strength up close, but lacks punch when used at a distance.

No matter how efficiently you dispose of the Assault Troopers, the aliens will eventually make off with Duke's most prized possessions—the twins.

04 The kidnapping of the twins (that was definitely strike three, aliens!) means it's time to backtrack through the area you just explored via RC Car, but this time at full size and packing outrageous firepower. Retracing your steps won't be as peaceful as the car ride here; shutters have closed in a few places and before you can pry them open, you must clear some rooms of encroaching baddies.

In this room, the ceiling gives way, allowing waves of Pigcops and Assault Troopers to spill into the casino. After they're all dead, the shutter blocking the way north can be pried open.

Two berserk Pigcops will be followed by two shotgun-wielding Pigcops, then six Assault Troopers! Grab the Beer from the center of the area and chug it down for a defense boost if needed.

Once the enemies are cleared out, take a moment to play the slots until you win to score an **Ego boost!**

05 Remember the first room where you had to drive helplessly past a couple of Assault Troopers? That's the site of the last stand for this part of the chapter. On the return trip, you'll find three shotguns scattered around the room and not one, but two bottles of Duke-brand Steroids! The fighting here is even more fast and furious than in the last room with the collapsing ceiling, as eventually six berserk Pigcops and six Assault Troopers will flood in from above. As before, once they're all put down, you can pry open the eastern shutter and proceed to the last portion of The Lady Killer.

The enemies here drop down from above. If you can defeat them early, more power to you, but don't neglect the enemies that are already at ground level.

BE WISE

Try to avoid accidentally walking over a spare shotgun if you're not low on ammo. It's best to pick up weapons only when you need them, so extra rounds aren't being lost into the ether.

Think of the room like a circuit and move forward in laps around its perimeter while clearing out the alien scum. This is better than backpedaling away from enemies, as you may bump into a Pigcop. Of course, you can also just pop both bottles of Steroids and beat everything into the ground, ensuring that you finish the "Duke Angry, Duke Smash!" **Achievement/Trophy.**

THE LADY KILLER, PART 3

OBJECTIVE: Search for Duke's chicks!

THE LADY KILLER CASINO

ENEMIES

[Assault Trooper]

[Rats]

[Pigcop]

[Assault Commander]

WEAPONS AND EQUIPMENT

[AT Laser (from Assault Troopers)]

[Pistol]

[Trip Mine]

[Beer]

[Shotgun (from armed Pigcops)]

TROPHIES & ACHIEVEMENTS

NAME	DESCRIPTION
Hippy Stomper	Foot stomp 12 creatures.
Trapper	Kill 10 aliens with Trip Mines.
Sticky Bomb Like You	Put a Trip Mine on a live enemy.
Full Body Tourettes (PS3)/ FBT (360)	Get knocked down 10 times.

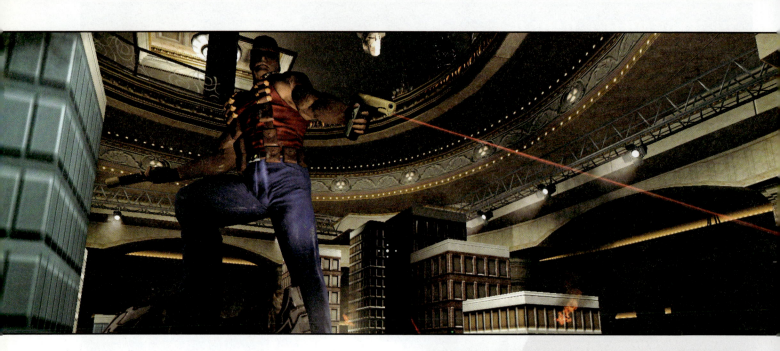

01 Back at full size and full strength, it's time to finish cleaning out Duke's casino before anything can be done about his missing babes. The first time you passed the Duke statue, it was a towering monolith you couldn't interact with at all. This time, Duke can play with himself—so to speak. You need to climb onto the Duke statue to access the second floor, but this requires repositioning the statue's pose.

To do so, turn the statue so its back is facing the real Duke, then raise the statue's left arm up as high as possible (see screenshot). Now it's time to trigger the Duke statue exhibit's "alien attack" display, which allows you to hop atop the skyscrapers. From here, you can jump onto the Duke statue's lower arm and clamber over its shoulders and head to the raised arm, and then on to the second floor.

02 A second floor storage closet reveals a vent shaft that leads into service tunnels. Unfortunately, the aliens have booby-trapped them from start to finish with laser Trip Mines. These mines can be detonated safely from a distance by shooting the mines directly, or tossing an object through the path of the beam.

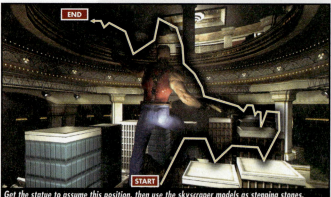

Get the statue to assume this position, then use the skyscraper models as stepping stones. Follow the path outlined here to access the next floor.

HIPPY-STOMPER

There are quite a few rats in this area. If you opt to stomp the rats rather than toss them into the Trip Mine beams, you'll earn progress toward the "Hippy Stomper" **Achievement/Trophy.**

These corridors contain EDF Ammo Crates, your first encounter with them. These boxes of bounty allow you to replenish ammo for Duke's two primary weapons as often as you like.

Duke must detonate the mines somehow, so shoot them with any weapon. If the explosion causes a fire, just destroy a nearby fire extinguisher to progress.

03 Having just acquired your first Trip Mines, now is a good time to get acquainted with using them. Duke will be greeted by a lone berserk Pigcop in the next room, followed by a group of Pigcops. If you plan to use Trip Mines against them, then set them up right away as they require a few seconds to activate. There are **Achievements/Trophies** to unlock both for killing 10 total enemies with Trip Mines and for sticking a Trip Mine to a live enemy.

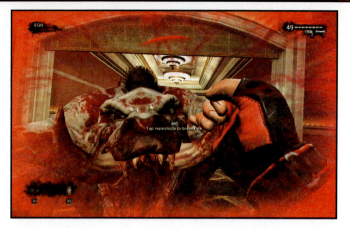

TRICKY TRIP MINES

Note that if you place a Trip Mine on a charging Pigcop, you're just going to create a hazard to Duke's health as well. That porky foe won't stop charging until the mine detonates!

The EDF soldiers see their small talk around Duke disturbed by the arrival of an Assault Commander. Assault Commanders are the highest-ranking soldiers in the Cycloid army, and they are capable of mutating human troops into Pigcop swine. The EDF soldiers are no match for Assault Commanders and the two EDF soldiers are instantly transmogrified into shotgun-packing Pigcops. Duke Nukem is more than a match for the alien commander, though. The Assault Commander will attack primarily by firing missiles from its bottom, plus it will occasionally mix in a charging blade attack that is capable of knocking down Duke on contact.

If you have Trip Mines remaining, toss one at the ground close to where the Assault Commander is hovering to inflict some heavy damage.

First, however, focus on eliminating the shotgun-toting Pigcops. Disposing of these foes means you won't get caught too close to one while strafing around the Assault Commander's rockets.

On his own, the fight with the Assault Commander is manageable as long as you stay on the move. Strafe one direction or the other continuously in the open spaces, keeping the enemy in your sights, and the Assault Commander will miss with his rocket blasts.

This fight presents a good opportunity to unlock the "FBT/Full Body Tourettes" Achievement/Trophy. Allow the Commander to knock Duke down with his spinning blade charge. Duke will eat floor and you'll be one tumble closer to the Achievement. Remember to give Duke's Ego time to recharge in between takedowns.

If you're having trouble with this fight, keep Duke hardened with Beer. There's a can on either side of this area.

ESCAPE FROM LAS VEGAS

"SCREW THE DAM, WHERE ARE THEY TAKIN' OUR CHICKS?"

As General Graves briefed Duke at the end of the previous chapter, the aliens are pushing on two diabolical fronts. For one, they've taken Hoover Dam and are using its hydroelectric power to open a wormhole in the sky, allowing aliens to continue pouring through to Earth despite Duke's destruction of their mothership. But, what's worse is that the aliens are kidnapping Earth women and taking them to the Duke Dome, for reasons so far unknown. Duke's a red-blooded, able-bodied American man and no matter how awesome he is, he can still only be at once place at a time, so the choice is obvious—Duke's going for the chicks!

GEARS OF DUKE

OBJECTIVE: Rejoin with EDF Captain Dylan and head towards the Duke Dome.

01 02 ITEM CRATE X2 04 05 06

03

ITEM CRATE X2
(UNDER OVERPASS)

ITEM CRATE X2

AMMO PILE

END

START

THE VEGAS STRIP

ENEMIES

[Pigcop] [Assault Trooper Captain] [Assault Trooper]

[Pigcop Captain] [Battlelord]

WEAPONS AND EQUIPMENT

[Ripper] [AT Captain Laser (from Assault Trooper Captains)] [Pipe Bomb]

[Trip Mine] [Steroids] [RPG]

EGO BOOSTS

REQUIREMENT	TOTAL EGO BOOST
Kill Battlelord	+3

TROPHIES & ACHIEVEMENTS

NAME	DESCRIPTION
Bucket Head	Find all three helmets in the single-player campaign (first of three is at the beginning of this chapter).
Pit Champion	Defeat the Battlelord in Las Vegas.

Just outside his casino Duke meets up with Dylan, an EDF specialist brought in by General Graves because of his experience with Duke and his zeal as a soldier. It's just outside the casino that you'll fully begin to appreciate the devastation caused by the initial alien attack and the subsequent crash of the mothership. And, while the alien mothership may be down, plenty of aliens remain on the ground with lots of surviving alien aircraft providing cover.

BATTLELORD

Once all the lesser aliens are cleared out, a giant Battlelord will arrive. This enormous alien warrior carries a huge machine gun, capable of intense firepower. It also rushes forward and kicks cars toward Duke when they're in the way. The Battlelord's enormous gun also has an attachment that fires homing mortars. At first, the boss won't use this attack and instead will only charge, kick cars, or fire its gun. After the Battlelord loses about one-fourth of its health, it will occasionally launch homing mortars. Beware, as these projectiles can track Duke even when he's behind cover or the central pillar! When the Battlelord has about half of its health remaining, it'll fire homing mortars constantly.

The most direct way to damage the Battlelord is with shots from an RPG. Sprint to one of the EDF Ammo Crates if you run out of rocket-propelled grenades.

Dance around the central pillar, keeping the Battlelord just out of sight except when you want to pop out and fire an RPG rocket. You can also use Pipe Bombs and Trip Mines liberally to set traps that the Battlelord is guaranteed to walk into. Don't bother with the Pistol, Shotgun, or Ripper…only explosives can inflict damage against this boss.

If you can hide behind the central pillar long enough, you can set traps using Trip Mines and Pipe Bombs while the Battlelord searches for Duke.

Once the Battlelord's health has been totally drained, it will collapse. Now it's time to approach and enter the "use" command to initiate a strength tap. Complete it successfully and Duke will break off and jam one of the creature's horns into its eye, which opens the way to land a knockout humiliation blow on the creature's tenders. Upon defeating the Battlelord, you'll gain an **Ego boost** and a **Trophy/Achievement** and finish the chapter. The Duke Dome is nearby…

If you fail the strength tap, the Battlelord will regain approximately one-fourth of its health. Don't fail the strength tap!

02 While approaching a crane, you'll encounter two Assault Trooper Captains making off with the Holsom twins. The Holsom twins are taken inside the Duke Dome. There's a crane here equipped with a wrecking ball, but the battery is out. You need to search a nearby construction yard to find a spare battery. Access the construction yard by running across the crane's arm and leaping to the top level of the nearby construction scaffold.

Two Assault Trooper Captains will attack as Duke nears the crane. Ignore them and sprint across the crane arm.

03 You must shoot the red barrels from within a suspended freight car to jump from the first yard to the second one. In the second yard, there are several RPGs and an EDF Ammo Crate. Nope, nothing is going to happen here. Once you're outfitted with an RPG, clamber to the top of the structure and take the spare crane battery. An alien gunship attacks. Nothing is ever easy.

The second yard has quite a few spots that can be used for cover. This will come in handy very shortly.

The enemy gunship hovers over the passageway to the north. Depending on the difficulty level, it will take approximately two to four RPG rockets to swat down this pesky fly.

As the gunship takes damage, it will start to smoke. Don't be afraid to take breathers to replenish Duke's Ego and try to pick up extra RPGs only when your ammo is completely dry. That way, you won't have to worry about sprinting to the EDF Ammo Crate, which is totally exposed out in the open.

When the gunship flies away, the fence door is blown off, allowing exit from this yard. A fallen I-beam also creates a path that will allow Duke to jump over the fence. Either way, he can return to the crane.

Insert the spare battery into the crane to restore electricity.

Position the wrecking ball even with the cracked portion of the wall, then steer the crane away, then back toward the wall to build up momentum for the ball to do its damage.

Angle the crane arm just over the newly-opened gash in the Duke Dome wall, then run across the crane arm to gain entry.

04 With the spare battery in tow, you can power the crane back on and use the wrecking ball to bash your way into the Duke Dome.

Nail the wall four times with the wrecking ball and the wall will give way.

CHAPTER 07

THE HIVE

THE HIVE, PART 1

OBJECTIVE: Track down the Holsom twins and the Alien Queen.

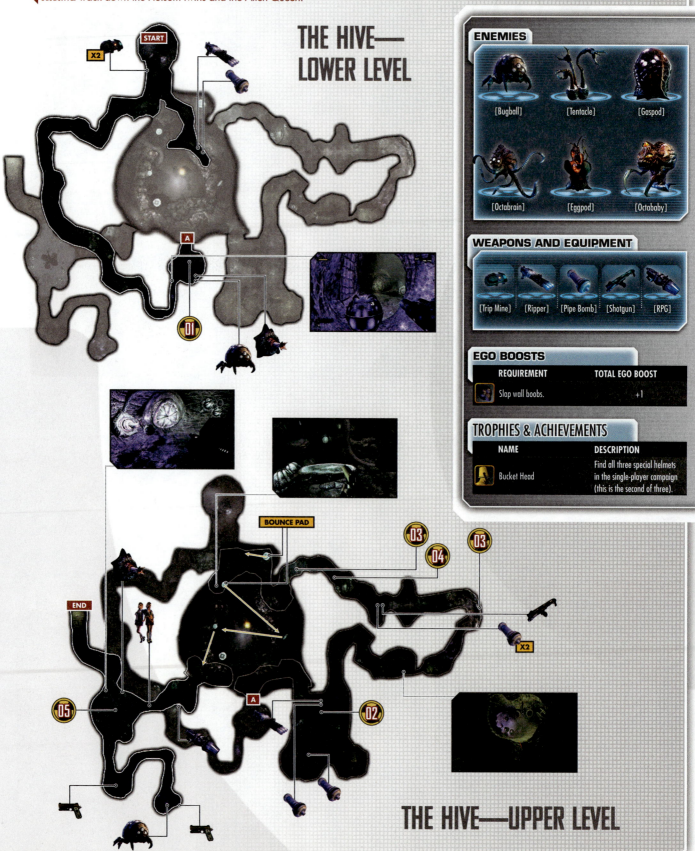

THE HIVE— LOWER LEVEL

THE HIVE—UPPER LEVEL

ENEMIES

[Bugball]   [Tentacle]   [Gaspod]

[Octabrain]   [Eggpod]   [Octababy]

WEAPONS AND EQUIPMENT

[Trip Mine]   [Ripper]   [Pipe Bomb]   [Shotgun]   [RPG]

EGO BOOSTS

REQUIREMENT	TOTAL EGO BOOST
Slap wall boobs.	+1

TROPHIES & ACHIEVEMENTS

NAME	DESCRIPTION
Bucket Head	Find all three special helmets in the single-player campaign (this is the second of three).

Deep underneath the Duke Dome, the intent of the aliens and the scale of their operation becomes more apparent. The Duke Dome has become their fortress, along with the caverns underneath it.

01 The aliens have begun sewing the world of humans in their own strange secretions, producing environments unlike anything terrestrial in origin. Breakable green membranes stretch across some passages. Some irising doors are ringed with tooth-like blockages, which must be opened by a glowing, blue Bugball...a socket near the toothy door will snare the Bugball and allow passage.

Toothed doors require a glowing Bugball to open. Bugballs also help light the way in the pitch-dark caves.

02 Once past the first sphincter-like doors, use Duke Vision and immediately search low and to the left. Look for a small passage to find some weaponry and a familiar helmet...

The tentacles are directed by seeking eyes. Shoot a tentacle to briefly disable just that tentacle. Shoot one of the eyes, however, to briefly disable all the tentacles it controls.

"That's one dead space marine."

You can't do anything for them.

03 This is your first glimpse of the actual plans of the aliens. It's a horrific sight—women are trapped in pods of alien design, while Pregnators forcefully impregnate some of them with alien parasites. In time, these parasites will grow so large and so violent that they will destroy the host and Octababies will emerge from the deceased female. A grotesque cycle.

Later, Eggpods will hatch into new Pregnators. Destroy the Eggpods before they hatch to avoid the possibility of more Pregnator pests.

04 Octabrains are a new type of enemy, higher up in alien hierarchy. These floating galactic invertebrates use their tremendous telepathic energy to hurl psychic blasts or toss objects from the environment. They will even use their kinetic powers to catch and return Pipe Bombs and RPG rockets!

Stick a Trip Mine to an Octabrain for a laugh.

Bounce Pads provide access to otherwise-unreachable heights. These contraptions allow leaps clear to the other side of the central chasm.

Bounce Pads don't require finesse; they will automatically transport Duke to the correct destination. You can even bounce Trip Mines and Pipe Bombs off them!

OCTABRAINS

Octabrains attack with a different approach than other enemies, so be mindful of this to avoid taking severe or fatal damage. Their primary attack is a psychic blast. They will launch this attack in front of Duke, so it's important to change speed and direction to avoid it. Most enemies attack by shooting directly at Duke, thereby turning strafing into a foolproof defense. Octabrains force you to strafe in a given direction just as a foe releases its energy blast, then immediately strafe in the opposite direction to make the blast miss and avoid the splash damage. On the other hand, you can simply shoot the Octabrain as it charges up the psychic blast. This will cause it to stop, reposition, and try again.

Occasionally, Octabrains will harness their powers and gather an object from the environment and toss it at Duke. Unlike the other attack, they will launch the object directly at Duke. So, strafing is good here again, but the force and velocity of their tosses with some objects make strafing a dicey proposition. Turn and sprint laterally or get behind cover. Some objects can also be destroyed with gunfire while in mid-air, if your aim is true. An Octabrain telekinetically controlling an object from the environment cannot be interrupted with attacks. Interrupting them works for their psychic blast, but not for their object-tossing.

05 Grind the Octababies underfoot for their devious act and proceed to the next chamber. If you still don't have the **Achievement/ Trophy** for stepping on little creatures, you will eventually. Bound babes in this part are on the verge of bursting, so kill them or risk dealing with a mess of new Octababies each time a host's lovely chest gives way.

The aliens must really have wanted to piss Duke off. Well, they got what they wanted.

There is a blocked door and socket leading north to the exit. Retrieve the Bugball from the south passage to open the way. Watch out when returning with the Bugball, as several Octabrains will attack. The RPG near the Holsom twins may seem appealing, but you might want to reconsider— Octabrains will hurl any rockets right back at Duke!

THE HIVE, PART 2

OBJECTIVE: Track down the Alien Queen.

THE HIVE

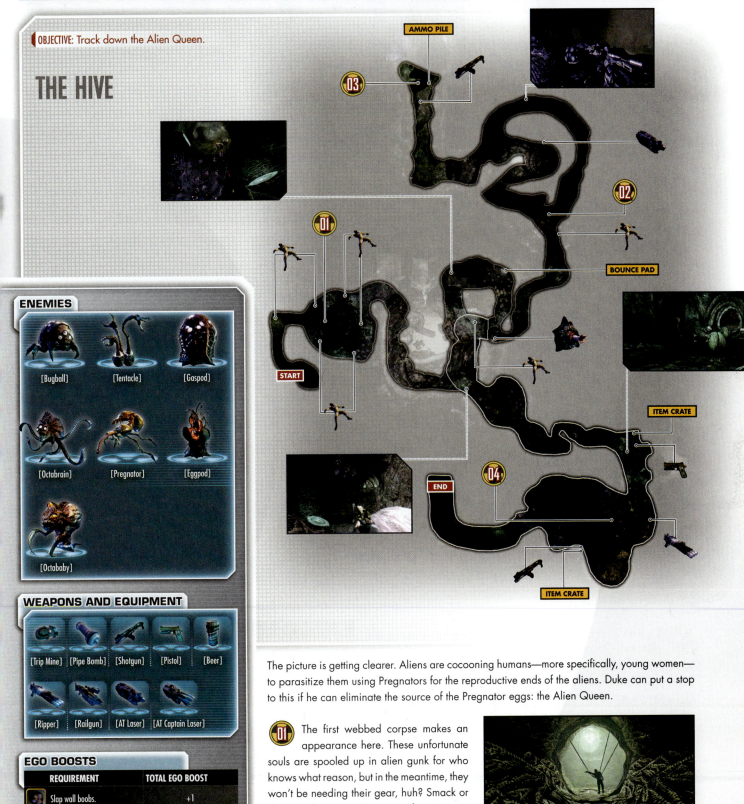

ENEMIES

[Bugball] [Tentacle] [Gaspod]

[Octabrain] [Pregnator] [Eggpod]

[Octababy]

WEAPONS AND EQUIPMENT

[Trip Mine] [Pipe Bomb] [Shotgun] [Pistol] [Beer]

[Ripper] [Railgun] [AT Laser] [AT Captain Laser]

EGO BOOSTS

REQUIREMENT	TOTAL EGO BOOST
Slap wall boobs.	+1

TROPHIES & ACHIEVEMENTS

NAME	DESCRIPTION
I Need a Towel	Get hit by 10 Pregnator bombs.

The picture is getting clearer. Aliens are cocooning humans—more specifically, young women—to parasitize them using Pregnators for the reproductive ends of the aliens. Duke can put a stop to this if he can eliminate the source of the Pregnator eggs: the Alien Queen.

01 The first webbed corpse makes an appearance here. These unfortunate souls are spooled up in alien gunk for who knows what reason, but in the meantime, they won't be needing their gear, huh? Smack or shoot each corpse piñata up to three times to snag spare weapons and equipment. After knocking around all the corpses, you should be filled to capacity with Pipe Bombs and Trip Mines and you'll have a choice pick of primary weapons. Note in particular the poor fellow who was carrying a Railgun.

109

02 You'll move on, exploiting Bounce Pads and eliminating Gaspods in a few places. The path to the south is blocked by a socket door, which requires a Bugball to open. The only way to go is north, so proceed that way and you'll find a spacious chamber that requires careful navigation.

Hair-raising jumps are required to ascend here. If you want an AT Captain Laser, check the bottom of the spiraling bone structure.

03 At the point furthest north, locate the glow of a Bugball just out of reach up the alien slopes. You'll also find an Ammo Pile and a Bounce Pad. Toss a Pipe Bomb off the pad and it will end up right next to the Bugball. Detonate the Pipe Bomb to make the Bugball roll down to Duke. Replenish your explosives at the Ammo Pile and get ready for quite a firefight.

Tossing Pipe Bombs off Bounce Pads is required for puzzles and combat scenarios at several points in the game.

On the way down the dark slope leading back to the spacious chamber, Duke will encounter four Octabrains. These fights all take place at close quarters, so you can easily toss a Trip Mine directly onto each Octabrain on the way down, if you want. Sticking a Trip Mine directly onto an Octabrain destabilizes its flight and sends it out of control. Calamari results.

Trip Mines kill Octabrains on contact.

Take caution when using Pipe Bombs against Octabrains—too late on the detonation or too close when it happens and this strategy will backfire.

Once inside the spacious chamber again, a trio of Octabrains will attack. Remember that Octabrains will suck in and then fling back tossed Pipe Bombs, but you can also use this to your advantage. Detonate a Pipe Bomb the instant the Octabrain sucks it in to turn the tables. Since three Octabrains attack together, you may get extra value out of Pipe Bombs thanks to splash damage. When the Pipe Bombs explode near the Octabrains, it will also destroy many of the Eggpod-like objects in the area that the Octabrains use as throwing weapons. When the threat is gone, push the Bugball further south to the socket.

04 Continue past the newly-opened door until Duke arrives at another large chamber. In this sectioned-off hive area, dozens of Eggpods surround several Podgirls and the whole mess is patrolled by Pregnators. The path to the west is blocked, so you'll have to kill about 10 Pregnators and an Octabrain to open the way.

THREE FOR THE PRICE OF ONE

The best place in the game to get the **Achievement/Trophy** for killing three enemies at once is here in this chamber. Toss a Pipe Bomb into a mess of Eggpods, Pregnators, and Octababies and set it off.

Pregnators fling goo bombs that deal damage and obscure Duke's vision.

Pregnators can pounce and grapple, searching for Duke's mouth with an unspeakable proboscis. A successful strength tap keeps the airway clear and makes the Pregnator dead.

CHAPTER 08:
QUEEN BITCH

KILLER QUEEN

OBJECTIVE: Kill the Alien Queen.

THE DUKE DOME INTERIOR

BOUNCE PAD

BOUNCE PAD

BOUNCE PAD

02

START

01

AMMO PILE

AMMO PILE

X3

ENEMIES

[Alien Queen]   [Pregnator]   [Octabrain]

WEAPONS AND EQUIPMENT

[RPG]   [Shotgun]   [Railgun]

[Ripper]   [Pipe Bomb]   [Trip Mine]

EGO BOOSTS

REQUIREMENT	TOTAL EGO BOOST
Punching bag.	+1
Slap wall boobs.	+1
Bicep curl.	+2
Bench press 600 pounds.	+3
Kill Alien Queen	+4

TROPHIES & ACHIEVEMENTS

NAME	DESCRIPTION
Full Body Tourettes (PS3); FBT (360)	Get knocked down 10 times.
I Need a Towel	Get hit by 10 Pregnator bombs.
Not Bad for a Human	Defeat the Alien Queen.

Here she is—the alien mother who has been producing all the loathsome Pregnator eggs. It's been a long time (not since the end of the episode "The Birth" in Duke Nukem 3D: Atomic Edition) since Duke has faced off against the brood mother for the Cycloid hordes. Let's knock out a chain of their family tree, shall we?

01 The way into the heart of the Duke Dome, where the Alien Queen is churning out her hideous offspring, is blocked from the inside. Looking through the office to the right of the door you can see the solution—if you can get explosives behind the doors. To the left of the door, alien secretions have tunneled a new hole in the wall, providing a view of a Bounce Pad. Toss a Pipe Bomb off this Bounce Pad, and the Pipe Bomb will end up just behind the barricade. If you run out of Pipe Bombs while attempting this, simply restock at the Ammo Pile in the office.

In the Duke Dome lobby, there are several weapons from which to choose. Pick up an RPG (remember that bosses are only susceptible to explosions) and another weapon to deal with lesser enemies while you focus on the boss. If you're going for the "Gunslinger" **Achievement**, remember to keep clutching Duke's golden pistol. Otherwise, you can take a shotgun or Railgun, depending on your preference. There's also a Ripper in the boss room.

EGO BOOSTS

Several **Ego boosts** are present here. If you missed them the first time, you can curl a dumbbell or pound a punching bag. Add at least 600 pounds to the barbell and you can accomplish an Ego-buffing bench press. Four hundred pounds of plates are next to the weight bench; the other 200 pounds are in a corner of the nearby office.

02 Step all the way forward into the Duke Dome proper to initiate the encounter with the Alien Queen. The Alien Queen is massive and heavily armored courtesy of the plates growing over much of her arms and head. Her only sensitive spots are her fleshy chest and face, which she normally protects with the harder portions of her body. To kill the Alien Queen, you must find a way to get her to expose herself so you can fire rockets into her softest parts.

ALIEN QUEEN

The most important weapons in this fight are Pipe Bombs and RPG rockets. You can refill Pipe Bombs at the Ammo Pile located dead center of the area, while an Ammo Crate allows you to refill RPG rounds on the left side. Trip Mines and the other weapon you're carrying only come into play while defending against the Alien Queen's servants.

The Queen guards her face and teats with her crab-like, rocky appendages. However, you can force aside her would-be wall by tossing Pipe Bombs off the Bounce Pads located on either side of the playing field. Detonate a thrown and bounced Pipe Bomb just after it disappears behind the Queen's wall of arms. This will cause her to reel briefly, just long enough to fire several RPG rockets at her chest and face. When she resorts to her defensive posture again, just use the same tactics.

Throw Pipe Bombs off the Bounce Pads to open up the Alien Queen's defenses.

With her chest exposed, the Alien Queen is vulnerable to RPG rockets.

The Queen will not attack until Duke strikes the first blow. After you've knocked aside her guard and fed her some RPG rounds, she'll begin retaliating. Her primary attack is a huge telekinetic blast that deals damage while knocking Duke down. The only way to avoid this attack is to be completely behind cover, out of the Queen's field of vision, when she unleashes the blast. Think of it as a supercharged version of the psychic blasts hurled by Octabrains.

The Queen will also use her arms and attempt to smash Duke. Sprint away from your current location when she's readying her smash to avoid it. Similarly, she will use her arms to smash Duke if he gets too close. There's no need to move forward until the end, so keep your distance. The Alien Queen will also spew out Pregnator eggs regularly, thereby unleashing another threat. Kill Pregnators as quickly as possible, before they become an overwhelming distraction.

Stay on the move and the arm smash shouldn't make contact.

Get behind cover to avoid the Queen's psychic roar.

Keep up the pace with rockets after the Queen completely lowers her guard, but watch out for Octabrains.

As she nears defeat, the Alien Queen goes on the offensive and forgoes defense altogether. She also stops summoning Pregnators and instead summons the real thing—full-grown Octabrains! Be very careful at this juncture. Although you need to use RPG rockets to inflict damage to the Queen, Octabrains make a habit of catching and throwing back RPG rounds! So try to kill any Octabrains that show up immediately, while avoiding the Queen's continued arm smashes and telekinetic blasts. Switch to peppering the Queen with more RPG rockets when no Octabrains are present.

Once the Alien Queen's health is totally depleted, she collapses. Quickly approach her mouth and win a strength tap to silence this filthy momma for good. Her calamitous death throes cause even more destruction in the Duke Dome and Duke himself is badly hurt in the aftermath...

CHAPTER 09:
DUKE NUKEM'S TITTY CITY

CANNONBALL RUN

"OUT OF THE FRYING PAN..."

Vegas is in ruins, but at least the mothership is down and the Lady Killer and Duke Burger are secure. Duke couldn't save all the babes, but perhaps he can still save the planet. The first order of business is to cover the distance between Las Vegas and the Hoover Dam, which the aliens are now using as a point of entry into Duke's world.

THE MIGHTY FOOT

THE MIGHTY FOOT, PART 1

OBJECTIVE: Secure a landing zone and begin heading toward Hoover Dam.

01

END

THE MIGHTY FOOT

02

START

ITEM CRATE

ENEMIES

[Pigcop]   [Pigcop Captain]   [Enforcer]

WEAPONS AND EQUIPMENT

[Pipe Bomb]

Finally, after an unexpected detour to Duke Burger, Duke has made it out of Las Vegas and is headed with the EDF toward Hoover Dam. The aliens have erected some sort of huge spire at the top of the dam and they're harnessing its immense hydroelectric power to generate a wormhole in the sky above Nevada and Arizona. Through this hole more aliens can pour through, making the loss of their mothership trivial.

You can't simply touch down on the dam, however. As an EDF soldier informs Duke, setting down close to Hoover Dam is off-limits because an alien Battlelord is shooting down anything that draws near. Instead, the EDF must set Duke down a short distance away from the Hoover Dam, meaning he'll need to travel the remainder of the way via his monster truck, the Mighty Foot.

01 Initially, Duke starts behind the helm of a grenade turret in an EDF gunship. Shell the highway below, as Pigcop Captains fire at the gunship with RPGs. After buzzing the highway, the EDF locate a solid landing zone near some buildings to the south, but the area is filled with Pigcops and Enforcers.

Like machine gun turrets, the gunship grenade turret will overheat and force a cool-down period if you just fire indiscriminately.

02 This wide-open area after the first big jump contains a downed EDF gunship. Take this brief respite to resupply with Pipe Bombs and primary weapons before attempting the second big jump. Next, proceed to the north, twisting through some valleys until the Mighty Foot reaches another jump. This one deposits Duke onto the highway.

Make a turbo jump from the south to reach the downed gunship.

Another turbo jump takes you over a gorge leaving the gunship area.

This is not a conventional highway on-ramp, but it'll do in a pinch.

03 The Vegas highways are even less friendly now than before the alien apocalypse. Instead of honking motorists and taxicab drivers jockeying for position, there are now Pigcops standing amongst abandoned cars ready to blow away anyone foolish enough to take the freeway.

Duke Nukem isn't just anyone, though, and the Mighty Foot is no ordinary car. Continue to cruise down the highway, running down foes, passing through a couple of tunnels, and making two big jumps. Eventually, though, the Mighty Foot will run out of gas. Now it's time for Duke to search the local area for a Gas can.

Up ahead, the highway has partially disintegrated and a crashed EDF gunship blocks the way across the only strip of road remaining. An EDF Ammo Crate indicates that something will be happening soon... Scoop up one of the Railguns and approach the barricade facing the far side of the highway to spot a truck barreling toward the gap. The truck crashes, offloading a cargo of several Pigcops.

Dispensing with the Pigcops should prove easy. Utilize the gap separating Duke from the pork and let 'em have it with the Railgun.

140

Next, an alien dropship swoops in and drops three bombs nearby before offloading a berserk Pigcop and two Enforcers on the far side of the chasm. The bombs, instead of having the intended effect of killing Duke, knock the crashed gunship off the highway. The way is now clear! Restock at the Ammo Crate, then cross the remaining strip of road to the other side. Note that the Enforcers here will drop their guns when killed, if you'd like an Enforcer Gun to tote around.

Dispose of the Pigcops that emerge from the crashed semi and let the alien bombs clear the way.

A LITTLE "BOOST"

There's only one building to explore here—the Hoover Dam Bypass Security Station. Before heading in that direction, though, proceed to the opposite end of the highway and check out the observation binoculars to gain an **Ego boost**. Next, bash open the padlock on the gate leading to the back of the security station. The door inside is blocked by boards, so hop on top of the nearby cable spindles, then drop into the security station via the windows in the roof. The Gas can required to refuel the Mighty Foot is here, along with a few other items of interest—some equipment supplies, a phone message (for the "Call Waiting" **Achievement/Trophy**) and two **Ego boosts** (look at the picture on one of the computers and toss one of the developer Frisbees).

With the Mighty Foot refueled and ready to rock, it's time to make a couple of jumps past the security station and further on down the road. Two alien fighters strafe the highway with laser bombs, though, knocking out large stretches of road. You must maneuver and deftly jump around the mess left behind.

CHAPTER 13:
GHOST TOWN

DUKE'S YOUR HUCKLEBERRY

OBJECTIVE: Continue progress toward Hoover Dam.

GHOST TOWN & OUTLYING AREAS

GHOST TOWN PROPER

ENEMIES

[Pigcop] [Pigcop Captain] [Rats]

[Enforcer] [Assault Commander]

WEAPONS AND EQUIPMENT

[Beer] [Shotgun] [Ripper] [Pipe Bomb] [Gas can]

EGO BOOSTS

REQUIREMENT	TOTAL EGO BOOST
Microwave something. (Not available in PS3 European version of the game.)	+2
Read Funbags magazine.	+1

TROPHIES & ACHIEVEMENTS

NAME	DESCRIPTION
Dead Useful	Kill 10 aliens with environmental explosives.

The scorched badlands around Vegas weren't the most hospitable place in the world even before the aliens attacked, but at this point it's positively hellish. What settlements and towns existed before have been overrun and the residents either killed or changed into Pigcops. Meanwhile, the wormhole above the dam is clearly visible. Duke must travel through a seemingly-abandoned town or two in the quest to reach the dam.

 The beginning of Ghost Town features several large jumps, including one that takes Duke through a wooden watchtower with a waiting Pigcop Captain. In the valley below, you'll find an old village devoid of human presence but swimming in Pigcops. The Mighty Foot can make short work of them.

You can enter a trailer atop a small hill on the west side by jumping on top of the tractor behind it, then jumping onto the roof. Inside, you'll find an Item Crate and a microwave. The microwave is useful in case you're still missing that **Ego boost**. For appropriate cuisine for the microwave, look no further than one of the rats scurrying about the trailer floor. (As noted previously, this is not an option in the PS3 European version of the game.)

LOOT AWAY

In previous Mighty Foot sections, enemies didn't usually drop their weapons when killed. During Ghost Town, they will. So feel free to take the RPG off the Pigcop Captain who was unfortunate enough to be watching guard in that wooden tower!

 After two more jumps, Duke arrives in the deserted town of Morningwood just as a couple of alien dropships vacate the premises. At first glance, there appears to be no enemies... but the truth is they're inside the saloon just waiting for Duke to step into the barrel of main street. The Mighty Foot once again runs out of fuel, so it's time to find another Gas can.

OBSERVING THE SABBATH

Before venturing into town, which triggers a lengthy battle against Morningwood's usurpers, take a moment to visit the quaint little church. Inside you'll find a dead Enforcer and his weapons. Search carefully amongst the smashed pews to find some unusual reading material, considering the location. Scope the magazine for an **Ego boost**!

When you're ready to fight, saunter down the main drag. Pigcops will flood into the street, starting from the saloon on the right and later from buildings on the far-left side of the street. Plenty of explosive barrels of TNT line the streets, so use them for progress toward the "Dead Useful" **Achievement/Trophy**, if you're missing it.

After killing several Pigcops, a shielded Enforcer pops open the attic door to the bar at the end of the road. Meanwhile, two more Pigcops hop down from a building just to the left of the barn.

THE IMMOVABLE OBJECT

How can an Enforcer be a tougher nut to crack? Having a full-body frontal shield might do the trick. The aliens seem to agree, because this particular Enforcer (those here and throughout the rest of the game) will sometimes protect themselves from all frontal assaults by using a huge shield.

The best way to crack such a shield is with explosive firepower—Pipe Bombs, Trip Mines, RPG rockets, Enforcer Gun bursts, and Devastator rounds all work well. The environment may help, too, depending on your location. Here in Morningwood, just grab one of the explosive barrels and toss it toward the shielded Enforcer.

Dust the Enforcer and his friends and they'll be replaced by yet another duo of normal Pigcops and a Pigcop Captain. As usual, the Pigcop Captain sports an RPG and fires down onto the street from the barn, the same spot the Enforcer occupied. After putting down these foes, the big boss finally appears. An Assault Commander smashes his way out of the barn, flanked by two berserk Pigcops.

There's no Shrink Ray handy to make this fight more manageable, but there's plenty of room to maneuver in the street.

03 The Assault Commander's grand entrance left the front doors of the barn demolished. Inside the barn, you need to find the Gas can. In order to do this, you need to move the hanging palette to the center, allowing you to lower a raised ladder, before moving the palette back to its original position.

Relative to the entrance, the Gas can is in the back-right corner, one floor up.

STEP #1: Climb the ladder on the right side and operate the crank to move the palette from the back of the barn to the middle. Jump onto the palette and then to the other side.

STEP #2: On the other side, turn left and climb the ladder to the attic roost. Turn another crank here to lower a ladder.

STEP #3: With ladders extending down from the attic roost to the walkways on both sides, return to the original crank, and move the first palette to the back of the barn. Now, climb up to the attic roost, descend the other side, and run all the way to the back. Hop onto the palette and then cross over to the Gas can.

With Gas can in hand, it's time to return to the Mighty Foot. On the way out of the barn, Duke notices a departing alien dropship. Did it offload reinforcements? Of course it did! Defeat the Pigcops that rush into the street and then gas up the truck.

SEARCH FOR GOODIES!

Before you use the Mighty Foot to blast through the barn, take a minute to explore the rest of the town. Almost everything is destructible (except the main buildings) and you can find some supplies tucked away in some areas.

It's normally not too difficult to reach Hoover Dam by road—until recently I-93 passed directly over the dam—but the highways are largely bombed out. Now it requires frequent off-road detours into the rocky, largely uninhabited and inhospitable lands surrounding the dam.

01 After a rip-roaring jump off a precipice into a shallow lake, Duke runs into a Pigcop and his captain using a billboard as a lookout. As it turns out, this billboard overlooks a long, unbroken stretch of highway that will take you much closer to the dam. It may seem like there's no way forward at first, but that's because the billboard will serve as a ramp. First, knock out one of the billboard's flimsy wooden supports to knock it down. Next, back up and boost forward over the slanted billboard to reach the highway.

02 While cruising on the highway, it quickly becomes apparent that Duke isn't alone. Pigcops have commandeered several flatbed trucks and are patrolling the road, ready to toss explosive barrels at any humans. While advancing along the highway, you must negotiate past these trucks as they swerve left and right to impede your progress. Also, some Pigcops will toss barrels at the Mighty Foot. All told, you must pass three trucks to continue.

Steer left and right along the road to avoid the tossed barrels.

When a truck begins to swerve one way, quickly boost past it on the opposite side before it can do any damage.

An alien fighter bombs the end of the highway, forcing Duke off the road again.

03 After the aliens force Duke back into the mountains by bombing the thoroughfare, alien dropships will start dropping off more Pigcops and then bombing to cause rockslides. Don't worry about the Pigcops and instead focus on the falling boulders. Either running into a boulder with force, or being hit by a boulder, causes very heavy damage to Duke. Two boulder strikes in close proximity can easily kill him. Avoid the obstacles and continue toward the final jump before the Mighty Foot runs out of gas yet again. What, again?

You can continue to plow through Pigcops and other enemies that get in the way.

Be very careful when approaching boulders. Duke can't withstand multiple strikes back-to-back.

After a final jump through a Pigcop Captain, the Mighty Foot runs out of gas again.

HIGHWAY BATTLE, PART 2

OBJECTIVE: Find more fuel for the Mighty Foot and continue onward.

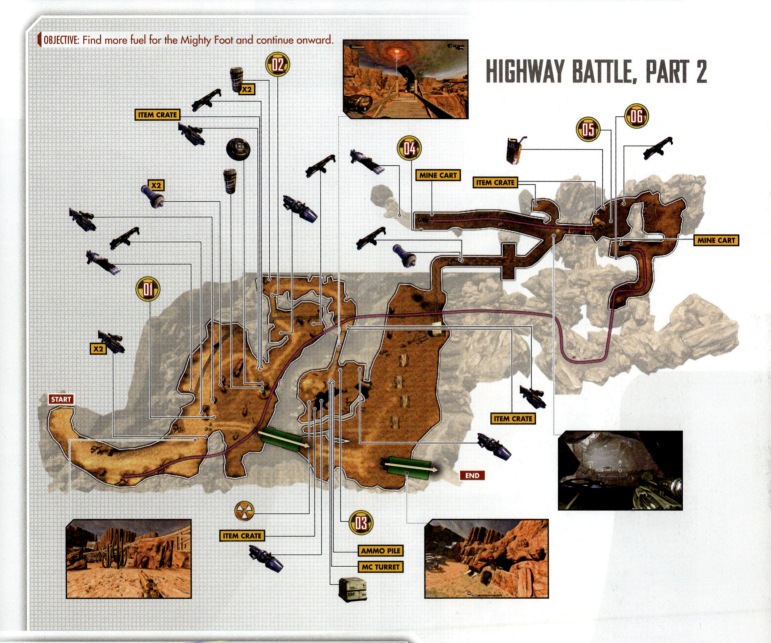

HIGHWAY BATTLE, PART 2

START

END

ITEM CRATE
X2
MINE CART
ITEM CRATE
MINE CART
ITEM CRATE
AMMO PILE
MC TURRET

ENEMIES

[Pigcop] [Pigcop Captain]

[Octababy] [Pregnator]

WEAPONS AND EQUIPMENT

[Railgun] [Ripper] [Beer] [Holoduke]

[Shotgun] [Pipe Bomb] [RPG] [Gas can]

TROPHIES & ACHIEVEMENTS

NAME	DESCRIPTION
Big Guns Big Ships	Blow up 5 enemy gunships or dropships.
Tosser in the Literal Sense (PS3); Downtown Barrel Beatdown (Xbox 360)	Kill 10 aliens with tossed objects.

The Mighty Foot runs out of gas near Anderson Mine, an area close to Hoover Dam. Duke must set out on foot to find more gas. At first, the search involves battling north toward and through a pass that eventually allows access to the turret the Pigcops will use to harass Duke right from the outset.

01 This area is full of wide-open areas and big firefights. Duke will be assaulted by multiple Pigcops, both up close and from far away. Initially, one Pigcop opens fire with a machine-gun turret from across a chasm, while three Pigcops leap across to get closer. Kill the Pigcop manning the turret from here (see screenshot; rely on the Railgun in this scenario), but note that replacement Pigcops will arrive.

After disposing of a gunner, just wait and snipe the replacements.

Take out all four turret gunners and no more replacements will appear until you progress further. As you approach a dilapidated house and wrecked truck, two more armed Pigcops attack along with a berserk Pigcop. Finally, just before the narrow pass that loops around to a bridge, a shotgun-packing Pigcop appears backed by another pistol-wielding comrade.

HOW DUKE LEARNED TO STOP WORRYING AND LOVE THE BOMB

The wrecked EDF gunship isn't sporting typical ordinance. Instead, it's outfitted with a bona fide nuclear warhead! You'd be advised against letting a stray round strike the red tip of this payload, unless you'd like to kill absolutely everything on the map—including Duke! Oh well, you may as well shoot the bomb once, just to check it out.

HIGHWAY BATTLE BEER CRAWL

There's nothing like guzzling a few cold beers in the great outdoors to bolster the spirit. This section contains some of the game's largest gun battles yet. This can be quite harrowing on higher difficulty

Don't miss these useful supplies when passing by this truck!

settings, where enemies can handle take more damage while Duke can absorb less. Luckily, several beers are littered about the area.

The first is located just prior to a ruined truck chassis (hidden in the bed of this same truck is a Holoduke—don't miss it!). There are two more beers just after cresting the next passageway through the mountains. Remember that you can only carry one beer at a time, so don't let them go to waste.

There's no reason not to keep Duke lubricated with liquid courage through the first stretch of this area. At the very least, you can down a couple, then save the last one for later. It may all depend on your ability and the difficulty setting.

02 Upon entering the narrow pass up north, two things will occur. First, Pigcop reinforcements will arrive behind Duke and man the machine-gun turret. As before, up to four Pigcops will take turns on the turret. At the same time, a Pigcop brigade will emerge from the channel. Two armored Pigcops with Rippers and two more pistol-toting Pigcops lead this attack. Keep a rocky cluster between Duke and the turret operators while fighting back the Pigcop charge.

ONE SHOT, ONE KILL. UNLESS YOU MISS.

The Railgun is a superb weapon, but its immense strength and powerful zoom come with a mild price: no weapon is thrown off course more than the Railgun if you get hit just before or while squeezing the trigger.

Taking a hit while firing the Railgun at long range basically guarantees that your shot will miss its intended target. Compensate for this by strafing or crouching behind cover in between shots. For each follow-up shot, step out or rise from cover, line up your shot quickly and fire, then duck behind cover again. This is also a great way to compensate for the frequent reloads required of the Railgun.

03 Once across the bridge, Duke finally arrives at the site of the downed EDF gunship. However, as a half-dozen Pigcops will attack from the east followed by an alien gunship. The Pigcops can be easily dispatched by an EDF gun emplacement, but not the gunship.

The ramshackle houses across the gap are loaded with red explosive barrels.

The bay of the crashed EDF gunship provides an ideal place to take cover from the alien gunship,

It's time to swap out the Railgun for an RPG and harness that firepower to bring down the alien bird. An Ammo Crate and Ammo Pile serve to keep Duke stocked on weapons while fending off the gunship. Once the gunship is destroyed, the wreckage of the fallen ship creates a ramp leading to the plateau adjacent the machine-gun turret site

04 After entering the mine (a crowbar would come in handy, eh?), Duke comes to another split in the ground that prevents access to a chamber that contains Gas cans. Head up the passage and locate a mine cart filled with three heavy blue barrels. Remove the barrels so the cart is light enough to push up the hill and into position. Get into the cart and pull the lever to release it down the hill.

After pushing the mine cart into place, jump inside and pull the lever to release it down the ramp and across the gap into the Gas can chamber.

05 Once Duke grabs a Gas can, several Octababies and Pregnators enter the chamber. While fighting these pests, the Pregnators will eventually damage the scaffolding in the chamber, allowing Duke to clamber up and out once the little aliens are all dead.

The scaffolding buckles enough to allow upward passage only after Duke squishes several of the Pregnators.

06 Another mine cart allows Duke a grand exit from the mine. This cart ride conveniently transports him back to the Mighty Foot and a couple of discourteous Pigcop valets. Afterward, it's simply a matter of gassing up the ride, then making a couple of small turbo jumps. Remember to collect any supplies or weapons in the outdoor area before leaving!

CHAPTER 15:

DAM TOP

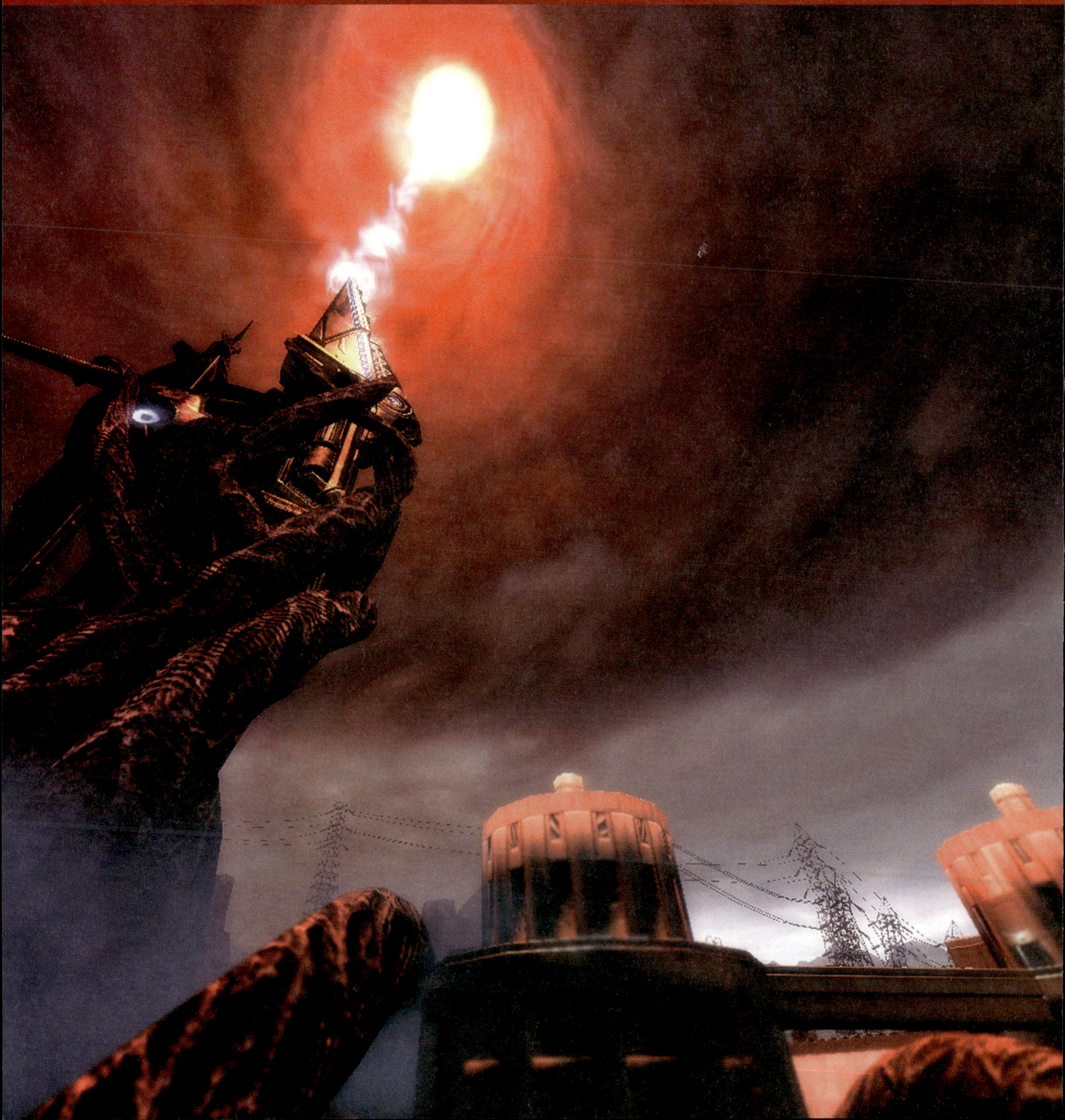

TAKING DOWN THE BATTLELORD

OBJECTIVE: Clear aliens from the top of the Hoover Dam, so allied forces can safely assault.

DAM TOP #1

START

01

A

DAM TOP #2

04 — ITEM CRATE — AMMO PILE

03 — LADDER

A

ITEM CRATE

END

ITEM CRATE

05

ITEM CRATE X2

ENEMIES

[Pigcop]	[Pigcop Captain]	[Enforcer]
[Assault Trooper Captain]	[Battlelord]	

WEAPONS AND EQUIPMENT

[Pipe Bomb]	[Trip Mine]	[Holoduke]
[Railgun]	[RPG]	[Enforcer Gun]

EGO BOOSTS

REQUIREMENT	TOTAL EGO BOOST
Throw paper airplane.	+1
Kill Hoover Dam Battlelord.	+4

TROPHIES & ACHIEVEMENTS

NAME	DESCRIPTION
A Good Dam Fight	Defeat the Battlelord on the Hoover Dam.

The Hoover Dam is finally within spitting distance. Only one stretch of dangerous driving remains before arrival, then the priority is to make it safe for EDF arrival. As a soldier noted a while back, an alien Battlelord atop the dam is making it impossible for airborne units to get close. Perhaps Duke should have a word with him?

The aliens continue to track Duke in the Mighty Foot, but they don't attack right away.

01 Duke is approaching the dam from the backside now, racing along Lake Mead. The rugged slalom course is mostly uneventful at first, save for the spectacular scenery of the alien's strange wormhole tower.

About halfway to the dam, several large boulders hurtle down the slopes toward the Mighty Foot. Although it may be mostly indestructible, big rocks are the Mighty Foot's Kryptonite.

You can afford one solid blow or two in a row, even on "Damn, I'm Good" difficulty, but you can't take three consecutive hard hits from rocks.

02 The crew of the alien gunship will attempt to take matters into their own hands, opening fire at the Mighty Foot. This is no time to stop, so put the pedal to the metal and rush onward before the gunship causes too much damage.

Soon, Duke's truck and the alien gunship will join the famous "Cosmic Ray Research" B-29 in a cold, watery tomb.

03 The aliens decide to hover just over the last jump the Mighty Foot will ever take. Here we see how truly tough Duke's favorite ride is, before it sinks into the drink along with the alien gunship wreckage.

Naturally, Duke bails from the doomed truck. Surface by holding the "Jump" button and locate the nearby ladder. Finally, the Hoover Dam! And Duke arrives just in time to get chewed out by the P.O.T.U.S. before he courageously flees the scene.

He's not very grateful, is he?

04 Continue on to access the main span of the Hoover Dam. Reuniting with Dylan is just like old times. Dylan will fight fiercely alongside Duke, with a strong gun and stronger language. The goal here is simple: clear the top of the dam.

"Good to f@$&in' see ya, Duke!"

The span has become the frontline in the battle of the EDF against the Cycloid invasion. You must fight several waves of Pigcops and Enforcers to reach the other side of the span. Before taking the fight to the aliens, though, locate the Holoduke tucked into the nearby Item Crate, but don't use it yet—it will be much more valuable against the upcoming boss.

Unload heavily on the shielded Enforcers to break their shields and expose them to damage.

Heavy munitions and Ammo Crates are readily available, so swap out your weapons accordingly. At the very least, make sure you have a fully-loaded RPG in tow, along with full stocks of Trip Mines and Pipe Bombs.

HOLODUKE HIJINKS

There's a very good reason why you should pick up the Holoduke and hang on to it until the boss fight. If you reach the boss checkpoint with the Holoduke in reserve but then die, then all the ammo and items in the area will reset when you reload the checkpoint and you'll still keep the reserve Holoduke! That means this area contains, in effect, two Holodukes. In fact, you could just die on purpose upon getting the boss checkpoint, ensuring that you have two Holodukes to use from the get-go!

DAMN, I'M GOOD...WELL, I'D BETTER BE.

At this part, the game's difficulty skews much harder for the "Come Get Some" and "Damn, I'm Good" difficulties, but especially for "Damn, I'm Good" where a direct Railgun shot won't kill a lowly Pigcop!

Starting with the ascent to the top of the dam, more enemies will attack at once, and in harder varieties (more fully-berserk Pigcops, shielded Enforcers, Pigcop Captains, and so on). You need to rely more on supplies and planning to finish off firefights. Hold on to Beers and Holodukes especially, as these can easily spell the difference between victory and defeat against multiple hardened foes.

THE MAN WITH THE GOLDEN GUN, ONGOING

If you're going for the "Gunslinger" **Achievement/Trophy**, then up until now you should have carried the golden M1911 pistol (first acquired in the Duke Cave) through every chapter. The pistol is normally a very serviceable weapon, but here it loses its punch. The Battlelord shrugs off bullets like a human shrugs off sugar ants, and you don't have time to play marksman lining up pistol shots against his Assault Trooper Captain escorts. So during the fight, swap the golden pistol for an Enforcer Gun or RPG and remember where you leave it. That way, you can retrieve it after the Battlelord falls.

One caveat, though: do not swap the golden pistol out for another weapon until after the Battlelord appears and you get the checkpoint for the boss fight! If you swap the pistol out before that checkpoint, you run the risk of losing the pistol forever if you die against the Battlelord.

05 The Battlelord appears at the end of the roadway and tosses its titanic gun on top of an EDF soldier, then climbs onto the dam. The Battlelord is accompanied by a flight of Assault Trooper Captains. At any given time, two captains will attack alongside the Battlelord— kill them and replacements will arrive. Luckily, Dylan will handle them although he will roam around a bit. Dylan is impervious to damage during this battle, so the more enemy attention he can capture, the better.

If the Assault Trooper Captains are focused on Dylan, ignore them. You have enough to worry about.

BATTLELORD

The Battlelord will primarily attack by firing its machine gun.

Although this Battlelord looks identical to the one Duke felled at the end of "Vegas in Ruin," this one is much tougher. Not only is the battlefield much narrower and less conducive to avoiding damage, but this Battlelord can take more damage. Duke needs to bring this brute to its knees for a strength tap challenge not once, but twice, to win the fight.

At the start, the Battlelord will remain near the crashed school bus (which contains an **Ego-boosting** paper airplane) at the back of the dam's roadway. If you approach, the boss will unleash a stomp attack and if you're in its field of vision, it will fire its gun, but it won't give chase yet.

You may have some entirely safe havens from which to pepper the Battlelord with rockets while he can't retaliate. Here, Duke is firing just over the top of a tipped police car.

The Assault Trooper Captains will almost certainly focus on Dylan. If you don't have an RPG, then grab one! An Enforcer Gun is a great weapon to pair with the RPG for this fight. The RPG allows Duke to fire at the Battlelord from across the span of the dam, while the Enforcer Gun can take out Assault Trooper Captains. The Enforcer Gun is also great when the Battlelord gets close enough for the missiles to lock onto the boss (although on higher difficulties, one of your prime directives is to avoid getting too close to the Battlelord if at all possible).

You can point the Enforcer Gun in the general direction of a nearby Assault Trooper Captain, then fire a single missile burst. Voila, a dead foe almost every time!

For most of the Battlelord's first health bar, he'll remain at the end of the dam, essentially serving as a colossal turret. Take this time to set a trap or two; utilize the presence of the truck and place Trip Mines neaby, high enough so that Duke can run underneath them, but in a perfect position for the Battlelord to set them off when he finally gives chase.

Remember to set traps before the Battlelord starts moving. Don't use Pipe Bombs or fresh Trip Mines once it's set up, as this will cause your explosives to despawn.

Here, kitty kitty...

When you're ready, take up a distant position near an EDF Ammo Crate and start unloading RPG rockets at the Battlelord. Once the Battlelord has only about two-fifths of its first health bar remaining, it starts moving forward. In addition to the machine gun, the Battlelord will start firing blue homing mortars. These mortars pose a threat even when Duke is completely shielded behind cover, so be ready to sprint laterally to avoid an incoming blue shell.

When the first health bar is depleted, the Battlelord will fall to its knees. Rush up and climb onto the Battlelord's head to trigger a strength tap challenge. Succeed, and Duke will tear out one of the Battlelord's horns before burying it in the monster's right eye. Well, there's still one eye left!

You must deplete the health bar another time, but this time the Battlelord will be more aggressive with its attack style. Consider using a Holoduke just as the brute recovers from Duke's first impromptu eye exam and unload everything you have right as the second health bar appears. Using the tip from "Holoduke Hijinks," you can immediately grab and activate a second Holoduke once the first one disappears, even if you entered the chapter with no Holodukes in reserve!

Bring the Battlelord to its knees twice and win both strength tap challenges to finish this intense battle. As the boss reels in pain, pummel the boss's groin to finish the job. Now, it's just a matter of rappelling down the side of Hoover Dam to gain entry into the interior. The final act of this alien drama is soon underway...

RECLAMATION

"AMERICA!"

The aliens came for our chicks. Well, they got some, sadly, but their mothership and queen were both destroyed. Despite the destruction of their transportation and their brood mother, the Cycloid can still perpetuate their presence. They're using the Hoover Dam, one of the great marvels of North American engineering, to power a wormhole through which they can travel. Well, Duke is finally at the dam. It's time to clean house!

THE SHRUNK MACHINE

THE SHRUNK MACHINE, PART 1

OBJECTIVE: Clean out the infested entryway to Hoover Dam.

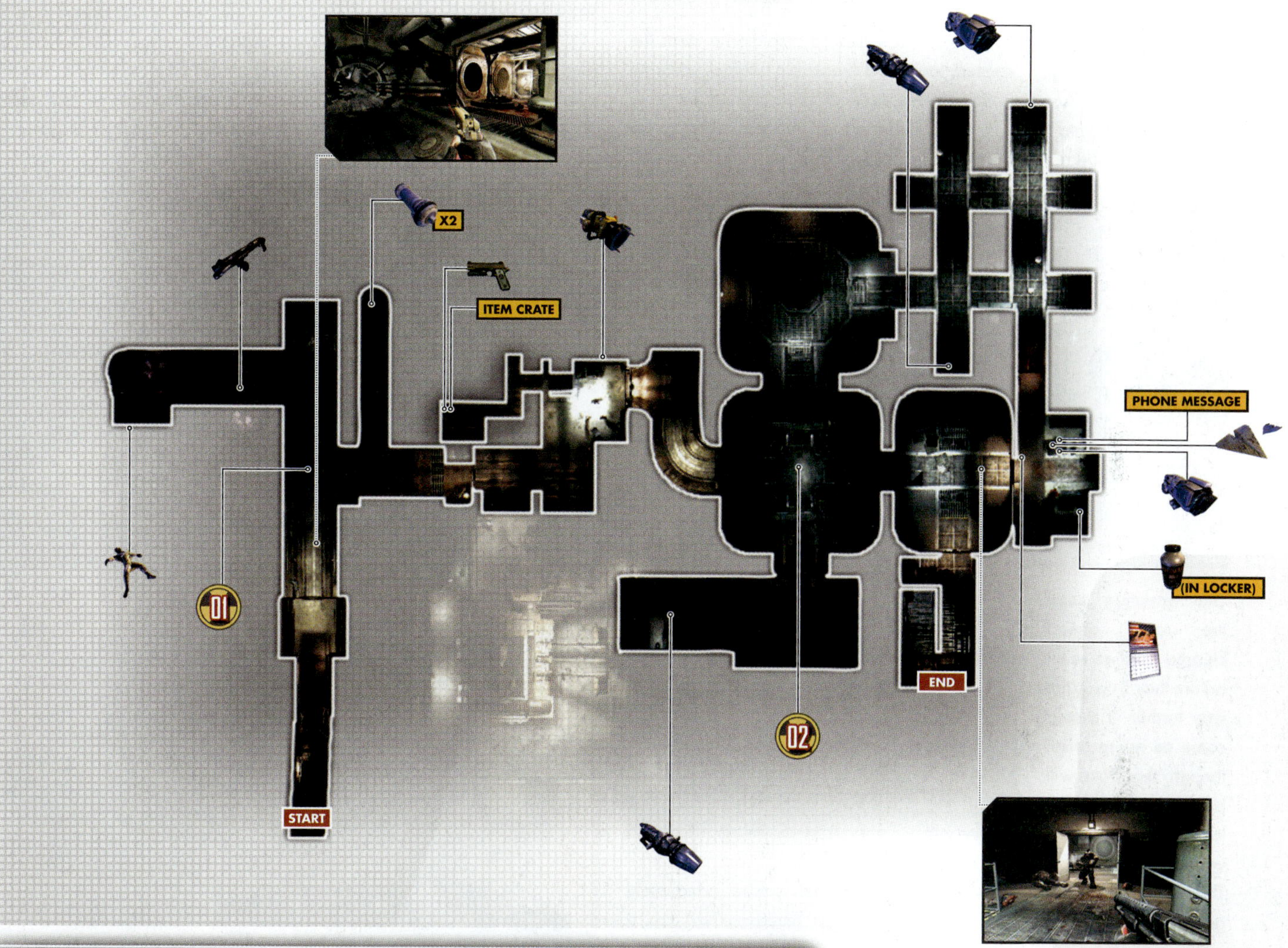

THE SHRUNK MACHINE, PART 1

X2

ITEM CRATE

PHONE MESSAGE

(IN LOCKER)

01

02

END

START

ENEMIES

[Tentacle]

[Octababy]

[Pigcop]

[Enforcer]

WEAPONS AND EQUIPMENT

[RPG]

[Steroids]

[Trip Mine]

[Shotgun]

[Pipe Bomb]

[Freeze Ray]

[Holoduke]

[Enforcer Gun]

EGO BOOSTS

REQUIREMENT	TOTAL EGO BOOST
Throw paper airplane.	+1
Look at wall calendar.	+1

TROPHIES & ACHIEVEMENTS

NAME	DESCRIPTION
Call Waiting	Listen to all phone messages.
I Need a Date	Look at every picture in the wall calendar.

The top of the dam is cleared now that the Battlelord is dead. Duke still doesn't know what the play is for dealing with the dam itself, though. For now, the goal is to track down General Graves.

 01 The left path from the start holds considerable supplies, so stock up if need be. Watch out for the Tentacles; shoot the eye on the left wall to buy some time to knock the corpse piñata around for an RPG, Steroids, and a Trip Mine. Shoot the eye again to get back out safely.

To the right, some workmen are trying to convince a soldier to clear the room ahead. Before you proceed, look for a breakable padlock securing a chain-link gate. Bust the lock and then the floor grate behind the gate, then duck down into the darkness and fend off a few Octababies in the crawlspace to find a Holoduke inside an Item Crate.

02 The infested room ahead, which is filled with Pigcops, is divided into quadrants. Upon first entering the room, several Pigcops will attack in the first wave (an assortment of both berserk and firearm-packing pork). Afterward, more Pigcops appear in the fourth of the quadrant that has a second-floor catwalk.

After eliminating all the Pigcops, return to the first quadrant, but be warned that two Enforcers will bash down a previously-locked door. When all of the baddies in the room are dead, a workman will open the way downstairs to the next segment.

Just keep moving in the dark vents behind the padlock, grab the Holoduke, and get right back out.

This hallway is a great place to hole up with the Freeze Ray and take down the first wave of foes. Enter the rooms to trigger the Pigcop attack and then retreat. Wait for them to round the corner one or two at a time, then freeze and smash.

The workmen need the room ahead cleared of alien scum before they'll open the way further. It should come as no surprise, though, that Duke will be in charge of this task instead of the unarmed EDF soldier.

Little skittish there, trooper? Take the Freeze Ray and do the EDF's job for them. Same s#!%, different day.

The Freeze Ray presents a new toy here. When you're adequately geared up, enter the room.

It's impossible to bait a couple of the Pigcops on the catwalk into following you down a dark hallway. When you finally go after them, watch out for a plethora of Pipe Bombs from above.

ICE TO MEET YOU

The Freeze Ray is a unique weapon that proves to be invaluable in close-range conflicts. This gun projects a short-range beam of icy energy, which deals a particular type of damage. We'll call this "ice damage." Once ice damage has built up to a certain amount, the enemy doesn't die—he is simply frozen solid! Now you can perform an execution to refill Duke's Ego. A melee attack or a shot from another firearm will also exterminate the enemy, although without the Ego recharge bonus.

Everybody chill.

The Freeze Ray cannot "run out" of ammo. Instead, it recharges freeze potential over time. If you're on-target with the beam, you can usually freeze four to five enemies in rapid succession before the Freeze Ray will require some "cool down" time. In the meantime, switch to another primary weapon while the Freeze Ray recharges.

Even Enforcers aren't immune to the Freeze Ray.

When the coast is clear, the workmen will open the way downstairs and onward. Before proceeding, though, check out the wall calendar and the paper airplane in the office to get **Ego boosts**. Listen to the phone message for progress toward an **Achievement/Trophy**, then grab the Steroids and resupply before moving onward.

THE SHRUNK MACHINE, PART 2

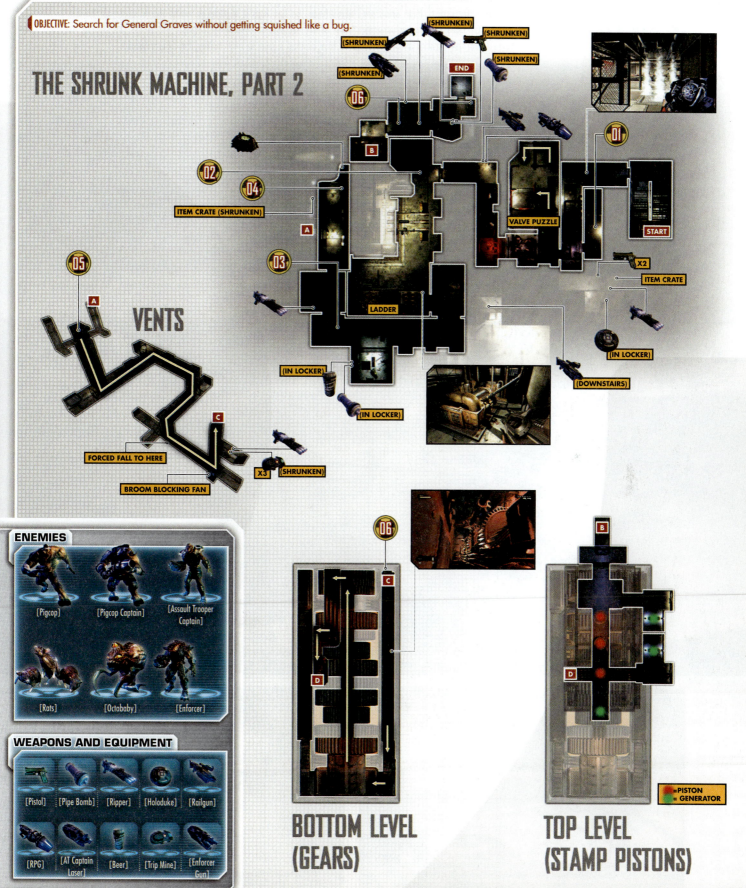

OBJECTIVE: Search for General Graves without getting squished like a bug.

THE SHRUNK MACHINE, PART 2

(SHRUNKEN)
(SHRUNKEN)
(SHRUNKEN)
(SHRUNKEN)
(SHRUNKEN)
END
06
B
02
04
ITEM CRATE (SHRUNKEN)
A
03
LADDER
01
VALVE PUZZLE
START
X2
ITEM CRATE
(IN LOCKER)
(DOWNSTAIRS)

05
A
VENTS
(IN LOCKER)
(IN LOCKER)
FORCED FALL TO HERE
BROOM BLOCKING FAN
X3 (SHRUNKEN)
C

06
C
B
D
D

ENEMIES

[Pigcop] [Pigcop Captain] [Assault Trooper Captain]
[Rats] [Octababy] [Enforcer]

WEAPONS AND EQUIPMENT

[Pistol] [Pipe Bomb] [Ripper] [Holoduke] [Railgun]
[RPG] [AT Captain Laser] [Beer] [Trip Mine] [Enforcer Gun]

BOTTOM LEVEL
(GEARS)

= PISTON
= GENERATOR

TOP LEVEL
(STAMP PISTONS)

The workmen have opened the way to an area outfitted with a heavy industrial machine, the gears deep in its belly powering stamp press pistons at the top. Traveling through this place eventually requires careful navigation inside this machine. Finally, there's a boss of a different kind waiting at the end...

Just as the alien infestation had spread through human structures elsewhere, so too has it started to warp the interior of the dam. The way forward is blocked in several places by odd fences constructed from alien secretions. None of Duke's weapons can harm the odd alien structures. Luckily, though, it's possible to redirect the flow of steam through a few busted pipes to melt away the blockages.

Run past the first steam vents when it's safe, then turn this valve slightly to melt away the first blockage. You don't have to turn it up all the way, just a single tick will do.

After clearing the first blockage, pop on Duke Vision before proceeding to find a hidden supply closet!

Past the first blockage sits another, but the solution isn't quite so simple this time. Although the steam can also be vented here, the pipes must first be repositioned so the steam is output over the alien growths.

STEP #1: *The pressure locks on a couple of pipes must be released and the pipes repositioned. The first release and pipe are to the right of the steam valve. Unlock the pipe, then push it counter-clockwise until it clicks into its new position.*

STEP #2: *The next pipe is in the back of the room. This one must be repositioned twice, though. Unlock and push it counter-clockwise until it clicks into position once, then crouch underneath the pipe to reach another pressure lock, then do it again.*

STEP #3: *Now it's time to return to the steam valve and turn it slightly, unleashing steam onto the next blockage. Once the alien gunk is destroyed, shut the steam off and proceed.*

02 Finding a Railgun and an RPG just lying around in the preceding hallway should indicate something… A whole mess of Pigcops and aliens are guarding the machine room. You should know how to make pulled pork from Pigcops and mincemeat from aliens by now, especially with a Railgun and an RPG handy. After all the enemies are slaughtered, refill your Railgun in the room underneath the catwalk if need be, then bash the board blocking the ladder release underneath the catwalk so you can ascend to the next floor.

Snap this board in half to release the ladder.

03 Round the first corner upstairs with extreme caution, as a Pigcop Captain lays in wait at the end of the corridor prepared to unleash some rockets. Take stock of the red barrel at the mouth of this hallway; even if a rocket misses its target, the exploding barrel will likely kill Duke. Charge into the room past the barrel and take down the captain right away. Another Pigcop around the next corner will drop a short-fused Pipe Bomb. Step back to avoid the splash damage, then rush forward and finish the job.

It's not a great idea to be near red barrels when swapping gunfire with foes. Either bait an enemy into firing and then step back out of the hall immediately, or rush past the barrel in the first place.

Watch out for the surprise Pipe Bomb right around the next corner.

04 There's nowhere to go but down in this room. To progress, you must use the Shrink Pad. A shrunken Duke will immediately get attacked by several rats, but they shouldn't pose much of a threat. After playing pest exterminator, explore the vent from which the rats emerged to find a tiny Item Crate. Unscrew the glowing nuts from a nearby grate and enter.

Not our idea of a good screw either, Duke.

05 There's another vent here leading downward. Upon entering, the fans will force Duke to the bottom. At this point (see screenshot), a fan backed by a blue-tinted light is blocked by a broom. Break the broom, and the fan's upward lift will carry Duke just outside the machine. While lofting upward, drift forward into a vent shaft for some shrunken supplies.

While inside the machine, you'll face quite an ordeal. To escape and continue onward, climb up and out of this mechanical beast.

STEP #2: Just inside, there's a long vertical shaft lined with three flat, spinning gear wheels. Coils behind each gear serve as ladders for a shrunken Duke; you'll need to cross each spinning gear to reach the next coil. At the top, a grate leads onward.

STEP #3: Drop down the grate opening to locate a small generator unit powering a fan. The spinning fan prevents passage, so shoot the generator with a shot from any weapon.

STEP #4: Fall down the shaft past the fan, deep into the churning transmission of the machine. Now make Duke mount the central arrangement of upright gear wheels by jumping onto a spinning gear on the side.

STEP #5: Now all that remains is crossing all the upright spinning gears! This insane feat will require some steady nerves. Fall off the side and Duke will likely end up in the smelting pit below. While some of the gears are lined up such that you can just run or jump across the tops of them, a few larger gears require that you pass through holes in their surface.

STEP #6: Here's an easy part. At the end of the machine's transmission, there are pipes leading upward. Use them to reach the machine's pistons.

STEP #7: Another fan blocks the path at the north end of the machine, so destroy the three small generators to stop the entire machine for good.

06 Finally out of the machine, all you have to do in the first room is climb out of it by smashing through the window above the door. Watch out for the Octababies feeding on the corpse of an EDF soldier, though!

Inside the room, get familiar with the oversized surroundings. There are some weapons sitting around, including an Enforcer Gun high up on a filing cabinet. To get it, open one of the file drawers and then push the EDF soldier's corpse close enough to the file drawer to hop onto the soldier and then onto the drawer. Next, hop onto the table and leap to snag the gun.

Although it's slow going, there's a very good reason to move the soldier besides getting the Enforcer Gun. You really don't want any obstacles near the metal case in the center of the room. At the very least, make sure the soldier's legs and torso are well out of the way of the area just around the cube.

Even if Duke is carrying two powerful weapons (for example, a Railgun and the Enforcer), swap one of them out for either a Ripper or shotgun. Make note of where you drop the weapon, though, as you must clamber onto a bucket to reach the elevator call button. After pushing the button, several Octababies will drop in from the vents and attack—plus the lights go out briefly! Cut loose with the Ripper or shotgun. The lights are only off for a brief moment and Octababy eyes glow in the dark. When the threat is dispatched, the elevator will arrive. It's time to grab your powerful weapon again and head for the metal cube...

Press the button, then hold off the Octababy invasion while waiting for the elevator.

ENFORCER

Although the elevator is here, there is an Enforcer inside. The central cube container is important because it's the only reliable cover in the room. Go anywhere else and the Enforcer will fire his missiles right at Duke. When the Enforcer gets close, he'll unleash a powerful stomp with potentially-fatal results. Continue to strafe around the cube and keep the Enforcer on the other side to remain safe. That's why it was important to clear the path around the cube earlier! Backing away from the Enforcer and getting stuck on the EDF soldier's body for even a split second may bring bad news for Duke.

Whenever possible, stay closer to the Enforcer's left foot than his right foot to keep him moving clockwise. This puts Duke at minimal exposure to his ferocious weapon.

Although all weapons are diminished in power while in a shrunken state, they still cause damage.

While backing away from the Enforcer, be ready to switch directions if he does. Ideally, make him go to his left (clockwise around the cube) as much as possible. By doing so, the last part of him to round cube corners will be his gun. This should provide time to pump shots into his body without fear of retaliation. Conversely, when the Enforcer is circling the cube to his right (counter-clockwise), the first thing around a given corner will be his Enforcer.

Stray explosions caused by the Enforcer's missiles may destroy the overhead lights, plunging the room into darkness. If this occurs, rely on Duke Vision or the light from explosions to find your way.

When the Enforcer dies, it's time to leave. Approach the elevator, but watch out for one last Octababy. Fortunately, the little monster's fall damages one of the railings inside the elevator, which allows Duke to climb up it. Standing on the far end of the broken rail causes it to move in the other direction. Now jump to the undamaged railings to access the elevator controls.

CHAPTER 17:
THE FORKSTOP

There
on and

02

provi...
Octa...
and a...
a lad...
inside...

03

end a...
Railgu...
but y...
piggi...
the an...
close...
as the...

After...
group...
as the...
norma...
Octab...
treme...

Fighting
barrels,
to defe...

Duke has finally made it to the generator room, where General Graves awaits. Hopefully, he has a plan to somehow destroy the alien wormhole.

01 Don't miss a phone message near the beginning. After crossing the threshold of the top level, proceed downstairs and find General Graves and his men. Graves reports that his engineers have determined that shutting down the dam's power production will also shut off the alien wormhole. However, EDF forces haven't been able to push past the infestation to make this happen. Duke must press on and succeed where the General's men have failed thus far.

"America is counting on you, Duke!"

02 Just past the General, Duke will enter the main chamber of the generator room. This area is literally overgrown with alien egg sacs, egg pods, and hideous tentacle growths. You must cross the bottom level and find a ladder on the other side to move forward.

In the center of the bottom section, an electric current is passing through but you can flank slightly to the right of the electricity by bashing through egg sacs. At the end of the run, there's a ladder leading up on the right.

03 Dismount the ladder to return to the top level. Use the control box to maneuver the hanging pipes up and to the right, then leap across to the pipes to the generator side. The first generator is relatively untouched, but it also doesn't lead anywhere. You must move to the next generator, upon which the alien tentacle growths have encroached. Climb the stairs to the top of this generator and notice that a lone portion of the railing is broken. Drop off the edge and land on a tentacle to walk across to the next generator.

The pipe should be moved as pictured here.

Climb this generator and hop onto a tentacle leading onward, but beware the electric sparks along the way.

After stepping off the tentacle back down next to the third generator, several Pregnators will attack. Kill them or ignore them; either way, your goal is to proceed to the fourth generator. At the top of the generator, leap onto the tentacles and use them to reach a catwalk on the wall above the fourth generator. Before you go that way, though, take a detour along the length of the tentacle in the other direction to find an Item Crate holding a Holoduke. When you're ready, follow the tentacle up to the catwalk and walk past the old man at the top of the generator room to the carriage.

Perhaps the best weapon against Pregnators (and other small foes) is the Freeze Ray, because it freezes them solid almost instantly.

TO MOVING CARRIGE

Climb this generator's stairs and jump onto the tentacles just above the railing. As always, watch out for electric arcs and don't miss the Holoduke!

04 Once on the motorized carriage, the old man will start moving it across to the other side. At about this time, a swarm of Assault Trooper Captains will attack! They're not much of a match for Duke Nukem and a Devastator with infinite ammo, though, and one way or another, that's what you'll have here. Whether it's from the Devastator in the companion barrel room, or the one in this area. Don't break too much of a sweat while fighting the captains, though, as they're just a warm-up. Behold, the return of the Octaking!

There are nearly a baker's dozen Assault Trooper Captains to crush with Devastator rockets. Stop by the Ammo Crate to refill rockets as needed.

OCTAKING

The Octaking was just being gentle the first time. Now that Duke's used to him, he's gonna get rough! At first, this boss just summons multiple Octabrains to fight for him. Quickly eliminate them using the Devastator and the Ammo Crate, or another weapon of choice. Note that Octabrains can't catch and return Devastator rockets!

Fire at the Octabrains at the start. The Octaking won't attack until he takes a bit of damage, so don't make things harder! Kill the minions before turning the Devastator on the king.

When the Octaking loses about 20% of its health, it starts unloading psychic blasts of energy. When the beast starts tossing objects, utilize the objects along the railing for brief cover, but remember that the Octaking's psychic blasts can still cause damage to Duke. Rely on lateral movement while on the carriage to avoid attacks as necessary.

The Octaking's psychic blasts are still huge and the splash damage is insane!

Yes, that's an entire generator hurtling toward the carriage. The Octaking will eventually toss huge objects to destroy the cover around the carriage.

The Octaking employs a new attack, too. The slimy beast will open its mouth wide and release several rockets in quick succession! Perhaps some of the Devastator rockets puncturing its hide aren't detonating, giving the Octaking a chance to return them to Duke. Now that's ingenuity.

When the Octaking's health bar is depleted, the beast collapses to the far deck with a missing brain lobe and a darkened eye. These grave injuries have robbed the Octaking of its powers of locomotion, but it retains some of its psychic faculties—the beast will haul in the carriage toward him! If it gets pulled far enough, the beast will explode and take Duke with him. Surviving is simple: unload everything in your arsenal on the Octaking to kill him for good!

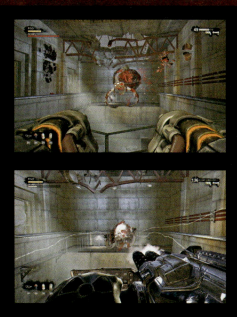

After the fight, the old man running the carriage will open the stairs from which Duke entered, allowing access to the level exit.

There's a bathroom in here in case you need to freshen up with **Ego boosts**. When you're ready to move on, plunge into stagnant water underneath the broken elevators in the elevator shaft.

HARDER DIFFICULTY SETTINGS

On "Come Get Some" or "Damn, I'm Good," this boss fight ranks up there as arguably one of the game's most challenging. There's a very good reason this chapter contains a Holoduke right before the carriage and a Beer on the carriage itself—you'll need them!

The first priority is to kill all the Octabrain minions right away. Although that's true on easier difficulties, it's a much taller order on harder ones. Psychic blasts just produce too much splash damage and are too difficult to avoid in groups—strafing back and forth to avoid one psychic blast may just cause others to hit. The splash damage alone from three or four Octabrains is virtually impossible to avoid. In addition, it's takes more to defeat the foes.

Here's where the supplies come in. When the Octabrains attack, activate the Holoduke on one edge of the carriage, then sprint to the EDF Ammo Crate. Unload on the Octabrains while they pepper the hologram. Stay away from the Holoduke, since the psychic blast splash damage will still hurt the real Duke. If the Holoduke runs out and there are still Octabrains in the area, then down the Beer. Taking even two psychic blasts back-to-back will probably result in Duke's death. When just the Octaking remains, the battle is more or less the same as the other difficulty settings, although the Octaking will withstand more punishment.

CHAPTER 19:
UNDERGROUND

UNDERGROUND, PART 1

OBJECTIVE: Search for a way to power down the dam.

WHITEBOARD

ITEM CRATE

END

LADDER

01

TURBINE
BLADE

(UNDERWATER)

START

(UNDER STAIRS)

RED TOOL CARTS

UNDERGROUND, PART 1

ENEMIES

[Octababy]

WEAPONS AND EQUIPMENT

[Pistol]   [Pipe Bomb]   [Railgun]

[Ripper]   [Shotgun]   [Freeze Ray]

EGO BOOSTS

REQUIREMENT	TOTAL EGO BOOST
Read Funbags magazine.	+1
Slap wall boobs.	+1
Look at picture on computer.	+1
Throw paper airplane.	+1

TROPHIES & ACHIEVEMENTS

NAME	DESCRIPTION
Drawings	Draw on whiteboard.

Duke has met General Graves and the shadow of a plan is in place. The President is off somewhere being useless; he's either lost his mind (bad), or is engaging in direct collusion with the Cycloid Emperor (worse!). Duke's mission is to plunge further into the dam and find a way to shut down the power. At the end of the generator room, Duke falls down an out-of-service elevator shaft into a watery abyss.

01 Duke emerges from the water on the turbine level underneath the generators. On the couch in the first room is a copy of Funbags magazine, good for an **Ego boost** if you missed it before. (Duke reads it for the articles.) Speaking of Ego boosts, there are some wall boobs (yes, wall boobs) behind the corpse piñata. A small fire blocks the way forward, so just shoot the fire extinguisher to subdue the flames.

Reading is fundamental.

Shoot the extinguisher to continue.

Penetrate a short distance into the area and locate the turbine powering a fierce-looking fan. As Duke approaches, a Pregnator hatches from an upside-down Egg Pod and falls straight into the blades. The turbine can be stopped by pushing three steel toolboxes into it (look for the red ones). Two of them are on the same level as the turbine, while the third requires traipsing upstairs, so you can push it off the ledge.

Two of the red tool carts are visible in this image (circled). The third is just down the hallway straight ahead.

You can walk upstairs and push the tool cart off the ledge, then push it into the turbine blade. Or, you can throw a Pipe Bomb at its perched location to make it fall down.

Snag a Freeze Ray from atop a ladder in the stairwell room if you want (this is the only instance of an enemy attack during this section). Also note that the final room contains a whiteboard, paper airplanes, and computers with pictures on them. If you've missed the attendant **Ego boosts** and **Achievements/ Trophies**, now's the time to get them.

A vent above some shelving leads out of this area, and on to the next part of this chapter.

UNDERGROUND, PART 2

OBJECTIVE: Continue deeper into the dam, searching for a way to disrupt power.

UNDERGROUND, PART 2

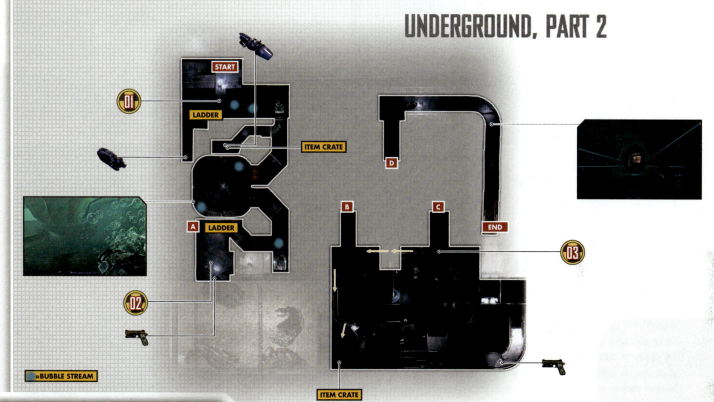

START
LADDER
ITEM CRATE
D
B   C
A   LADDER
END
02
03
=BUBBLE STREAM
ITEM CRATE

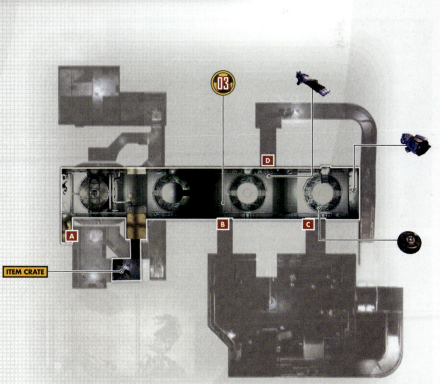

03
D
A   B   C
ITEM CRATE

ENEMIES

[Pigcop]   [Pregnator]

[Pigcop Captain]   [Enforcer]

WEAPONS AND EQUIPMENT

[AT Captain Laser]   [RPG]   [Pipe Bomb]   [Pistol]   [Steroids]

[Trip Mine]   [Ripper]   [Holoduke]   [Shrink Ray]

TROPHIES & ACHIEVEMENTS

NAME	DESCRIPTION
I Need a Towel	Get hit by 10 Pregnator bombs.

Down he goes, further along the dam's massive infrastructure. Descending in the dam also means plunging below the water line, so be prepared for more watery environments.

 There hasn't been much swimming yet, but that's about to change. Duke must stay underwater for sustained periods of time from this point forward. This is possible because of bubble streams. When near a bubble stream, Duke's air supply will replenish.

If you cannot reach the surface for air, a bubble stream will suffice.

FREEZE-FRAME!

Most weapons are unaffected underwater, with the exception of the Freeze Ray. Although you can shoot it underwater, the end result is that it will freeze Duke and not your intended target!

Climb the ladder at the start to acquire an AT Captain Laser. Further along, an RPG and Pipe Bomb are hidden along a diversionary route. There's no bubble stream down this hall, but there is a pocket of air to use; just surface above the console on which the RPG sits.

Past an airlock door that needs to be opened, you'll find the underwater aspect of a great turbine. Don't swim close to the spinning blades, or Duke will take heavy damage. The water in this area is turbulent, so be ready to adjust. Swim around the room to the other tunnel, but be prepared to fight some Octababies. If you have an RPG handy, use several rockets to clear away the threat. Take the next ladder to access dry ground again.

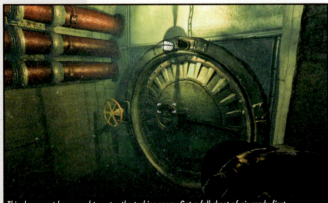
This door must be opened to enter the turbine room. Get a full chest of air ready first.

Octababies attack at the far side of the turbine room.

 Duke will spot an old friend through the window shortly after surfacing. Stick around a moment after the enemy leaves to hear what an old man in a porta-potty has to say about all this.

Inside the turbine housing again, the exit is just ahead and to the left. While crossing the turbines, though, an errant Pig-cop rocket destroys the next turbine, blocking the way forward, while also knocking out the power. It's time for Duke Vision!

The Cycloid Emperor! He's here!

 The destroyed turbine means it's time for a detour down the very hall from which the rocket emerged. At the end, Duke will get assaulted by a shotgun-packing Pigcop, a Pigcop Captain sporting an RPG, and several Pregnators.

At first, there is nowhere to go; the double-doors leading out of the room are shut tight. After defeating a few

You can plunder the Pigcop Captain's perch for an RPG and an Item Crate. Simply jump onto the pipes running along the room (refer to the map).

enemies, though, another Pigcop will smash down the door followed by a shielded Enforcer! Fight past these foes, then advance along a hallway filled with boxes and two explosive barrels to find the stairwell leading to the next chapter.

Before you leave the generator room for the last time, though, check out the catwalk above the end of the room. You'll see a Shrink Ray and a partially broken ladder. Grab those explosive barrels mentioned previously, stack them to create a ledge, then jump onto the ladder!

After killing some combination of three or four Pigcops and Pregnators, a shielded Enforcer will crash the party!

CHAPTER 20

THE CLARIFIER

❚ OBJECTIVE: Continue searching for a way to disrupt power.

WHITEBOARD

PHONE MESSAGE

(INSIDE LOCKER)

ITEM CRATE

A

01

PHONE MESSAGE

X4

(INSIDE LOCKER)

LADDER

X2

02

(INSIDE LOCKER)

(ATOP SCAFFOLD)

THE CLARIFIER, MAIN LEVEL

THE CLARIFIER, TOP TIER

END

A

FROM MAIN LEVEL VIA
THE SKYJACK VEHICLE

X2

=HEAVY BARREL

ENEMIES

[Pigcop] [Pigcop Captain]

[Enforcer] [Assault Commander]

WEAPONS AND EQUIPMENT

[Railgun] [Pipe Bomb] [Ripper] [RPG] [Shotgun]

[Trip Mine] [Holoduke] [Pistol] [Beer] [Steroids]

[AT Captain Laser] [Shrink Ray] [Freeze Ray] [Enforcer Gun]

EGO BOOSTS

REQUIREMENT	TOTAL EGO BOOST
Smoke cigar.	+1

TROPHIES & ACHIEVEMENTS

NAME	DESCRIPTION
Call Waiting	Listen to all phone messages.
Drawrings	Draw on whiteboard.

Some of the immense workspaces used in the construction of the dam remain relatively untouched since the dam's completion. After emerging from Pigcop-engineered detours in the underground guts of the generator, you'll have to explore these areas for some sort of solution to the problem—General Graves sent men ahead before Duke to find a way to interrupt the dam's power production...perhaps some EDF forces are still around, trying to complete their mission?

01 A couple of berserk Pigcops make an appearance in the first few halls. There are also several supplies and weapons to acquire. At the small office, notice a security camera feed—it looks like the Cycloid Emperor is taking an active role in exterminating human presence in the dam.

EGO, ANYONE?

Don't miss the phone message and the cigar.

Check out the desk in this office for an **Ego-boosting** cigar, as well as a phone message that goes toward the "Call Waiting" **Achievement/Trophy.**

The way out of the office is blocked by breakable boxes. Crush the boxes and enter the next corridor, but watch out for an armed Pigcop attack. Around the bend, you'll find a Pigcop Captain, an Enforcer, and a Ripper-toting Pigcop. Try to get up to where the Ripper-toting Pigcop is stationed. To do so, destroy the crates blocking the transit of the wheeled scaffold, then push it closer to the next level. When it's in position, simply climb the ladder onto the scaffold and then jump.

The wooden boxes don't provide much cover for either side.

Destroy the little box pyramid, then push the wheeled scaffold.

From up high, Duke has a great view of the entire area—a quarry construction area and the adjacent work area that supports it. A Pigcop is manning the crane's control deck. After defeating this porky foe, some nearby barrels will explode, crippling the crane in the process.

Another office in this area has a phone message, along with a Beer and a whiteboard.

The crane's cargo bed must be loaded with four heavy barrels to weigh down the arm enough so that you can use it to reach the area across the way.

The first heavy barrel is next to the cargo bed. Soon after, a worker smashes through the far wall while driving a skyjack vehicle in a desperate, doomed bid to escape some incoming Pigcops. These grotesque foes will spill into the area from the hole the doomed skyjack driver made. Defeat the Pigcops first, then focus on the skyjack.

STEP #1: Grab the barrel by the cargo bed and toss it in.

STEP #2: Acquire the skyjack from this poor soul (see screenshot to left). Kill the Pigcops who attack, then check the passage behind them for a Railgun and four Trip Mines!

STEP #3: Snag the heavy barrels from atop a small scaffold in the work area and the ones above the corridor. Get the Shrink Ray, as it will come in very handy soon.

STEP #4: When the barrels from up top are placed in the cargo bed, two groups of Pigcops will emerge from the sides. The area from which the second group appears contains the final heavy barrel.

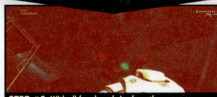

STEP #5: With all four barrels in place, the crane arm should be positioned such that Duke can climb the scaffold next to the crane, then jump across and run on the crane arm to the next area.

STEP #6: With the crane in position, use the ladders on the scaffold in the quarry area to climb up next to the arm, then jump onto it and use it to cross up and above to firm ground again. There's a Freeze Ray up here in case you want to take it to the next area.

THE CLARIFIER, PART 2

◀ OBJECTIVE: Rendezvous with Captain Dylan.

THE CLARIFIER

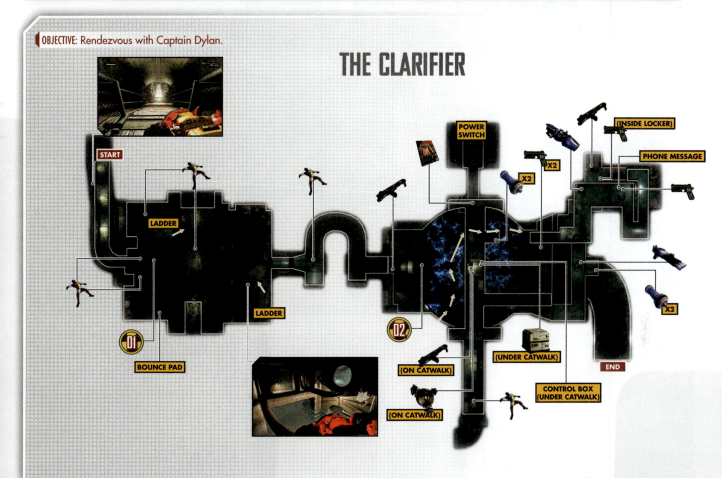

START

LADDER

LADDER

BOUNCE PAD

POWER SWITCH

(UNSIDE LOCKER)

PHONE MESSAGE

X2

X2

X2

(UNDER CATWALK)

END

CONTROL BOX (UNDER CATWALK)

(ON CATWALK)

(ON CATWALK)

01

02

ENEMIES

[Pregnator]   [Octabrain]   [Pigcop]

WEAPONS AND EQUIPMENT

[Pistol]   [Ripper]   [Shotgun]   [Pipe Bomb]

[Trip Mine]   [RPG]   [Wall Bombs]

EGO BOOSTS

REQUIREMENT	TOTAL EGO BOOST
Read Slutbutts magazine.	+1

TROPHIES & ACHIEVEMENTS

NAME	DESCRIPTION
Call Waiting	Listen to all phone messages.

We've seen some signs of EDF forces, but none are drawing breath. Some of the fiercest combat is ahead, with no solution in sight. Is no one left to show Duke the way?

01 The first room is a large chamber bisected by a large pipe. You need to use a scaffold's ladder on the left to climb up to the pipe from the first side, or jump off the bounce pad on the right. From the second side, another scaffold ladder lets you mount some crossbeams and then a tentacle on the other side to reach the pipe leading out of the room.

It's not this guy's day.

The catch here is that two Octabrains, a Pigcop, and numerous Pregnators fill the room. The Octabrains are the most dangerous foes. The Pigcop continually tosses Pipe Bombs from the other side of the big pipe, while the Octabrains will catch them and hurl them directly at Duke!

If you're running low on supplies, you can scavenge more from the hanging corpses.

A ladder on the far side allows access to the tentacle that crosses the supports.

02 Travel through the pipe to emerge atop a large, electrified pool of water. There's a familiar face on the upper tier of the catwalk, so getting there is the goal for now. Further along, you need to find a way to remove the electrical current from the pool, opening the way to the exit.

STEP #1: The first step is to cross the electric pool by jumping between pieces of floating debris.

STEP #2: Next is a series of hallways leading to the upper floor. There are several weapons to pick up along the way, plus a phone message for the "Call Waiting" **Achievement/Trophy.** The catwalk will collapse once you reach the second floor, but you can proceed via the other catwalk by crossing to it atop a double red pipe.

STEP #3: Other EDF forces did make it! Sort of. With the wall bombs in Duke's possession, the plan to stop the energy production is clear—just destroy the entire dam! Before descending to the first floor of the catwalk, search the end of Dylan's catwalk for some **Ego-boosting** reading material.

STEP #4: To reach the switch that shuts down the power, you must use the control box on the lower tier of the platform over the water and rotate it 180 degrees.

FIGHT!

As you start rotating the platform, several Octabrains will attack. Even though there's an EDF Ammo Crate in the middle of the platform, this fight can still be incredibly hard. There is almost no room to maneuver side-to-side to avoid psychic blasts or thrown projectiles. Defeat the Octabrains as quickly as possible and remember that shooting them when they charge up a psychic blast will interrupt their attempt. A Holoduke, a Beer—or both—can be invaluable here.

STEP #5: Once the Octabrains are all eliminated, rotate the platform the rest of the way. Flip the power switch to allow a non-fatal dip in the water.

STEP #6: Dive into the water and descend toward a wheel that opens a great water lock. Past the lock is the way to the next chapter.

BLOWIN' THE DAM, PART I

OBJECTIVE: Place Dylan's wall bombs.

BLOWIN' THE DAM (UNDERWATER)

SECOND

END

CEMENT SHOE CORPSE

AIR VALVE

04

02

FIRST

01

L

F

E

TREASURE CHEST

START

G

X2

K

I

H

C

AIR VALVE

B

J

H

D

05

J

A

AIR VALVE

GIANT CLAM (EMITS BUBBLE STREAM WHEN OPEN)

AIR VALVE

X2

03

BUCKET HEAD

AIR POCKET

= BUBBLE STREAM

Exiting The Clarifier puts Duke at the foot of the dam's lake side. The underwater dam wall is likely one of the best places to use dam-busting explosives. This entire section takes place underwater, so adjust accordingly.

ENEMIES

[Octabrain] [Energy Leech]

WEAPONS AND EQUIPMENT

[AT Laser] [Steroids] [Beer] [Pipe Bomb]

[RPG] [Shotgun] [Pistol]

EGO BOOSTS

REQUIREMENT	TOTAL EGO BOOST
Kill the Energy Leech	+4

TROPHIES & ACHIEVEMENTS

NAME	DESCRIPTION
Bucket Head	Find all three helmets during the single-player campaign.
Pescaphobe	Kill all the catfish in the underwater level.
Beating the One Eyed Worm	Defeat the Energy Leech.

CATFISH GUMBO

There are 15 catfish in this level. Fry them all in one run to unlock a **Trophy** or **Achievement**. Most of the catfish are within viewing distance of the main path over the yellow air pipes. A few, however, are off the beaten path. The catfish are marked on the map with callouts, which point to the matching images that follow.

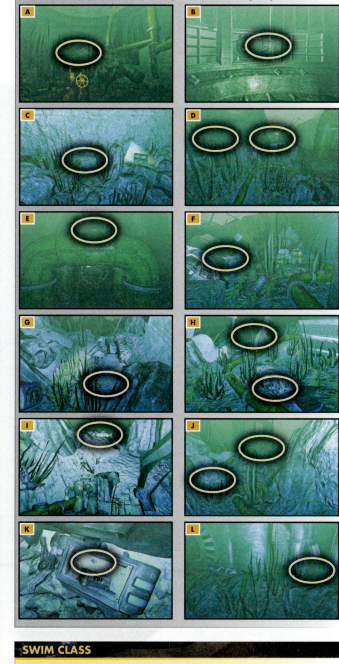

SWIM CLASS

When swimming, remember that you can rapidly ascend or descend by holding either the "jump" or "crouch" buttons. The distance you can travel underwater is limited by Duke's lung capacity. His current supply of oxygen shows up as a gauge at the bottom of the screen. When this runs out, Duke starts taking damage.

01 So, where does the air come from? Almost exclusively from bubble streams of oxygen, which vent from a cluster of air outflow pipes. You need to move the area of venting pipes forward by opening air valves along the length of the pipes. This will cause sections of pipe further along to start venting bubble streams, while shutting off the previous ones. Keep this in mind if you aren't done exploring a section to your satisfaction, since you cannot backtrack.

Turn the air valves to advance the venting of air along the yellow air pipes.

TODAY'S SPECIAL—CATFISH!

One catfish is in the chamber with the first air valve. Open it up with the wheel, then ascend out of the chamber through the busted window. Another catfish is just outside the window. Off to the right and slightly behind the outflow tower are a treasure chest and another catfish.

02 First, as you progress along the pipe, an Octabrain will emerge from a freight container in the path ahead. Octabrains are annoying enough on land, and doubly so underwater. About the only upshot is the lack of hard objects for them to toss in the murky depths; they may often settle for tossing corpses or plant matter, and this fleshy material doesn't transmit enough kinetic force to hurt Duke.

This area also contains two catfish in plain view and a secret to the south. Take a deep breath, then swim over a wrecked yacht and into the husk of a smashed tower to find an enormous clam. This clam emits bubble streams, but only when it's open. The RPG here is fool's gold; you won't get any use out of an RPG here at the moment. Further along, there's a grating that serves as an ideal spot to place a wall bomb. Directly above the pipes in this area is yet another catfish.

03 Another catfish is swimming along the route to the second air valve. Don't turn the air valve before you're done with the previous area (did you check the clam and the treasure chest? Did you kill all the catfish so far?), as there's no going back. Once the valve is turned, two Octabrains will attack.

After turning the second valve, it's time to swim south toward an eerie light to find the pipe again. The light turns out to be illuminating a poor soul wearing cement shoes. To the right of the corpse is a catfish hiding in the reeds in total darkness (use Duke Vision to find it).

Remember that shooting an Octabrain as it charges up a psychic blast interrupts the attack.

After finding the yellow air outflow pipes again, take a moment to refill on oxygen, kill the two catfish, and look to the south to find another semi-distant light. Although the light seems to point to an EDF soldier's corpse, it's really pointing beyond it. Swim in that direction to find a pocket of air underneath a ruined outflow tower. One of the helmets required for the "Bucket Head" **Achievement/Trophy** is found here.

If you find the murky depths too dark for comfortable navigation, flip on Duke Vision. This will also help you find a hidden catfish close to this corpse.

This is the one place where Duke can draw breath from open air rather than out of a bubble stream.

04 After turning the third air valve, two more Octabrains attack. This section of the chapter doesn't have much in the way of armaments, so you must make due with what's available. On the bright side, if you acquired the Shotgun from the freight container it works well against these brainy foes. Just past the Octabrain assault, be on the lookout for two more catfish.

Trying to set up the second wall bomb incurs the wrath of the Energy Leech.

05 The fourth air valve is here. Don't forget to find the last two catfish; one is next to an Ammo Crate in a downed Wasp gunship, while the other is to the right of the second wall bomb grating. Turn the air valve, filet the last two catfish, then set the second wall bomb on the grating. The dam is toast! Well, maybe it's not quite that simple.

ENERGY LEECH

While attempting to place the second wall bomb, the Energy Leech surges forward for a grand entrance. This boss fight presents quite a challenge, as you also need to keep an eye on Duke's air supply all the while trying to down this incredible beast. At least ammo is not a concern; two RPGs and two EDF Ammo Crates are available.

The Energy Leech attacks mainly with an electrical, spit-like attack. Avoid this by strafing constantly while returning fire with the RPG.

The water presents an extra challenge. The buoyancy of swimming through liquid slows down Duke's movement and removes his ability to sprint. So when the beast attempts one of its attacks, strafe from one Ammo Crate to the other, moving in one direction most of the time to avoid incoming attacks while returning fire with rockets.

When the Energy Leech's health is totally depleted, it's time to approach it and initiate a strength tap challenge to deal the finishing blow! This last assault will annihilate the Energy Leech and cause significant damage to the dam. With the boss dead and shredded, the tunnel through which it came is accessible. Swim back into the dam...

When the Energy Leech rears up, it's getting ready to use its entire body for a brutal bash attack. Again, avoid this by strafing in one direction. Don't stop moving!

After taking lots of damage, the Energy Leech will occasionally draw in water, hoping to bite any adversaries it draws in. Either swim away from the suction, or interrupt it with a rocket down the monster's throat.

BLOWIN' THE DAM, PART 2

OBJECTIVE: Get the hell out of the dam!

BLOWIN' THE DAM—THE ESCAPE

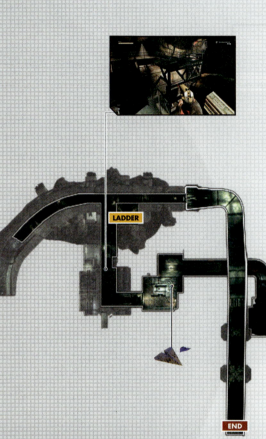

LADDER

END

01
START

03

X2

02

X2

04

ENEMIES

[Pigcop]   [Pigcop Captain]

WEAPONS AND EQUIPMENT

[Ripper] [Pipe Bomb] [AT Captain Laser] [Pistol] [Shotgun]

EGO BOOSTS

REQUIREMENT	TOTAL EGO BOOST
Read 69MM magazine.	+1
Throw paper airplane.	+1

Between the damage done by Dylan's wall bombs and the Energy Leech battle, the dam is in serious trouble. The wall integrity is compromised and water is coursing through the infrastructure of the dam. The structure can't hold out for long against the inexorable weight of all the water, so it's time to get out—fast!

01 The dam is just starting to crack, but the progress isn't going to get any slower...it's time to get out of here! If you've missed 69MM magazine before, now is the time to get it—this **Ego-boosting** publication is behind a fence in this room (see screenshot, below left).

Follow the arrow to get out!

Evacuation route signs guide your way.

The water level will begin rising quickly. Bring along the Ripper found in the first stairwell and ascend past the rising water in the stairwell and the hallways ahead. The emergency evacuation route signs point the way.

02 While approaching the bridge in a large chamber on a catwalk, falling debris and an explosion causes it to collapse. After doubling back slightly, locate the red pipes and cross to the other side of the bridge.

The red pipes still provide a way across; otherwise, you can wait for the water level to rise high enough in order to pass.

BOOM GOES THE DYNAMITE!

Watch out if you think you can just go down the red pipe path first. Red explosive barrels will fall from the ceiling, causing a potentially fatal explosion. Nope, you have to check the bridge first!

The bridge is out.

03 Round the corner and a Pigcop Captain will fire an RPG round just as the ceiling collapses. Leap over the hole in the floor left in the little piggy's place and prepare for a harrowing hallway. While ascending this curving stairwell, barrels will plummet down the stairs. The barrels alternate between normal ones and explosive ones; regardless, any barrel will cause damage if it hits Duke. To avoid damage, look for small cubbyholes to duck into and recharge Duke's bruised Ego. You must balance this against the constant rising of the water, though.

You can take a breather by ducking to the side, but this gives the rising water a chance to catch up.

With a weapon like the Ripper, you can shoot and destroy red barrels before they get close enough to pose a problem.

04 At the top of the barrel hallway, you'll encounter the Pigcop who's been tormenting Duke. Deal with this foe appropriately and leave the room quickly. The water stops rising at the top of the curved hallway, but a shutter will fall and trap Duke if you don't progress in a timely manner.

Soon after, two Pigcops emerge through a set of double doors. These are the last bastion of the Cycloid defense and it doesn't even matter—the dam is toast either way. Dispose of them and enter the next chamber. The bridge is out again, but that doesn't matter. Either jump down or find the nearby ladder to descend to the ground so you can access a ladder on the far side. Collapsing debris has knocked a walkway down into an outflow channel—and just in time, too…

Duke arrives at an outflow pipe just as a torrent of water approaches. Conveniently enough, Duke is ejected far from the dam as it crumbles into the water.

THE AFTERMATH

▌OBJECTIVE: Defeat the Cycloid Emperor!

THE FINAL BATTLEFIELD

START

01

X2
[DURING LAST PHASE]

X2
[DURING LAST PHASE]

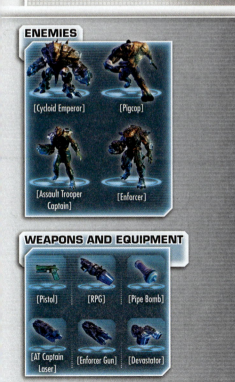

ENEMIES

[Cycloid Emperor]   [Pigcop]

[Assault Trooper Captain]   [Enforcer]

WEAPONS AND EQUIPMENT

[Pistol]   [RPG]   [Pipe Bomb]

[AT Captain Laser]   [Enforcer Gun]   [Devastator]

The dam is dust, the wormhole is closing up, but things aren't quite over yet. Both sides have a champion left with a chip on his shoulder and a score to settle. It's time for the final showdown of Duke Nukem against the Cycloid Emperor!

01 Duke returns to consciousness with an EDF soldier attempting to revive him. The soldier apprises Duke of the situation and hands Duke his signature golden M1911 pistol. Now it's off to get dressed down from the P.O.T.U.S.

The destruction of the dam didn't completely eradicate the alien threat as it turns out. The Cycloid Emperor is here, ready to exact revenge for its thwarted schemings.

CYCLOID EMPEROR

In many ways, the Cycloid Emperor is similar to the Cycloid featured in the game's first chapter of the game. This beast is huge, tough, and out for blood. This time, however, this massive beast isn't going to fight alone and it has more tricks up its cybernetic sleeves.

Take me to your leader, indeed.

Duke starts out armed only with his golden Pistol, which is completely ineffective against the lumbering king of the aliens. On the other hand, the Pistol is efficient against the Pigcops.

The Cycloid Emperor will wander around the battlefield while firing dual rockets from afar.

These Pigcops, unlike the others, come equipped with RPGs. Avoid the Emperor's attacks and wait for the alien gunships to drop off Pigcops to kill, then loot their weapons and use their RPG rounds to unload into the Cycloid Emperor.

The Cycloid Emperor can also speed across the area using the blue thrusters attached to its limbs.

When Duke runs out of rockets, just avoid the Emperor until more Pigcops arrive. Loot their RPGs for more ammo to pump into the alien ruler. Once the boss's first health bar is drained, the Cycloid Emperor will fall to the ground. Approach the boss and initiate a strength tap challenge to pull part of the life support mechanism off its mechanical suit. That's far from all it will take to finish the job, though. The Emperor will get back to its feet and redouble its efforts to down Duke!

By raising its mechanized fists above its head and then bringing them down with great force, the Emperor can cause electrical shockwaves that travel along the ground toward Duke.

This is the only place where normal Pigcops will sport RPGs.

The Emperor's life bar must be drained three times. Each time you must win a strength tap challenge to proceed to the next phase of battle.

It's time for round two. You're still relegated to looting fallen Pigcops for their Pipe Bombs and RPGs, but now new threats arrive to complicate matters. Occasionally, Assault Trooper Captains and Enforcers will appear on the battlefield. Of course, the Enforcer Guns make for great weapons against the Emperor, while AT Captain Lasers can help you hold the Emperor's lesser friends at bay.

Pound-for-pound, Enforcer Guns are arguably even better than RPGs against the Emperor. However, using an Enforcer Gun requires that the user be much closer to the enormous brute— RPG rounds track at distances that Enforcer Gun missiles do not.

The Emperor's homing mortar shower can be devastating if Duke gets caught in the center of the blast.

Meanwhile, the Cycloid Emperor will start using a homing mortar attack that involves launching a cluster of mortars skyward. If the Emperor managed to track Duke before the mortar launch, the mortars will all come straight down with great force right on top of Duke. Try to avoid the Emperor while he's scanning for targets, or sprint like crazy away from your current location as the mortars rain down.

Deplete the boss's health bar a second time and the Cycloid Emperor collapses once more, susceptible to yet another strength tap challenge. But wait...this guy still wants to fight! The Emperor will attack with more gusto than ever, while even more reinforcements arrive as back-up. Look for Pigcops, Assault Trooper Captains, Enforcers, and even shielded Enforcers during this stage!

STRENGTH TAP CHALLENGES: THEY MEAN IT THIS TIME

Strength tap challenges have been pretty lenient up to this point. No longer! Mash the "use" button as quickly as possible to ensure you win strength tap challenges against the ruler of the aliens.

The Cycloid Emperor also begins using another attack. Rather than scanning for precision with a mortar salvo, the Emperor will cross its arms and send two targeting lasers in a big "X" around him, and mortar rounds will go off along the ground on the path of the lasers almost immediately.

This attack has little warning, but if Duke is far away from the Emperor, it will be a non-issue.

After a brief battle, an EDF Wasp gunship soars in majestically to drop off much-needed supplies near the center of the playing field. The gunship drops off two EDF Ammo Crates and two Devastators! Now it's really time to cut loose.

Grab a Devastator right away and get to work at depleting the Cycloid Emperor's final health bar. With a Devastator in hand, it should also become much easier to defeat the Emperor's minions. An Enforcer Gun also becomes much more appealing when nearby Ammo Crates can constantly reload it!

By standing near the Ammo Crates with an Enforcer Gun, you can fire the Enforcer Gun at will while using the Ammo Crate compartment as cover from the Emperor!

Remember to keep the golden pistol in your arsenal while completing this final chapter in order to complete the "Gunslinger" Achievement/Trophy.

The Cycloid Emperor can finally be killed with another successful strength tap after he falls down a third time. His gigantic, solitary eye pops from its socket in his huge skull.

Once infinite ammo is on your side thanks to the EDF Ammo Crates, it's time to unload with the Devastator and Enforcer Gun.

Approach the Emperor's body and make good on Duke's promise at the beginning of the fight.

Finally, a gunship will swing in low and offer Duke an escape route.

That's it! The dam is busted, the wormhole closed, and the king is dead! But, wait... which king?

Defeating Duke Nukem Forever on any difficulty unlocks the opportunity to play the hardest difficulty, "Damn, I'm Good". Completing every chapter on this difficulty setting will unlock an **Achievement** or **Trophy.** Difficulty Achievements and Trophies stack—that is, if you finish the game on "Come Get Some" your first time through, you'll also unlock rewards for completing both lesser difficulties.

Watch the credits all the way through for an Achievement or Trophy thanking you for your patience while contemplating the monumental endeavor that is Duke Nukem Forever.

Finish the game on "Come Get Some" difficulty or better and you'll also unlock a number of new ways in which the game can be played! Under "Extra Game Settings" you'll be able to find toggles for some very interesting parameters:

Invincibility; Infinite Ammo; Instagib; Mirror Mode; Grayscale Mode

The scale of each character's heads can also be adjusted! Finally, there's a toggle to revert the Freeze Ray to its behavior in Duke Nukem 3D, in which it bounces freezing crystal particles off walls, rather than focusing freezing power in a short-range beam.

The level cap in *Duke Nukem Forever* is set to 42. All players begin their multiplayer career as a level 1 Duke, but it doesn't take long to achieve several level promotions and be well on your way to level 42. And the more levels you earn, the more items you unlock for the My Digs mode.

OVERDRIVE MODE

Overdrive awards double XP and +10 XP per hit.

One quick glance at the level requirements is all it takes to see that the climb from level 40 to level 42 is incredibly steep. Fortunately, all is not as it seems. Players are sent into Overdrive Mode upon reaching level 40 (shortly after declining the option to Prestige—because it's dumb!). Overdrive Mode grants players 10 XP for every hit they successfully land on other players; even non-fatal bullets that only slightly damage the enemy will earn 10 XP. Furthermore, all combat XP awards (e.g. kills, assists, captured babes) are doubled.

GAMEPLAY MODES

There are four multiplayer game modes, each playable with up to eight people. All modes can be played on each of the 10 included maps, except for Capture the Babe which can't be played on Duke Burger, Erection Site and Hollywood. The rules are the same for every map although weapon placement, interactions with the environment, and power-up availability does change.

> **MAP-SPECIFIC TACTICS**
>
> The "Multiplayer Maps" chapter in the guide packs over 50 pages of strategies and tips specific to each map. The sections that follow contain numerous tips for each individual gameplay mode, designed to help newcomers and veterans alike get up to speed with Duke's unique brand of multiplayer.

DUKE MATCH

Free-for-all mode. No teams, every Duke for himself.

It's kill or be killed when playing Duke Match. You have no teammates to watch your back and the only objective is to kill as many players as possible before the designated score or time limit is reached. Scoring is based purely on kills, but deaths are tallied too (how else would you get to brag about your impressive kill/death ratio?). Killing an enemy counts as +1 kill, while being killed by an enemy or performing a suicide counts as +1 death. It's really straightforward.

VICTORY FORMATION

The player who creates the match can set the following win conditions:

- **Score:** 10, 20, 30, 40, 50, 60, 70, 80, 90, 100, or No Limit (player with the most points when time expires wins).
- **Time:** 10, 15, or 20 minutes.
- The default setting is 20 points and 10 minutes. The first to reach 20 points wins, or whoever has the most points after 10 minutes.

Be ready for some close-quarters encounters, especially in the vicinity of weapon pick-ups and spawn points.

CORE TACTICS

Fast and Deadly: Multiplayer combat in *Duke Nukem Forever*, especially in Duke Match mode, is extremely frenetic. Players who move slowly, run in straight lines, or are too deliberate in their choices won't last long. Stay on the move, grab the power-ups and weapons as you see them, and always be ready to fire, jump, turn, and fire again!

Learn the Hot Routes: Experienced players know the surest way to get yourself killed is to wander the map aimlessly looking for people to shoot. It's much safer—and more effective—to follow one or two specific routes that link preferred power-ups and weapons. It's better to focus on efficiently slaughtering everything in a small portion of the map, than it is to wander at length. This book lists one "Hot Route" for each of the 10 maps in the following chapter. Learn them, understand why they work, and then experiment with a route of your own that suits your individual style of play.

Respawn Quickly: There's no tactical advantage to delaying your respawn during Duke Match. Get back in the game quickly to make sure you don't miss out on any of the action. The only exception to this rule is if you're playing one versus one and you're trying to cling to a narrow lead during the final seconds of the match.

Don't Be a Hoarder: Death happens. It's a reality when playing multiplayer that you're going to be killed and killed often. And you can't take a collection of Pipe Bombs and Trip Mines with you to that magical penthouse in the sky. Make sure you're smart about how you use them (and remember where you put them), but don't hold onto the Trip Mines and Pipe Bombs for too long, or else you may never get the chance to use them.

Finish the Fight: Some may disparage this tactic by calling it "kill stealing," but others like to think of it as taking care of unfinished business. Always be on the lookout for two players engaged in a shootout...and open fire! Chances are one or more players are low on health and is ready to fall. A Pipe Bomb will often take out both of them, as will a few rounds from the Ripper or a volley of rockets from the Devastator. Don't underestimate the effects of splash damage on weakened enemies.

TEAM DUKE MATCH

Team-based death match. Players are divided into red and blue teams. Team with the most kills wins.

Team Duke Match is played very similarly to standard Duke Match, except players are divided into two teams. Players can switch teams before the match begins, should that need arise. Score is kept for individual players, but it's the total kill tally for the team that determines the victor. Killing an enemy earns you +1 kill and +1 team point. Dying or committing suicide counts as +1 death for the player, but does not impact the team score.

VICTORY FORMATION

The player who creates the match can set the following win conditions:

- **Score:** 10, 20, 30, 40, 50, 60, 70, 80, 90, 100, or No Limit (team with the most points when time expires wins).
- **Time:** 10, 15, or 20 minutes.
- The default setting is 50 points and 10 minutes. The first team to reach 50 points wins, or whichever team has the most points after 10 minutes.

Alert teammates to the enemy's whereabouts and try to flush foes toward teammates with the Railgun or RPG.

CORE TACTICS

Red & Blue All Over: Players receive red and blue shirts (and names in the HUD) based on their team. Members of the opposition are not always red, nor are you always blue. Pay close attention at the start of the match to determine whether to shoot the red or blue players, as this changes from match to match. If you forget, look at the score on the upper part of the screen—your team will be on the left-hand side.

Stick Together: The reason you play Team Duke Match is to work as a team, so put your lone wolf instincts to rest for a while. Work with your teammates, perhaps in pairs or as a group, and gang up on isolated enemies. Move through the map as a pack, but keep some distance between team members, or else you'll get wiped out by a single attack.

Dominate the Power-Ups: One of the best ways to dominate a game of Team Duke Match is to make sure your team acquires every Whiskey, Statue, Jetpack, and Holoduke as soon as it appears. As powerful as some weapons are in the right hands, consistently gaining temporary invincibility and invisibility goes a long way to achieving victory.

Camp One, Rush Three: It won't work on every map, but teams with an expert sniper or player who consistently manages to secure the RPG should consider using three players to draw the enemy's attention and flush them toward a hidden sniper. This also works with Trip Mines and Pipe Bombs.

HAIL TO THE KING

Team-based attack and defend game. Teams compete to maintain control of a capture point to achieve victory.

Hail to the King pits two teams against one another to determine which side can maintain possession of a randomly relocating capture point the longest. The capture point appears as a large yellow Duke Nukem logo when neutral. The color changes to that of the controlling team once a player enters the circle. The player must stand in the circle for 2 seconds to earn 1 team point. Teams earn points faster by having multiple players in the circle simultaneously. Killing an enemy also earns 1 team point.

The capture point is considered contested and returns to yellow as soon as a player from the opposing team enters the circle. Even if there are three players from the red team in the circle, it only takes one player from the blue team to enter the capture point to change it back to yellow. Teams only score points when a member(s) of their team is alone inside the circle. Points stop accruing the moment all players leave the circle. The control point randomly moves every three minutes. Most maps have between four and six possible capture point locations.

VICTORY FORMATION

The player who creates the match can set the following win conditions:

- **Score:** 50, 100, 150, 200, 250, or No Limit (team with the most points when time expires wins).
- **Time:** 10, 15, or 20 minutes.
- The default setting is 100 points and 10 minutes. The first team to reach 100 points wins, or whichever team has the most points after 10 minutes.

Avoid bunching your entire team up inside the capture point. It's more effective to have one or two outside the circle to defend the point.

CORE TACTICS

Beer Me! Hail to the King is the only game type that has the Beer power-up. Beer provides Duke with an increase in strength and reduces the amount of damage he suffers from enemy attacks. Sure, the blurred vision is a drawback, but don't go near the capture point without first popping the cap on a tall frosty one.

Divide & Conquer: Launch a coordinated attack to capture the point, then quickly spread out. Too many teams make the mistake of huddling together in the circle, making them a prime target for a Pipe Bomb or RPG. Spread out within the capture point (use available cover if possible) and position one or two teammates outside the circle, in a position where they can provide fire on the attacking enemy's flank.

Something Sticky: Place Trip Mines on objects and walls just outside the capture point to catch enemies as they rush in to attack the point. Conversely, when attacking a heavily fortified capture point alone, throw a Trip Mine onto an enemy before the opposing team sends you packing. The Trip Mine will go off as soon as one of his teammates intersects the laser, killing multiple enemies.

Leave Early: The capture point changes every three minutes, not after a set number of points have been recorded. Start turning your attention to the next possible capture location when there's approximately 10 seconds left on the current point. It's much harder to take a point after a team has sufficiently set up a defense on it. Getting a head start on capturing the next position, particularly in the early or middle stages of a match, is more valuable than trying to milk a few more points out of an expiring capture location.

CAPTURE THE BABE

Team-based capture the flag game. Teams compete to kidnap the opposing team's babe and return her to their own base.

Capture the Babe is a team-based game mode that blends aggressive offensive play with the need to protect your team's babe. The babe (one of the Holsom twins) is assigned a red or blue sweater and stands atop a small platform at each team's base. Teams must balance the desire to capture the other team's babe with the need to protect their own. Points are accrued by picking up the enemy babe and carrying her back to your team's base. Your babe does not need to be present in order to score a point. Teams gain 1 team point each time the opponent's babe is returned to their team's babe platform. Kills and deaths/suicides alter individual stats, but do not factor in the team's score.

The babe may not weigh much, but she's no paperweight. The babe carrier's mobility is somewhat diminished (runs slightly slower, jump height is reduced) while carrying her and he can no longer crouch or use the

Jetpack. He can, however, continue to use Bounce Pads. Fortunately, the Garter Pistol makes up for these deficiencies! The babe carrier automatically switches to the pint-sized pistol known as a Garter Pistol, which is the only weapon available to the babe carrier. It may not look like much, but this pint-sized pistol can kill an enemy with a single shot!

Prevent the other team from scoring by killing the member running off with your team's babe. The babe automatically falls to the ground after the babe carrier is killed. She will automatically warp back to her team's base after 10 seconds, but she's still vulnerable to being stolen during this time. She'll also warp back to the home base if a friendly team member runs up to her and touches her. Of course, an enemy can also approach and carry her away for the point.

VICTORY FORMATION

The player who creates the match can set the following win conditions:

- **Score:** 5, 6, 7, 8, 9, 10, 11, 12, 13, 14, 15, or No Limit (team with the most captures when time expires wins).
- **Time:** 10, 15, or 20 minutes.
- The default setting is 5 points and 10 minutes. The first team to capture the opponent's babe 5 times wins, or whichever team has the most points after 10 minutes.

The opponent's babe won't put up a fight, but she will fidget and try to block your vision. Deliver her a spank on the butt to get her hand out of your face.

CORE TACTICS

Shrink to Kill: It's best to avoid attacking an enemy babe carrier with a Ripper, Pistol, or some other gun that won't deliver an instant kill—you don't want to give him a chance to fire with the Garter Pistol. On the plus side, you can achieve an instant kill with the Shrink Ray! The babe doesn't shrink along with her kidnapper. Instead, she immediately falls on him and delivers fatal damage!

For Personal Defense Only: The Garter Pistol is a powerful hand cannon of a pistol, but it takes a while to reload it. Only fire it when needed and line up the shot well. Chances are you won't get a second shot off.

Escort Service: Never leave the babe carrier to fend for himself on the return trip. Even when armed with the Garter Pistol, it's just too easy for enemy players to gang up on an isolated player. Coordinate with your teammates so there's always one or two players in the babe carrier's vicinity to intercept opponents attempting to rescue their babe.

Heed the Cues: Pay attention to the audio/visual cues made by the announcer so you know when the other team has stolen your team's babe, if she has been returned, and if the other team scored. You'll also learn when your team has recovered your babe or kidnapped the enemy babe, perfect for those times when your teammates have their microphones turned off.

Offense Wins Championships: It's only natural to want to stick around and keep that pertly little babe company. Although it's not a bad idea for one player to patrol the area just beyond the home base, you must repress any chivalrous instincts you may have and refuse to camp the home base. Lone wolf defenders are likely to be overrun by the enemy, therefore being of little service to their team. And more importantly, matches are consistently won by the most aggressive team. Charge the enemy base, steal their babe and trust that you'll likely get a chance to down one or two enemies en route. Let them worry about defending the babe from your team; keep up the pressure and show them who's boss!

Cold Showers: Even better than blowing an enemy into little chunks of meat is freezing him solid...and walking away. That's right, don't deliver the fatal blow! Resist the urge to execute the enemy (or trample a shrunken foe), as it takes longer for them to return to action while frozen/shrunk than it does to respawn after being killed. Freezing (or shrinking) even one enemy will give your team an advantage. Freeze two in place simultaneously and you'll have a four-on-two fast break to victory. Throw it down, big Nukem!

WEAPONS & POWER-UPS

The following pages detail the multiplayer-specific uses and statistics for each weapon and power-up in the game. Nearly all of the pieces of equipment discussed on the following pages behave very similarly to their use in the single-player campaign. Please refer to the "Weapons & Abilities" chapter in this guide for more information.

DUKE'S MP ARSENAL

BODY SHOTS FTW!

There are no target-specific damage multipliers at work in multiplayer mode. Headshots inflict the same amount of damage to the enemy as shots fired at the torso or limbs. Make it easy on yourself and aim for those steroid-infused pectoral muscles!

RELOAD OFTEN

Not every weapon needs to be reloaded—some carry their full capacity in a single clip—but it's important to press the Reload button after every encounter when using the Pistol, Shotgun, Ripper, and Railgun. There's no excuse for running into combat with a weapon half-loaded. Reload every chance you get!

PISTOL

The pistol can be fired as fast as you can pull the trigger and it takes only three hits to kill an enemy. Its 8-round clip capacity is enough to kill two enemies without reloading, provided you hit your mark. The pistol delivers consistent damage across its effective range (point-blank to infinity), although it's lack of a scope makes it difficult to aim at long range. The pistol is a quality short-to-medium range weapon that compliments slower, heavier weaponry well.

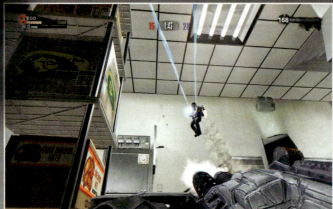

STATS	
Damage per Shot	40.0
Rounds per Clip	8
Rate of Fire	400rpm
Max Ammo Capacity	64
Maximum Range	Infinite
Splash Damage Radius	N/A
Respawn Time	20 seconds

RIPPER

Duke's trusted machine gun is known as the Ripper, a high-velocity weapon of mass dismemberment. Although each individual bullet only inflicts 18 points of damage, it takes just 0.36 seconds and six direct hits to kill a foe thanks to the weapon's ridiculous firing rate. The Ripper isn't the most accurate weapon, but firing in small bursts goes a long way to increasing accuracy and conserving ammo. Better still, even a short burst will likely discharge enough bullets to drain an enemy of its Ego. Fire longer bursts at closer range to ensure you deliver the fatal attack before the enemy does. The Ripper is one of the most effective weapons to use when countering a Jetpacking enemy.

STATS	
Damage per Shot	40.0
Rounds per Clip	8
Rate of Fire	400rpm
Max Ammo Capacity	64
Maximum Range	Infinite
Splash Damage Radius	N/A
Respawn Time	20 seconds

SHOTGUN

The Shotgun is a devastating weapon at close range. Each shell disperses 10 pellets and each one is capable of causing 40 points of damage. The pellets release in a tight area at close range, but they spread out as they travel away from the muzzle. The damage of each pellet also diminishes with distance as it approaches the maximum range of 50 feet. The odds of a one-shot kill is virtually 100% at close range (possible max damage of 400), but those odds diminish as the target gets further away. The spread of the pellets and decreasing damage per pellet may require two shots to deliver fatal damage beyond 25 feet.

STATS	
Damage per Shot	40.0 per pellet, 10 pellets per shot
Rounds per Clip	7
Rate of Fire	60rpm
Max Ammo Capacity	28
Maximum Range	50ft
Splash Damage Radius	N/A
Respawn Time	20 seconds

RAILGUN

The Railgun is Duke's dedicated sniper rifle, capable of firing an energy spike that can travel through multiple enemies without damage reduction. The Railgun is a one-shot kill weapon with excellent zoom capabilities thanks to its powerful optical scope. Note that peripheral vision is considerably limited while utilizing the scope, leaving the user vulnerable to flanking attacks. It's possible to shoot with the Railgun without using the scope, although getting an accurate shot is more difficult. The Railgun's relatively slow firing rate and small clip capacity renders it a risky weapon to use in a mobile, close-quarters engagement.

STATS	
Damage per Shot	135.0
Rounds per Clip	3
Rate of Fire	40rpm
Max Ammo Capacity	12
Maximum Range	Infinite
Splash Damage Radius	N/A
Respawn Time	20 seconds

FREEZE RAY

The Freeze Ray is that rare weapon that allows the user to actually see where the projectiles are heading. The Freeze Ray fires a steady stream of ice that delivers 320 damage per second, assuming a constant direct hit. Rather than kill the enemy, the Freeze Ray immobilizes the enemy within a block of ice, leaving the enemy defenseless for roughly 8 seconds. Attacking players can deliver a fatal blow with another weapon by striking the frozen foe with a melee attack, or by delivering an execution attack (approach closely and follow on-screen button prompt to perform the execution).

Executions are glorifying to perform, but time consuming. It's safer to just melee the enemy for the kill. Better yet, leave him frozen and continue fighting—it's more advantageous in objective-based modes to leave enemies frozen in place than to kill them and allow a speedy respawn.

STATS	
Damage per Shot	5.3 stream, 320 damage per second
Rounds per Clip	200 (regenerates)
Rate of Fire	Continuous
Max Ammo Capacity	200 (regenerates)
Maximum Range	56 feet
Splash Damage Radius	N/A
Respawn Time	20 seconds

STATS	
Damage per Shot	N/A
Rounds per Clip	10
Rate of Fire	80rpm
Max Ammo Capacity	10
Maximum Range	Infinite
Splash Damage Radius	N/A
Respawn Time	20 seconds

SHRINK RAY

The Shrink Ray fires a relatively slow, green projectile that instantly shrinks its target in size making them susceptible to a foot stomp. Better still, you can leave them in miniature form to delay their return to action for approximately 10 seconds.

The Shrink Ray is the ultimate weapon in Capture the Babe. A shrunken player cannot pick up the babe, plus shrinking the babe carrier causes the babe to fall and instantly crush the player! Shrinking an enemy also lessens their weapons and only the Freeze Ray maintains its effectiveness while in this state. When a shrunken player plants Trip Mines, they will remain tiny even after the player returns to full size. As is the case with the Freeze Ray, oftentimes it's far more advantageous to leave enemies in a shrunken state rather than kill them. This is particularly true in objective-based modes.

AT LASER

The AT Laser fires a three-round burst of lasers with pinpoint accuracy. The weapon can be fired 20 times before running out of battery power (no reloading is required). The AT Laser can kill an enemy with a single burst, provided at least two of the three lasers hit their mark. All three lasers fire in the direction where the reticle is placed when the trigger is pressed, but this limits the AT Laser's effectiveness against enemies moving perpendicular to the player. The AT Laser excels in duels at medium range, or when targeting a distant, yet stationary, foe.

STATS	
Damage per Shot	50
Rounds per Clip	60
Rate of Fire	180rpm for 3 round burst
Max Ammo Capacity	60
Maximum Range	Infinite
Splash Damage Radius	N/A
Respawn Time	20 seconds

RPG

The RPG is one of the most imposing weapons in Duke's arsenal because of its tremendous blast radius and potential to deliver deadly damage to multiple enemies with a single rocket. Although its ammo capacity is limited to five rockets, the RPG is consistently the most pursued weapon when matches begin.

Part of the RPG's allure is its homing ability. Aim the RPG at an enemy, then watch the reticle achieve lock-on status and turn red. The rocket will track the player mid-flight, even as the player runs, or flies, away. The RPG's homing capability can handle open terrain with ease, but players can evade the rocket by running around sharp corners or by taking cover behind a pillar. Lastly, always consider your distance to the target before firing the RPG, as suicide-by-RPG is a common occurrence.

STATS	
Damage per Shot	135.0 per homing rocket
Rounds per Clip	5
Rate of Fire	60rpm
Max Ammo Capacity	5
Maximum Range	Infinite
Splash Damage Radius	12.5 feet
Respawn Time	20 seconds

ROCKET JUMP!

One of the staples of old-school *Duke Nukem* is the ability to use the RPG to perform a rocket jump. This technique allows you to use the propulsion of the rocket to send Duke flying high into the air. Perform a rocket jump by angling the RPG toward the ground at no more than a 25-degree angle, then leap into the air and fire the weapon. The closer you are to the epicenter of the explosion, the higher Duke will go. Duke will incur about 20% less damage when a rocket jump is executed at the correct angle, otherwise he will feel the entire wrath.

Use this powerful technique to avoid enemy attacks, take shortcuts to higher ledges and balconies (such as the Whiskey power-up on Morningwood) and to just look like a bad-ass. But remember, the RPG only has 5 rockets. Use them wisely!

DEVASTATOR

Pound for pound, the Devastator is the most lethal weapon in the game due to its high rate of fire and sizable blast radius. This weapon is essentially a fully-automatic, double-barrel rocket launcher. Hold the trigger to fire alternating rockets from the left and right chambers at the rate of four-per-second. Although the damage caused by an individual rocket is a fraction of that of the RPG, there's no need to fire one rocket alone. Aim at a target's feet to ensure the rockets don't sail past their mark to score the kill.

The Devastator's sizable clip of 69 rockets should provide enough firepower for the 20 seconds it takes for the weapon to respawn. This formidable weapon is extremely effective when fighting in confined spaces, provided you are outside the splash damage radius. The Devastator is also very efficient against a Jetpacking enemy.

STATS	
Damage per Shot	25
Rounds per Clip	69 (of course)
Rate of Fire	240rpm
Max Ammo Capacity	69
Maximum Range	Infinite
Splash Damage Radius	9.4 feet
Respawn Time	20 seconds

ENFORCER

The Enforcer can be considered a rocket-based upgrade to the AT Laser. It fires in a three-round burst (one burst per second) and has an unlimited effective range. That's where the similarities end, though. The Enforcer fires three heat-seeking rockets that, unlike the RPG, don't require a target-lock on its mark. They instantly home in on any nearby heat source. The Enforcer's rockets inflict 30% more damage than the Devastator and explode on contact, delivering that damage across a radius of 8 feet.

The Enforcer is commonly found in miniature form on multiplayer maps, necessitating a brief exploratory stint in a shrunken state. Even though the weapon's splash damage is less effective in wide-open spaces, the heat-seeking properties of the rocket give it a better chance of hitting their mark. Players can evade the Enforcer's heat-seeking projectiles by quickly turning sharp corners or by taking cover on the far side of a pillar.

STATS	
Damage per Shot	40 per heat-seeking projectile.
Rounds per Clip	15
Rate of Fire	180rpm
Max Ammo Capacity	15
Maximum Range	Infinite
Splash Damage Radius	8.0 feet
Respawn Time	20 seconds

EXPLOSIVES

TRIP MINE

Trip Mines allow the player to set explosive traps for their enemies throughout the map. Trip Mines stick to any surface, including teammates, enemies, and the babe. Once affixed to a surface, the Trip Mine beeps shortly and then arms itself as a laser extends outwards from the device. The Trip Mine remains active until someone breaks the laser, thereby causing the explosives to detonate. Up to four Trip Mines can be placed by each individual player simultaneously. All deployed Trip Mines disappear from the map once the player who placed them is killed. Trip Mines have a wide blast radius and pack enough punch to instantly kill any player caught within it.

The key to using Trip Mines is to place them low on walls so that opponents can't see the lasers. Avoid triggering an enemy's Trip Mine by leaping over the laser, or by standing back and shooting the Trip Mine to detonate it. Pipe Bombs are also effective at destroying Trip Mines. Try placing Trip Mines on the floor near weapon/power-up locations, near the babe platform, or on enemies! Trip Mines thrown at Bounce Pads will automatically land and arm themselves at the Bounce Pad destination.

STATS	
Damage per Shot	125
Rounds per Clip	N/A
Rate of Fire	N/A
Max Ammo Capacity	4
Maximum Range	N/A
Splash Damage Radius	6.25 feet
Respawn Time	20 seconds

PIPE BOMB

STATS	
Damage per Shot	125
Rounds per Clip	N/A
Rate of Fire	N/A
Max Ammo Capacity	4
Maximum Range	N/A
Splash Damage Radius	16.25 feet
Respawn Time	20 seconds

Pipe Bombs are remote-detonated explosives that pack as much punch as a Trip Mine, but these devices boast an expanded blast radius. Players can carry and/or deploy up to four Pipe Bombs at once. Once a Pipe Bomb has been thrown, the player automatically swaps his weapon for a remote control detonator. This allows the player to spring explosive traps for enemies by scattering multiple Pipe Bombs around a high-traffic area (think capture locations in Hail to the King matches), then detonate them simultaneously with a press of the Fire button. Pipe Bombs persist on the map until detonated or until the player who threw them is killed.

Pipe Bombs come in handy when fighting a group of enemies or when you're simply outmatched by an opponent. Quickly toss the Pipe Bomb, back away, and then press the Fire button. Pipe Bombs can be thrown a considerable distance by leaping into the air while throwing. Pipe Bombs generally follow the arc set by the reticle, making it possible to lob them into the air at Jetpacking enemies. Try throwing a Pipe Bomb at a Bounce Pad to make it bounce a considerable distance and height.

ENVIRONMENTAL EXPLOSIVES

Trip Mines and Pipe Bombs aren't the only explosives in *Duke Nukem Forever*. Be on the lookout for red barrels, as these flammable containers are highly explosive and can be used to kill unsuspecting enemies. The locations of each explosive barrel are indicated on the accompanying multiplayer maps. Try targeting them when an enemy is nearby, especially the barrels near weapon spawn locations.

POWER UPS & EQUIPMENT

Multiplayer games also feature multiple power-ups and pieces of equipment that can be used to great effect. While the Jetpack, Beer, and Holoduke are stored in Duke's inventory to be used on command, the golden Statue and Whiskey pick-ups take effect immediately.

JETPACK
■ **Respawn Time:** 30 seconds.

The Jetpack is exclusive to multiplayer mode and grants the player the ability to fly above the map and inflict mayhem on those below. Put the Jetpack to use by leaping into the air, then double tap the Jump button to engage the thrusters and take flight. Release the Jump button to descend, but be careful as Duke can easily suffer damage from a long fall if you cut the engines too soon. You can soften the landing by re-engaging the engines to slow his descent.

The Jetpack comes with a sizable tank of fuel, enough to last for nearly 30 seconds of continued use. It's possible to extend your time in the air by feathering the thrusters and setting down atop elevated rocks and ledges. Not only does this help conserve fuel, but it's a great way to gain an element of stealth. The Jetpack is very loud and highly susceptible to weapon fire, so it pays to be as discreet as possible when using it.

HOLODUKE
■ Respawn Time: 10 seconds after hologram disappears.

The Holoduke is another sought-after piece of equipment. When put to use, it creates a holographic version of the player's character who runs around the map, shoots at enemies, and even taunts them. The hologram is somewhat robotic in its movements, but it will fool players more often than not.

The real advantage to using the Holoduke is that it provides the player roughly 15 seconds of near-invisibility. A player using the Holoduke will have a slight shimmering effect, but it is difficult to spot at distance. Combine the Holoduke's cloaking ability with the holographic Duke to fool enemies. Watch as they rush the hologram, granting you clean shots at their flank. The Holoduke is particularly useful when trying to steal an opponent's babe in Capture the Babe matches, or when camping a particular sniping position.

STEROIDS
■ **Effect Duration:** 21 seconds.
■ **Respawn Time:** 30 seconds.

Not satisfied with the weapons you currently have? Feel like turning someone's face to hamburger? Want your fists to crackle and spark with lightning? If so, then Steroids are the answer! This "medicine" greatly increases Duke's speed and drastically intensifies his punching power. Taking Steroids instantly incurs a 25% damage penalty, but players on Steroids can often-

times overwhelm other players. This is particularly true against players with precision weapons such as the Railgun, Freeze Ray, or Pistol—Steroids have the added effect of making the player immune to Shrink Ray attacks. Gulp down a jar of Steroids and then head for a nearby enemy. Hold the Fire button to make Duke throw alternating left and right jabs. Duke can kill an enemy with a single punch while on Steroids.

BEER

- **Effect Duration:** 21 seconds
- **Respawn Time:** 30 seconds

Beer is only available during Hail to the King matches. Players can pick a can and use it to gain a slight increase in Duke's strength. More importantly, the Beer lessens the amount of damage the player incurs during combat. Unfortunately, drinking the Beer causes the player's field of vision to blur, making it tougher to run in a straight line. Aiming also gets more difficult.

One of the best times to drink a Beer is when you're trying to defend a capture location, as the increased damage resistance will help stave off enemy attacks. Additionally, your team will continue to score points by maintaining sole possession of the capture point. Players under the effects of a Beer appear on-screen with bubbles rising from their head. Burp.

WHISKEY

- **Effect Duration:** 15 seconds
- **Respawn Time:** 120 seconds

The golden bottle of Whiskey (which is available on most maps) will quite possibly be the single most sought-after power-up in the game, as it offers 15 seconds of uninterrupted invincibility! The effects begin the moment the player touches the Whiskey pick-up. The player glows an orange color, indicating that he is invincible to everything except damage from a fall. It's entirely possible to fall to your death while under the influence of the Whiskey, so be careful. Finding ways to pair the Whiskey power-up with a weapon like the Devastator or Ripper goes a long way to padding that kill/death ratio.

STATUE

- **Effect Duration:** 15 seconds
- **Respawn Time:** 30 seconds

The golden Statue power-up grants the player double damage for the currently equipped weapon. The effects of the Statue are immediate, so make sure to have a loaded weapon and a target or two in mind before touching the Statue. Players enjoying the benefits of double damage will have a green glow on their weapon, indicating that the effect is active.

Many of the weapons in multiplayer mode are capable of one-hit kills, but the double damage effect successfully extends the blast radius, making weapons like the RPG and Enforcer even deadlier. The effect also makes it easier to achieve a Shotgun kill against an enemy at range, as each pellet has double damage. The Statue makes it much easier to kill enemies with the Pistol, Ripper, and AT Laser as well. The only weapon that doesn't enjoy a noticeable benefit from the effect is the Railgun, which is not only a one-hit kill, but causes no splash damage.

CASINO

TEMPT YOUR FATE AT THE LADY KILLER CASINO.

Lady Luck better be smiling down on Duke tonight, as the action at the casino is about to really heat up. The Lady Killer Casino contains three floors of atriums, maintenance corridors, and casino rooms, making it one of the largest and most complex of the 10 maps. It's so large in fact that it's the only map that has a sizable portion cordoned off during standard Duke Match battles—the blue team's side of the map is off-limits in non-team matches.

Pipe Bombs and Trip Mines play a big role in combat at the Casino, particularly along the balconies encircling the central atrium and in the maintenance corridor. The numerous ventilation grates provide shortcuts from one level to the next, both for shrunken Dukes and full-grown Nukems! Many of these lead to ceiling-mounted grates that can be shot, creating an escape route for a shrunken Duke. Although the weapons are spread far and wide across the map, the primary power-ups are located in the atrium, along the balcony and atop the two bronze statues in the middle. Lastly, there are two secret areas on this symmetrical map, but they are both empty save for Capture the Babe matches when they contain an Enforcer.

DUKE AND TEAM DUKE MATCH

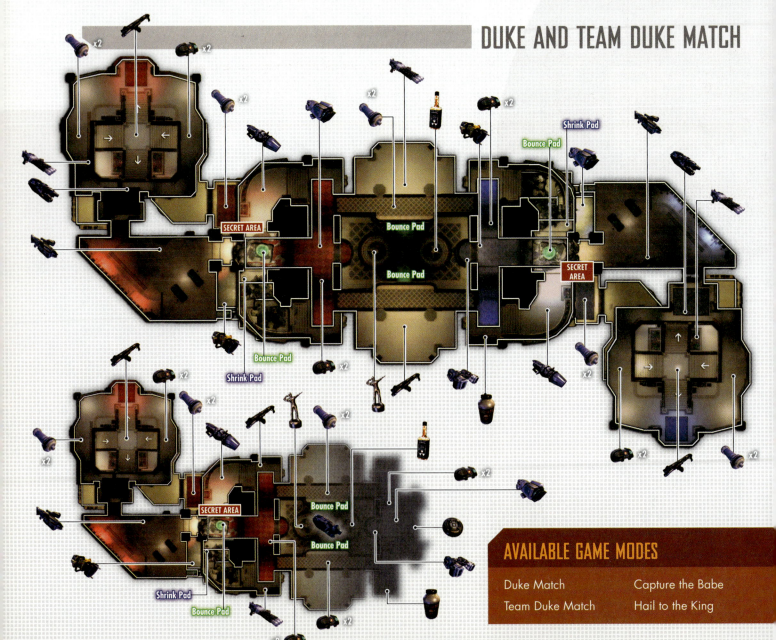

AVAILABLE GAME MODES

Duke Match	Capture the Babe
Team Duke Match	Hail to the King

GENERAL TACTICS

BOUNCE A QUARTER OFF IT

The Statue and Whiskey power-ups (or two Statues during CTB matches) sit atop the bronzed backsides of the babe statues in the central atrium. The gold tint of the power-ups blends in rather well against the bronze statues, thus making them easy to miss. And even when you know they're there, they can still be difficult—and downright dangerous—to obtain.

For starters, don't run to the statue in hopes of leaping and grabbing the power-up. Not only is it too high to reach, but you'll be a sitting duck for other players. Instead, use one of the Bounce Pads to quickly gain access to the balcony, then turn to the left or right and locate the gap in the glass railing near the power-up you crave. Run and leap through this opening onto the bronzed beauty to claim the power-up. Always look for Trip Mines before you leap, though!

Head to the balcony, grab the Holoduke and Devastator and leap off the railing down onto the Whiskey power-up.

ROCKET JUMP

If there's one place in the casino where it's okay to perform a rocket jump, it's in the atrium. Try to perform one to get a power-up atop a statue, but remember that it's not the best idea. The RPG comes with very limited ammo, so why waste it when you can just use a Bounce Pad to get there?

EYES IN THE SKY

Players who enjoy launching surprise attacks, or who are handy with the Railgun, are in for a treat near the craps tables. Lay claim to the Railgun and circle back around to the main floor of the atrium. Descend the stairs in the corner to the maintenance corridor and shoot the grate on the wall, then crouch down and enter the vent. Duke will fall and hit a hidden Bounce Pad inside the ductwork, which will catapult him upwards to the vent on the wall in the corner of the gaming room. Shoot or melee out the grate and wait inside the ductwork for an enemy to enter the room.

Keep the Railgun's laser sights fixed on the Railgun pick-up near the slot machines to get an easy kill. Be sure to place a Trip Mine inside this section of ductwork before fleeing, as it's an unavoidable booby trap for those who may enter later.

Hang out inside the vent overlooking the gaming room and Railgun to get the drop on an enemy. Even Pipe Bombs work well if you don't have a power weapon.

WEAPONS & POWER-UPS

The casino's low ceilings forsake the Jetpack for obvious reasons, but every other weapon and power-up is in play with the exception of the Enforcer during standard Duke Match games. Each of the team-based modes feature a wealth of weaponry (including pairs of RPGs, Railguns, and Enforcers), but Capture the Babe is the only mode that also features two Devastators!

Everything is equal for both teams on this symmetrical map, but that's not the case during individual games of Duke Match. Players who spawn on the ground floor of the atrium should immediately head for the RPG in the red curving hallway, while those who spawn upstairs should head to the blue side to pick up the Devastator and Holoduke. It can be easy to miss the Statue and Whiskey on this map; use the Bounce Pads to reach the balcony, then run and leap onto the large bronze statues to get the power-ups.

WEAPONS/POWER-UPS MATRIX

NAME		DM	TDM	CTB	HTTK
	Shotgun	2	3	3	3
	Ripper	2	3	3	3
	Railgun	1	2	2	2
	AT Laser	1	1	2	2
	Freeze Ray	1	1	2	2
	Shrink Ray	1	1	2	2
	Enforcer	-	2	2	2
	Devastator	1	1	2	1
	RPG	1	2	2	2
	Pipe Bomb	6	8	12	10
	Trip Mine	6	8	8	10
	Steroids	1	1	1	1
	Holoduke	1	1	1	1
	Jetpack	-	-	-	-
	Beer	-	-	-	27
	Statue	1	1	2	1
	Whiskey	1	1	1	1

Advancing on the enemy's babe is an important part of CTB matches, but it's also vital that some players defend the base. The large number of weapons on this map makes it possible in a number of ways, but some weapons are more powerful than others. Discuss with your teammates who will get the Enforcer from the mini-route and who, if any, will go for the Shrink Ray. Additionally, note that the Whiskey is no longer atop a bronze statue; instead, it's on the floor in between the statues. Although it's dangerous to run along the bottom of the atrium with the enemy's babe, the Whiskey power-up is invaluable to a babe carrier if you can get it.

HAIL TO THE KING

Casino is sure to become a favorite map for Hail to the King fans, as the plethora of Beer and Shotguns makes for an exciting match. Both teams have immediate access to an abundance of weapons, but the blue team has a quick route to the Devastator, whereas the red team is closer to a Holoduke. Whichever member of the red team gets the Holoduke should immediately deploy it and hunt down the enemy with the Devastator before the red teammates try to capture the point.

Use the Devastator to protect your teammates as they capture the point. Stand outside the circle, preferably just out of sight, and use it to blast enemies trying to steal the point.

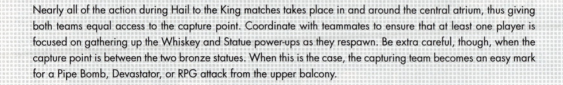

SECRET AREA

Bounce Pad

Shrink Pad

x2

Bounce Pad

Bounce Pad

Shrink Pad

Shrink Pad

Bounce Pad

SECRET AREA

x2

x2

x2

x2

x2

x2

x2

Nearly all of the action during Hail to the King matches takes place in and around the central atrium, thus giving both teams equal access to the capture point. Coordinate with teammates to ensure that at least one player is focused on gathering up the Whiskey and Statue power-ups as they respawn. Be extra careful, though, when the capture point is between the two bronze statues. When this is the case, the capturing team becomes an easy mark for a Pipe Bomb, Devastator, or RPG attack from the upper balcony.

DUKE BURGER

A BURGER RESTAURANT FEATURING MINI-DUKES.

Welcome to the kitchen of Duke Burger, a Duke-themed fast-food restaurant serving up a pile of rocket-fueled explosiveness. Some restaurants may think bigger means better, but it's the little things that matter most here at Duke Burger! And that's not just a marketing spiel dreamed up by some suits in a boardroom, it's the literal truth at Duke Burger.

All players participating in the action at Duke Burger do so as mini-Dukes, permanently shrunken in size. Don't confuse one of the action figures for an enemy—the rocket you waste may be your last! There are no Shrink Rays or Shrink Pads at Duke Burger, nor can you play Capture the Babe on this map, but the shrunken size of the competitors opens up a world of new possibilities. For starters, everyday kitchen appliances become a lot more interesting when you risk being trapped inside them. And the grill and deep fryers are positively lethal to players who fail to hop across the safety of the burger buns. A large number of Bounce Pads, a Jetpack, and towering shelves and cabinets all provide ample opportunity to get an elevated view of the battlefield—and with no risk of suffering fall damage thanks to Duke's shrunken stature.

DUKE AND TEAM DUKE MATCH

AVAILABLE GAME MODES

Duke Match	Hail to the King
Team Duke Match	

GENERAL TACTICS

KITCHEN NIGHTMARE

The dishwasher and microwave ovens can be used to trap enemies as they go for the power weapons inside. Shoot the spatula on the wall next to the open microwave door to fling the door shut when an enemy is inside. Similarly, target the large green buttons on the front of the dishwasher and near the shelves to the left to drop the doors and activate the dishwasher. You need to be quick, as it doesn't take long to grab a weapon and escape the trap, but snaring a foe inside an appliance is one of the most satisfying kills you can get. The AT Laser, Ripper, Pistol, and Railgun all offer pinpoint accuracy for shooting the button or spatula.

WEAPONS & POWER-UPS

There may not be as many weapons at Duke Burger as compared to other maps, but only the Shrink Ray and Enforcer are missing in action. Although they may be all accounted for, the RPG and Devastator are located inside the restaurant's booby-trapped microwave and dishwasher, respectively. Enter at your own risk, and be fast about it!

The weapon and power-up locations are identical for all three modes with one exception: the Ripper is positioned a few paces toward the center of the map during Hail to the King matches. There is no Whiskey on this map either.

WEAPONS/POWER-UPS MATRIX

NAME		DM	TDM	CTB	HTTK
	Shotgun	2	2	-	2
	Ripper	1	1	-	1
	Railgun	1	1	-	1
	AT Laser	1	1	-	1
	Freeze Ray	1	1	-	1
	Shrink Ray	-	-	-	-
	Enforcer	-	-	-	-
	Devastator	1	1	-	1
	RPG	1	1	-	1
	Pipe Bomb	4	4	-	4
	Trip Mine	4	4	-	4
	Steroids	1	1	-	1
	Holoduke	1	1	-	1
	Jetpack	1	1	-	1
	Beer	-	-	-	10
	Statue	1	1	-	1
	Whiskey				

FISH IN A BARREL

Take advantage of a player's fear of being trapped inside the dishwasher or microwave by lining each appliance with Trip Mines. This way, not only will you score a kill even when you don't see an enemy enter either trap, but you can even steal kills from players about to shoot the spatula or button. The Trip Mine will go off and kill the enemy before the trap can be sprung by someone else!

DEATH FROM ABOVE

The Jetpack offers skilled players an advantage on this map, not only because of its ability to keep a player above the fray, but it affords a player the chance to snipe atop boxes and jars that are otherwise out of reach. To get the Jetpack, go to the southeast corner of the map and leap

across the dishes in the sink to reach the Bounce Pad. Turn and face the sink and leap for the narrow edge of the bulletin board. Run along the bulletin board to the Jetpack atop the shelf in the corner.

The edge is not as narrow as it looks. Run along the top of the bulletin board to reach the Jetpack in the corner.

Sporting the Jetpack, immediately fly toward the grill and pluck the Statue off the burger bun for double damage. Continue flying north to grab the RPG from inside the microwave to gain some added firepower. Continue to soar in the air, fire the RPG, and enjoy double the normal damage across the blast radius.

Make mine a double—damage that is!

THE UNFRIENDLY SKIES

The going will certainly be rougher for those being harassed by an aerial assailant, but all is not lost. There are multiple ways to down a Jetpacking opponent, provided the flier tends to stick to the same area. One way is to use a Bounce Pad to get as high as possible and throw Trip Mines against the wall just below the ceiling. Many flying players tend to glide toward corners of the room, then strafe around with their back to the wall. Trip Mines will be harder to detect and less expected near a corner, where players will likely be strafing with their backs to them.

HOT ROUTE

The compact layout of Duke Burger makes it difficult to focus on a singular path without either covering too much of the map or not enough. Although many players will opt for a route that utilizes the Jetpack, Statue, and RPG, there is an alternative. Enter the storage room upon spawning and use the Bounce Pad to reach the Railgun. Next, run along the upper shelf to the Bounce Pad leading up to the secret area and the Holoduke. Return the way you came, slip through the hole in the wall to the other shelves and start sniping while invisible. Drop to the floor, grab the Ripper for close-range defense, and return to the storage room to repeat the route. The key is to utilize the Holoduke and Railgun together while maintaining an elevated position until it is no longer advantageous.

SECRET AREA

Bounce Pad

Bounce Pad

Bounce Pad

x2

WIPE YOUR FACE

Although it won't inflict any damage, one way to annoy elevated enemies (or any, for that matter) is to target the jars of condiments on the shelves. It only takes a single bullet to shatter a jar of sauce and the contents will splatter across the screen of any nearby players, briefly obscuring their view.

COOKING UP S'MORES

The Railgun is a popular weapon on this map—and for good reason. There are numerous positions to set up camp and do a little Railgun sniping. None of the locations are entirely foolproof, especially against an airborne foe, but some spots do afford a moderate amount of concealment.

The first thing to do is get the Railgun. Enter the storage room in the southwest corner of the map and use the Bounce Pad to reach the top of the shelf. After picking up the Railgun, head to the east atop the shelves beyond the hole in the wall. Next, leap at an angle toward the large mayonnaise jar on the shelf in the middle. This provides a good spot from which to snipe, as it affords a view of the Jetpack pick-up, the Statue, and the other shelves near the grills.

Another favorite spot from which to snipe is atop the dishwasher. Get the Jetpack and fly back across the map to the dishwasher and land on top. The raised doors provide protection from the left and right and the wall offers cover from behind. This position is vulnerable to Pipe Bombs and an aerial attack, but only once the Jetpack respawns. Take aim at any opponents near the microwave, by the secret area, and near the stoves.

Use the Holoduke for camouflage and move behind the large tub of mayonnaise to the right with the Railgun for a guarded sniping position overlooking the microwave.

SECRET AREA: HOLODUKE

The secret area is inside the ventilation system within the ceiling. There are two entrances to it, both courtesy of Bounce Pads in the center of the room, high atop shelving between the storage room and dishwasher. Use one of the uppermost Bounce Pads to enter the ductwork in the ceiling and grab the Holoduke. Now quickly run for the Holoduke inside the secret area immediately after acquiring the Railgun inside the storage room. It's also possible to fly to the secret area using the Jetpack.

HAIL TO THE KING

All of the capture points in Hail to the King at Duke Burger are on the kitchen floor spread around the vicinity of the grills. Pipe Bombs, Beer, and Steroids all come in handy in this mode, as much of the combat takes place at a very close range. The Shotgun and Ripper are also quite useful. It's all but impossible to guard the capture point from all approaches, so spread out across the edge of the capture zone and face outwards to spot opponents. Look for areas within the capture point that have overhead cover, as the best way to flush out an enemy is from the sky.

Teams can get off to a quick start by dominating the airspace above the capture points. Don't give the enemy an easy target on the floor—remove the aerial threat!

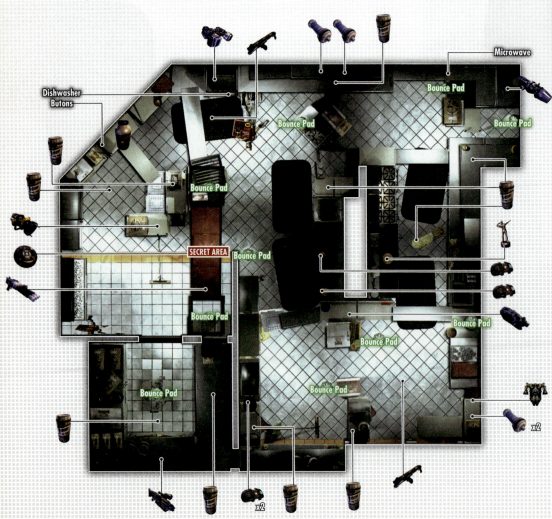

You don't need to be in the capture point to be a contributing member of the team. With so much attention placed on securing the points, it's often quite easy to run the perimeter of the map collecting power-ups and heavy weapons. A player in an elevated position with the Holoduke, Jetpack, Railgun and/or Devastator or RPG can be every bit as beneficial to their team as the players down on the ground contesting the point.

If multiple enemies are approaching when defending the capture point, remember to drink a Beer. The extra damage resistance will offset the blurred vision.

ERECTION SITE

AN ABANDONED CONSTRUCTION YARD.

DUKE AND TEAM DUKE MATCH

The only thing more fun than holding a shootout in an office building is doing it in one that is still under construction. Erection Site is a sprawling construction project that consists of three structures placed around the perimeter of a dirt clearing. The largest building (the one to the south) is three stories tall, including the ground-floor parking garage. The other buildings are somewhat smaller, but all are tall enough to transform the exterior into a veritable shooting gallery. The crane in the center of the map can be moved, but not without some risk. Would-be crane operators must remain in the cockpit while the crane is being rotated, providing any nearby sharpshooters with plenty of time for a headshot. Run along the crane's lengthy boom for quick access to the southern and western building.

The vertical, asymmetrical nature of the map precludes Capture the Babe matches, but this same feature only adds to the excitement when playing Hail to the King. Weapons and power-ups are in abundance, provided you know where to look—and have practiced your rocket jump. And though it may seem as if Trip Mines and Pipe Bombs are in short supply, there's actually a very large stash of them underneath the foreman's trailer by the crane. Use either of the nearby Shrink Pads to top off your supplies. Lastly, the stairwells, elevator shaft, and ventilation system provides ample opportunity for mayhem.

Rotate Crane

Shrink Pad

Bounce Pad

Shrink Pad

x4 Mini

x4 Mini

SECRET AREA

Bounce Pad

Bounce Pad

SECRET AREA

x2

Shrink Pad **Shrink Pad**

x2

Mini

AVAILABLE GAME MODES

Duke Match

Team Duke Match

Hail to the King

MY, WHAT A BIG CRANE YOU HAVE!

The crane in the middle of the map can rotate roughly 70 degrees, ranging from the upper edge of the building on the west side to the third floor window of the building to the south. To move the crane, simply climb into the operator's seat and pull the levers. The crane will slowly rotate in place from one building to the other. Note that Duke can't exit the chair until the crane comes to a stop, so this move certainly carries some risk with it. Climb onto the crane and run along the boom for quick access to the top of either structure. Getting onto the crane can be accomplished from the ground, but it's easier to do so by leaping from the second floor of the building to the north. Lastly, be extra careful when leaping from the crane to the building on the west side of the map, as it's a tough jump that often ends in a player falling to his death.

WEAPONS & POWER-UPS

The quantity and locations of the weapons is identical across all three modes with the only exception being an added Shrink Ray on the upper floor of the southern building during Hail to the King matches. The only change to the power-up placement is the switching of locations for the Holoduke and Steroids.

This map is a sniper's dream come true, so players must be cautious when venturing into open spaces. Two Railguns spawn on opposite sides of the map, one on the third floor of the southern building and the other on the ground near the northern structure. The RPG is located inside the foreman's trailer, whereas the Devastator is located high inside the western structure. The RPG is required to access the secret areas in order to obtain the Statue or Whiskey power-ups. Similarly, players will need the Shrink Pad to access the miniature Enforcer within the elevator car—drop onto the elevator from above to get the power-up (Holoduke or Steroids).

WEAPONS/POWER-UPS MATRIX

NAME		DM	TDM	CTB	HTTK
	Shotgun	2	2	-	2
	Ripper	2	2	-	2
	Railgun	2	2	-	2
	AT Laser	1	1	-	1
	Freeze Ray	1	1	-	1
	Shrink Ray	1	1	-	2
	Enforcer	1	1	-	1
	Devastator	1	1	-	1
	RPG	1	1	-	1
	Pipe Bomb	6	6	-	6
	Trip Mine	6	6	-	6
	Steroids	1	1	-	1
	Holoduke	1	1	-	1
	Jetpack	-	-	-	-
	Beer	-	-	-	15
	Statue	1	1	-	1
	Whiskey	1	1	-	1

GENERAL TACTICS

GO SMALL FOR BIG BANGS

There are four Shrink Pads on the map, two near the foreman's trailer and two by the elevator shaft inside the southern building. Use either Shrink Pad near the trailer to gather the Pipe Bombs and Trip Mines beneath the trailer. The effect lasts long enough for Duke to collect all eight explosives before returning to normal size, but you must hurry! Use the mound of dirt to leap over the orange fence and immediately place a Trip Mine inside the trailer to snare players going for the RPG.

Use the Shrink Pad on either side of the trailer to get small enough to access the Trip Mines and Pipe Bombs underneath the trailer.

TINY TARGETS

It may sound risky, but one of the safest ways to move about in the clearing is when Duke is small. Consider using a Shrink Pad to safely cross the yard when making your way toward the Railgun to the north, especially if there's a sniper in one of the secret areas. You may still get shot at, but your chances of being hit will be—like Duke—a whole lot smaller.

TRIP MINE THE STAIRS

One of the best uses of the Trip Mines on this map (aside from inside the trailer near the RPG) is inside the stairwells and along the walls where the Bounce Pads send players hurtling through the air. Remember that players often move quickly through the stairs to return to the action and it's easy to catch them off-guard with a Trip Mine. Similarly, players are completely at the mercy of gravity when using a Bounce Pad—they can't help but hit the Trip Mine if one is placed where they land.

While in a shrunken state, you can access the Enforcer that is located inside the elevator in the parking garage area of the southern structure. Use the Shrink Pad in the garage and quickly run down the ramp to get the weapon. Don't try to run back up the ramp and out of the elevator just yet, as Duke will be killed if he returns to size while on the slanted board. Instead, wait to return to normal while on the floor of the elevator, then use the Shrink Pad inside the elevator car to shrink again and safely ascend the ramp.

SECRET AREA #1 STATUE

The more strategically advantageous of the two secret areas, this one is located high atop the building in the northwest corner near the row of port-a-potties. Acquire the RPG from inside the foreman's trailer and either run along the crane or use the Bounce Pad on the third floor of the southern building to reach the middle floor of the northwest building. Climb the stairs to the roof and face north. Use the RPG to rocket jump onto the roof directly adjacent to the railing near the stairs (expert Duke-athletes may be able to leap from the railing onto the roof) to access the secret area and grab the Statue. This is a fantastic sniping position!

SECRET AREA #2: WHISKEY

The second secret area is in the southwest corner of the map atop the building enshrouded by the alien tentacles. Acquire the RPG from the foreman's trailer in the center of the map and approach the tentacle behind the Bounce Pad. Run up along the tentacle toward the second floor of the building next to the Bounce Pad, then turn and rocket jump onto the roof in the corner. There is a Whiskey power-up in the corner, behind the air conditioning unit and tentacle.

Be wary of where you stand when the effects of the Shrink Pad elapse. Use the Shrink Pad inside the elevator to safely exit.

With the Railgun at the ready, crouch in this corner near the Steroids to have a clear shot at the secret area and at anyone searching for the Railgun.

SNIPE THE SNIPERS

Expect to encounter two prominent approaches to this map: there are those who will stick to the interiors and use weapons like the Shotgun, Devastator, and Freeze Ray at close range and then there will be the snipers. A sniper armed with an RPG and the Railgun can dominate the map from atop the northwest secret area (with the Statue), so it's important to know how to counter this. One way is to climb the alien tentacle in the southwest corner to the building and lob Pipe Bombs. This is admittedly a dangerous technique, but it can work. Another somewhat risky tactic is to use the Railgun on the ground to try and snipe from the northern building. Fortunately, there is another option.

Head to the southern building, climb the stairs to the middle floor, and enter the elevator to get the Holoduke. Ascend to the top floor, deploy the Holoduke and grab the Railgun while invisible. Shoot out the vents on the floor to the east, crouch down, and move a few rooms over to acquire an angle on the sniper. Others will no doubt make their move on the third floor Railgun (some possibly through the nearby window via the Bounce Pad). Stick to your corner position near the Steroids power-up and shoot them, too. Place Trip Mines nearby to cover your back.

RUN FAST, BOUNCE HIGH

To succeed at Erection Site, it's vital to know the fastest paths to the most powerful weapons and, just as important, the elevated positions on the map. There's simply no time to waste figuring out how to reach the Devastator or how to quickly reach the Railgun on the third floor.

Start by committing the ways in and out of the western structure to memory. It's three stories tall and only the lowest level is accessible from the ground. The second level can be reached by running along the alien tentacle in the southwest corner of the map. From there, you can grab the Devastator and head up the stairs to the third floor. It's also possible to reach the third floor directly via the crane or by using the Bounce Pad atop the southern building. Descend the stairs or use the ductwork to drop down to the Devastator.

There are two ground-level entrances to the southern building, with stairs in each corner leading to the second and third floors, but there are easier ways up. The Bounce Pad in the southwest corner will catapult players to the middle floor of the southern building. Conversely, the Bounce Pad in the northeastern corner of the yard (beyond the crane) will send players flying through a third-floor window near the Steroids power-up. It's also possible to run along the crane when it's facing south and enter the third floor near the Railgun.

HOT ROUTE

This is an ideal route to take when the crane is angled toward the west. Head straight to the trailer and grab the RPG. Loop around the crane in a counter-clockwise direction to obtain the Railgun, then leap onto the back of the crane and run up the boom to the roof of the western building. Use the RPG to rocket jump onto the roof to claim the Statue, then start sniping with the Railgun. Keep this up until you run out of ammo, then use the Statue's double-damage to add to the splash damage from the RPG. Descend the stairs to the middle level, swap the RPG for the Devastator, and battle back to the start of the route.

x4 Mini

x4 Mini

SECRET AREA

Shrink Pad

Shrink Pad

HAIL TO THE KING

x4 Mini

SECRET AREA

Rotate Crane

Shrink Pad

Bounce Pad

Shrink Pad

x4 Mini

Bounce Pad

Bounce Pad

SECRET AREA

x2

x2

Shrink Pad

Shrink Pad

x2

Mini

x2

This is a great map for Hail to the King when there are large teams and everyone knows their way around the map. The capture points shift between locations on the ground near the crane to the roof of the western building to various places inside the southern structure. Despite the map's size, most of the capture points are hemmed in rather tightly, allowing little room for players to take a defensive role outside the capture point without having to move too far away. This makes having a supply of Pipe Bombs (or the RPG) even more important than normal for attacking teams.

One of the unique aspects of Hail to the King matches is that it brings the large second-floor room into play. This area beneath the collapsed third floor of the southern building doesn't see much action during Duke Matches. The hole in the third floor provides an excellent opportunity for attacking teams to launch their assault undetected. Secure the Pipe Bombs in the southwest stairs and ascend to the third floor. Toss the Pipe Bombs down at the defending team inside the capture point, then use the additional Shrink Ray to miniaturize anyone who survives the explosions.

Don't be afraid to set traps at the capture points. Throw a Pipe Bomb and wait to detonate it when the other team gets there. This works especially well against over-aggressive teams.

HIGHWAY NOON

A BRIDGE AND GULLY ON A NEVADA HIGHWAY.

DUKE AND TEAM DUKE MATCH

The alien invasion wreaked havoc on this lone stretch of highway in the desert—now how is anyone supposed to get to Duke's casino? There's no time to worry about that now, however, as there's a battle to fight amongst the collapsed roadway and toppled cars. Highway Noon provides a little something for everyone (the Jetpack isn't available during Capture the Babe matches). The network of paths crisscrossing beneath the highway provides a chance to escape the upper level combat, but isn't without its own set of risks.

Bounce Pads, narrow paths of concrete, and even tilted shipping containers combine to give players a number of ways across the map, but it only takes one false step to send someone falling to their demise. Unlike on many maps, the Whiskey, Statue, and Holoduke are right out in the open. The only power-up that can be tricky to find is the Jetpack, which requires a lengthy leap from the highway to the rocks far to the north. Combine the RPG with the Jetpack and show the opposition what road rage is all about!

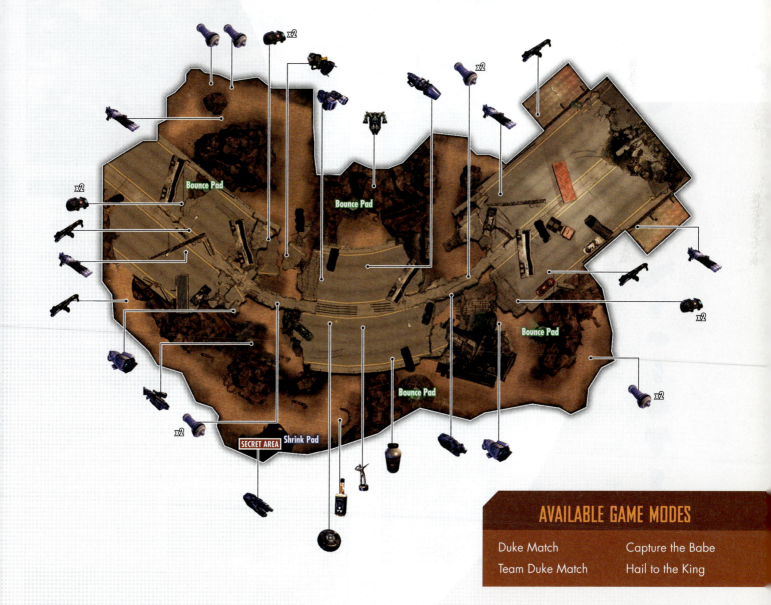

AVAILABLE GAME MODES

Duke Match	Capture the Babe
Team Duke Match	Hail to the King

WEAPONS & POWER-UPS

Every weapon in Duke's arsenal is in play during each gameplay mode, although players will need to utilize a Shrink Pad to access the Enforcer inside the secret area. The western side of the map contains twice as many Trip Mines as Pipe Bombs, while the eastern side has the opposite set-up so adjust your tactics accordingly.

The big rush early in matches will be for the RPG and Holoduke, which are located in the center of the map. Don't be afraid to hang back and let the dust settle before moving in with the Ripper or Shrink Ray. Those on the west side of the map can use the early rush as a chance to access the Enforcer from the secret area.

WEAPONS/POWER-UPS MATRIX

NAME		DM	TDM	CTB	HTTK
	Shotgun	4	4	4	4
	Ripper	4	4	4	4
	Railgun	1	1	1	1
	AT Laser	1	1	1	1
	Freeze Ray	1	1	1	1
	Shrink Ray	2	2	2	2
	Enforcer	1	1	1	1
	Devastator	1	1	1	1
	RPG	1	1	1	1
	Pipe Bomb	8	8	8	8
	Trip Mine	6	6	6	6
	Steroids	1	1	1	1
	Holoduke	1	1	1	1
	Jetpack	1	1	-	1
	Beer	-	-	-	9
	Statue	1	1	1	1
	Whiskey	1	1	1	1

GENERAL TACTICS

LONG DISTANCE ASSAULTS

Weapons with lock-on and homing capabilities (like the RPG and Enforcer) are very powerful on this map given the lengthy sight-lines. Both of these weapons (and the Railgun to an extent) can be used with great success, provided that you're careful when lining up shots. Stay clear of the middle section of the highway unless blind-firing the weapon. These weapons have excellent range but the RPG's lock-on takes a few moments to acquire its target. Move to the side of the map where there's some protection from sneak-attacks when taking this kind of shot. This is also true for sniping and using the Enforcer. The Enforcer can be fired from the hip rather well against close-to-medium range opponents, but it's always wise to take that extra moment to aim the shot when using a weapon with such limited ammo.

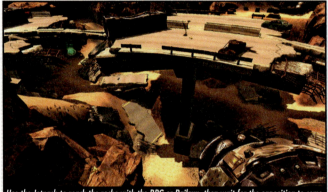

Use the Jetpack to reach the rocks with the RPG or Railgun, then wait for the opposition to come looking for a weapon in the center.

BECOME THE INVINCIBLE ENFORCER

The Whiskey's proximity to the Enforcer makes the two an obvious pairing. Just don't grab the Whiskey before trying to get the Enforcer in the secret area. The Whiskey protects against shrinkage, even when you're standing atop a Shrink Pad. Grab the Enforcer, exit the secret area before returning to size, then grab the Whiskey if it's there.

ALL TRIPPED UP

Enemy attacks can come from a lot of directions on this map, but there are several natural chokepoints where Trip Mines can be used to great effect. Placing Trip Mines doesn't have to come at the expense of using the other weapons, or attacking your foe directly, but it's a tactic that can generate a number of extra kills.

For starters, players spawning near the eastern tunnel should immediately grab the Trip Mines near the edge of the highway collapse. Turn to the left and place one on the end of the jersey barrier to catch players flying up to the road from the Bounce Pad far below. Another key spot for a Trip Mine is between the gap in the barriers on the central portion of highway, near the Holoduke and RPG.

It doesn't matter what mode you're playing, a Trip Mine set at the end of the barrier will kill anyone who uses the Bounce Pad directly below.

HOT ROUTE

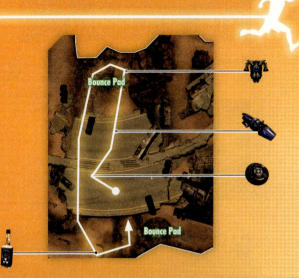

The Jetpack provides the ability to fly anywhere on the map, but it's also an easy target for skilled players. Stick close to the rocks and Whiskey to make the most out of this route. Sprint to the middle of the highway to lay claim to the Holoduke. Instantly deploy it, jump the barrier, and grab the RPG while continuing to sprint north toward the gap in the guardrail. Leap from the highway to the Jetpack on the rocks and take to the sky. Fire the RPG at any enemies you spot while invisible and begin flying south across the map. Swoop down to claim the Whiskey as it reappears and find a spot on the rocks from which to fire the RPG at players who shoot at the Holoduke. Save some fuel to return to the highway and start the lap over. Pick a different spot on the rocks to land near the end of the route each time, or else players will memorize your path.

Trip Mines placed inside the red shipping container are very difficult to spot—until it's too late.

Take the Devastator, hit the Bounce Pad and start firing! There's almost always at least one or two players near the RPG and Holoduke. Come prepared or don't come at all!

Lastly, placing a Trip Mine on the rocks near the Jet Pack is a surefire way to gain some extra kills. The players who already have the Jet Pack and are swooping in for a re-fueling may see the Trip Mine and shoot it, but those leaping from the highway bridge will have little chance of avoiding it. There are countless other spots to place Trip Mines as well, but these tend to catch enemies without fail.

SPEAKING OF FALLING...

It is possible to descend the side of the cliffs without freefalling to your death. Look for an area with some small protrusions and attempt to bounce from one to the other on the way down. It won't be pretty, but it's a lot better than ending up in a pile of gibs.

FALLING UPWARDS

The four Bounce Pads make it possible to quickly grab one of the weapons or power-ups off the ground below the highway, then return to the upper level where most of the action is taking place. Although useful during Duke Matches, the Bounce Pads to the east and west are most beneficial during Capture the Babe and Hail to the King matches. On the other hand, the Bounce Pads in the center of the map are great for sending players into the thick of combat whether they're prepared for it or not.

The angled red container is a perfect spot to toss a Trip Mine, as many players use it to escape from danger, camp out, or even reach the upper roadway without using a Bounce Pad. The container's red paint helps conceal the laser too!

Use these Bounce Pads wisely and be sure to have the Devastator on hand for those opponents sure to be lurking above. It's fine to hit them while wielding the Shotgun or Ripper, as long as you gain the benefits of the Statue before hitting the Bounce Pad. The north-central Bounce Pad lands players near the RPG, while the south-central Bounce Pad sends players towards the Whiskey.

RUN & GUN

Success at Highway Noon isn't entirely reliant upon the powerful weapons. In fact, it's entirely possible to accumulate a number of kills with just the Shotgun and Ripper, provided you move smartly. One way to accomplish this is to move quickly and erratically to avoid becoming an easy target for any Jetpacking rocketeers or snipers. Move quickly between the cars and toppled buses and look for recently spawned enemies. Avoid the crossfire zone in the center of the map where players with more powerful weapons are likely to be and try to keep the action in front of you. Follow the path down to the lower level in hopes of catching enemies off-guard as they go for the Devastator or other weapons.

Moving swiftly amongst the cars and buses near the spawn points creates an opportunity to get the drop on enemies coming up from below.

SECRET AREA: ENFORCER

This secret area is among the tiniest in the game and amounts to little more than a pocket of air within the wreckage of the alien ship on the south side of the map. Hop onto the Shrink Pad near the crash site and jump across the metal crates toward the wreckage.

Leap onto the alien ship and pick up the miniature Enforcer. The ceiling within this portion of the wreckage is tall enough so that Duke won't get crushed upon returning to normal size.

CAPTURE THE BABE

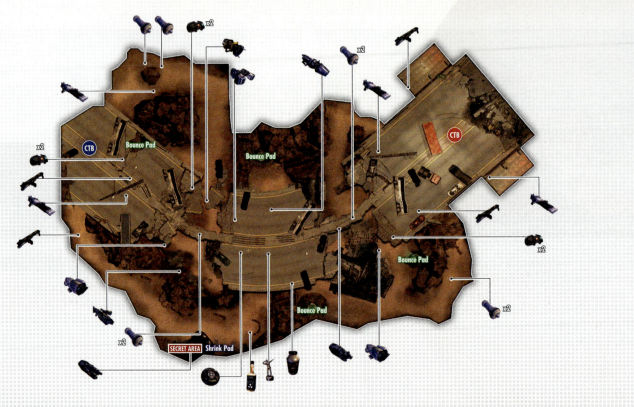

The only difference in weapon and power-up placement in this mode is that there is no Jetpack, so all other tactics are still fair game. And because there's no Jetpack, people tend to forget about the rocky perch where it normally rests, thus making it a decent spot from which to snipe. Of course, most of the action in Capture the Babe takes place around the capture points and on the highway between them. Players on the blue team should use the Trip Mines near their spawn point and place numerous traps around the babe. Have two players share this responsibility so that a single death doesn't remove all four Trip Mines from play. Those on the red team have fewer Trip Mines at their immediate disposal, but they possess arguably tighter chokepoints through which to funnel enemies.

Split your team in such a way that one player's primary role is to secure the Devastator and defend the babe. Use the Bounce Pad on the north-central side of the map to return to the middle, hopefully behind the enemy as they advance on your team's babe. The others should attempt to move as a group along the edge of the map to the enemy babe. Stay clear of the highway when carrying the babe, as that area is just too exposed.

Stay off the highway bridge when trying to capture the enemy babe. Take the longer way, stick close to the rocks, and make sure you have an escort.

HAIL TO THE KING

The capture points are spread far and wide on this map, ranging from near each team's spawn point to the top of the bridge near the RPG, to multiple spots beneath the highway. This reduces the effect of Trip Mines, as there are just too many variables to predict where the enemy is coming from. That said, the Pipe Bombs are really helpful in flushing enemies out of a capture point. Highway Noon has fewer Beer pick-ups than many of the other maps, thus making it unlikely that you'll encounter entire teams with resistance bonuses.

One of the key challenges every player must overcome is simply determining the location of the new capture point. The on-screen indicator certainly helps, but the multiple elevations on this map can make finding it rather difficult. A team with a Jetpack has a decided advantage simply because the flying player can identify the capture point and inform the rest of his team.

Pair the Jet Pack with the RPG or Devastator and take the point!

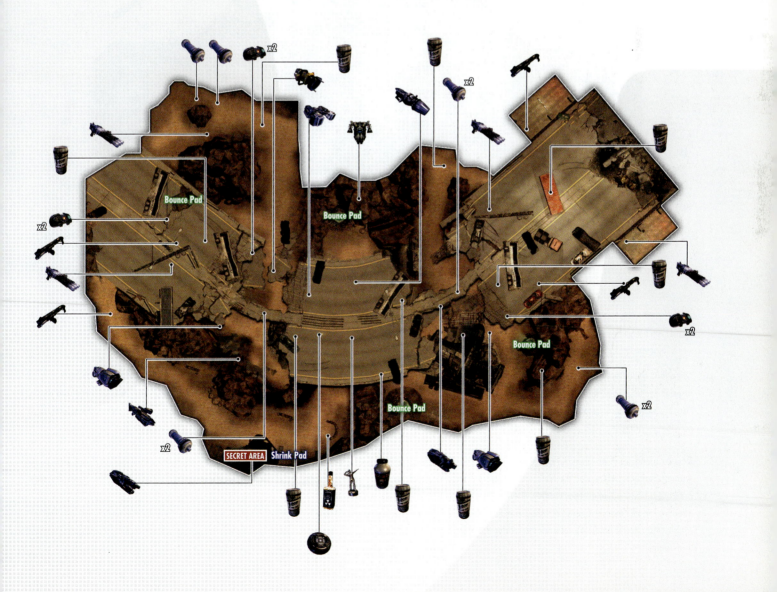

HIVE

AN UNDERGROUND ALIEN LAIR BELOW THE DUKE DOME.

DUKE AND TEAM DUKE MATCH

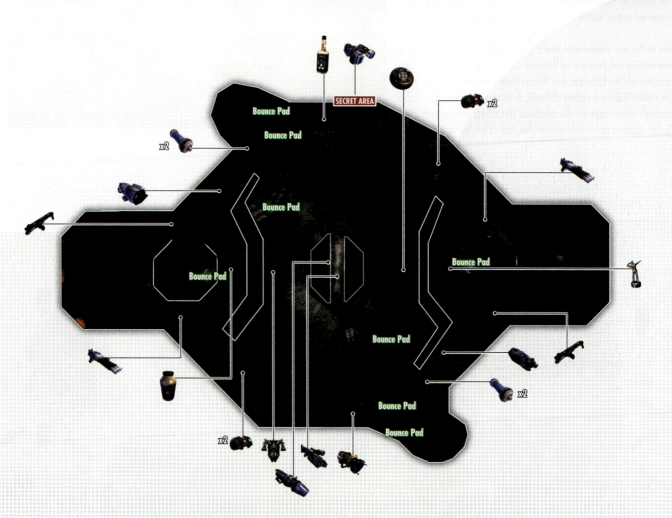

The aliens have been exterminated, but there are still plenty of pests occupying this underground Hive. Carved out of the bedrock and lined with alien organic matter, this symmetrical map provides players with an intimate encounter of the shooting kind. Players can immediately start off in any of three directions en route to a large cavern where a network of paths wraps around and through a central spire. Alien tentacles pierce the rock in a number of places, providing daring shortcuts across the chasm.

Despite being set in an alien burrow, the Hive map offers quite a bit of headroom. So much, in fact, that there's even a Jetpack available for those who want it! Surviving the war in the Hive requires agility, knowledge of the jumps you can make—and can't—and the sense to always toss a Pipe Bomb before entering a narrow tunnel. The Shotgun, Ripper, Freeze and Shrink Rays draw most of the attention on this map because the others are so hotly contested and the map is noticeably smaller than many others. But it's not the weapon that you will use, but how you will use it that counts!

AVAILABLE GAME MODES

Duke Match	Capture the Babe
Team Duke Match	Hail to the King

GENERAL TACTICS

TOXIC TO THE TOUCH

The western and eastern ends of the map (the team spawn areas) offer players three paths toward the center: south, north, or drop into a pit and take a lower tunnel to the south. This tunnel leads to the same place as the upper path, but it contains several bulbous alien life-forms. Although not hostile, these putrid specimens grow and burst as Duke draws near, thereby emitting an ink-like torrent of spray. The material isn't deadly, but it can inflict a small amount of damage if caught in close range.

Whatever they are, they sure are gross. Shoot them so they don't burst.

Target these alien pustules while firing at an enemy if one happens to be in the area, as the spores they release will inflict additional damage. Similarly, you may consider shooting these growths at the start of the match, especially in Capture the Babe games, to prevent the enemy from doing the same.

WIN THE INITIAL RUSH

Many players, especially in Team Duke Match games, will race straight for the RPG in the middle of the map right at the start. The quickest way to get there is to run to the left from the team spawn area (applicable for both sides), drop off the upper ledge and use the Bounce Pad nearest the edge of the chasm to catapult to the base of the spire (the other Bounce Pad simply returns the player to the top of the ledge). Enter the tunnel on the bottom to grab the RPG. Of course, the enemy will be doing the same thing so pick up a couple of Pipe Bombs on the way and toss them ahead of you. It's also a good idea to pick up the Shotgun near the spawn area in case the Pipe Bombs don't get the job done. Whatever you do, don't fire the RPG inside that tunnel!

The RPG is just the type of weapon that often leads lambs to slaughter. Approach carefully and consider tossing a Pipe Bomb for safe measure.

WEAPONS & POWER-UPS

Matches played at the Hive map yield a sense that there aren't that many heavy weapons available. The truth, however, is that every weapon and power-up except for the Enforcer is in play, albeit not in great numbers. The RPG and Railgun are positioned inside narrow tunnels in the center of the multi-level spire, forcing players to put up a fierce fight for them.

The other primary heavy weapon, the Devastator, is tucked away in a secret area that is only accessible via the Jetpack. The narrow tunnels and walkways often push enemies into closer proximity than on other maps. This not only increases the value of the Shotgun and Ripper on this map, but the Steroids as well. This is a great map for those looking to pad their puncher's stats.

WEAPONS/POWER-UPS MATRIX

NAME		DM	TDM	CTB	HTTK
	Shotgun	2	2	2	2
	Ripper	2	2	2	2
	Railgun	1	1	1	1
	AT Laser	1	1	2	2
	Freeze Ray	1	1	1	1
	Shrink Ray	1	1	2	1
	Enforcer	-	-	-	-
	Devastator	1	1	2	1
	RPG	1	1	1	1
	Pipe Bomb	4	4	4	4
	Trip Mine	4	4	4	4
	Steroids	1	1	2	1
	Holoduke	1	1	1	1
	Jetpack	1	1	-	1
	Beer	-	-	-	8
	Statue	1	1	1	1
	Whiskey	1	1	1	1

CAMPING THE RPG

The RPG sits in the middle of a lengthy, narrow tunnel but there is a small alcove adjacent to it where players can stand out of sight and wait for opponents to rush by. It's a relatively safe place to be if you simply must find a spot to camp. The biggest drawback in doing so, however, is that crafty players will often toss a Pipe Bomb toward the RPG before rushing in just in case someone is doing just this thing.

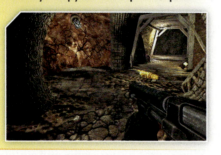

The race for the Railgun can also be fierce, although it requires a bit more finesse to reach. Go along the right-hand path while exiting the spawn area (grabbing the Ripper in the process) and continue past the Trip Mines and across the bridge to the middle level of the central spire. The path naturally spirals downward to the left, but don't descend! Instead, crouch and enter the much smaller opening in the middle of the spire. The Railgun is straight ahead. Be on the lookout for enemies crouching at the entrance to the tunnel from the opposing side and open fire with the Ripper.

Always stand back before entering the tunnel to make sure someone isn't entering from the other side.

MIND THE GAP

Knowing how and where to leap onto the tentacle above the Bounce Pads is extremely valuable. Players will often spot the Whiskey, Devastator, or RPG (depending on game mode) and fruitlessly try to use the Bounce Pads, only to end up heading in the wrong direction. Players spawning near the blue side should always go for the item on the tentacle, as it is always either the Whiskey or the Devastator. Players spawning on the red side may want to leap to the southern tentacle when playing Capture the Babe or Hail to the King to get the Devastator or RPG, respectively. This tentacle is home to the Freeze Ray during Duke Matches.

For starters, without the Jetpack or an incredibly accurate rocket jump, each tentacle is only accessible from the side opposite the nearby Bounce Pads. From the spawn area, head to the right (toward the Trip Mines) and stop at the start of the bridge leading across the chasm. Note the gap in the rocks where the path bends. This is your takeoff point. Run and leap from the edge of the rocks to the tentacle. It's not an easy jump, but it's not impossible. From there, run off the far edge of the tentacle to land near the Bounce Pads.

You'll be ready to really open a can on someone if you manage to score both the Statue and Whiskey at the start of the match!

EXPLOSIVE TAKEOFFS

The gap in the rocks where players must run and leap for the tentacle (particularly on the north side) is an excellent place to put a Trip Mine. The draw of the Whiskey or Devastator often proves too glaring and players commonly overlook the laser directly in their path. There's enough time before the Trip Mine arms itself to throw it in place, then run through the opening to get the Whiskey. Placing Trip Mines inside the tunnels leading to the RPG and Railgun is also effective.

JETPACKING TO NEW HEIGHTS

Players spawning near the red team spawn have a slight advantage in reaching the Jetpack, as they can use the Bounce Pad to land just steps away from it. Those spawning on the blue side must leap across the tentacle to reach that same Bounce Pad (or take the long way around). Either way, the Jetpack is incredibly valuable on this map, not only because it allows the player to reach the Devastator inside the secret area, but because it grants the player access to areas otherwise unreachable.

A great spot to access, if you have the Railgun, RPG, or Devastator, is the tentacle that wraps around the central rock spire. Land on the tentacle to conserve fuel and use a heavy weapon to attack the enemies far below. Run along the curving tentacle to move to the far side of the spire to avoid return fire. This position is vulnerable to enemies attacking with the Railgun or RPG, but is virtually safe from other attacks due to its location.

Run along the tentacles wrapping around the rocky spire to launch attacks on enemies on all sides of the cavern far below.

The Jetpack also makes it possible to land on either of the higher tentacles. This is another spot that people don't expect players to shoot from even though its low enough to be effective even with the AT Laser or Ripper. Lastly, using the Jetpack to hover high above the outlet from the enemy spawn area places you essentially behind the enemy as they make their way toward the Trip Mines nearest their spawn area—rain fire down on them as they emerge from the tunnel.

Use the Jetpack to chase down enemies wherever they go in the central cavern. Don't let them escape!

240

HOT ROUTE

Grab the Whiskey from the northern tentacle and use the nearby Bounce Pad to make a quick run for the Jetpack. Use the power of the Whiskey to reach the secret area and grab the Devastator. Now fly to the upper tentacles wrapping around the rocky spire. Attack enemies on the north side of the spire, then circle around and soar to the upper tentacle in the southeast corner. Attack from here until it's no longer safe (or you're out of Devastator ammo), then return to the Jetpack to refuel and perform another lap.

SECRET AREA

Bounce Pad
Bounce Pad
Bounce Pad
Bounce Pad
Bounce Pad

CAPTURE THE BABE

The multiple routes leading to and from each team's base and across the map make games of Capture the Babe quite interesting, as one wrong guess can spell the difference between victory and defeat. Nevertheless, there are certain paths that make more sense, depending on whether or not you have the babe. Resist the temptation to place the Trip Mines along the right-hand path leading away from your spawn area, as it's unlikely that the enemy will be coming from that direction—it requires too much circumnavigation.

Instead, you can expect the enemy to arrive at your base via the hole in the center of the spawn area. Once in possession of your team's babe, they often exit through the upper left-hand path, use the Bounce Pad to access the center of the map, then Bounce Pad up to the tunnel on the other side to return to their base.

It doesn't matter which way the babe carrier goes when he has an escort wielding a Devastator!

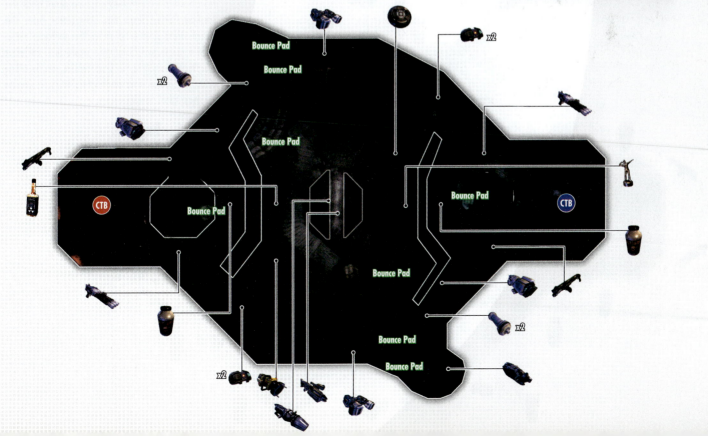

Bounce Pad
Bounce Pad
x2
x2
Bounce Pad
CTB
Bounce Pad
Bounce Pad
CTB
Bounce Pad
x2
Bounce Pad
Bounce Pad
x2

SECRET AREA: DEVASTATOR

The secret area is accessible during all modes except Capture the Babe. To reach it, rush to the lowest area in the center of the map and run to the west side near the wooden walkway to find the Jetpack. Turn to face north (lower end of the stairs) and fly to the top of the cave where an organic radial door is located. Open the door to enter a very small secret area housing a Devastator.

HAIL TO THE KING

The weapons may have moved around a bit on this mode, but they're all still there—the RPG was moved from the lower tunnel to the southern tentacle. There are five capture points on this map: the aforementioned lower tunnel, one at each of the team spawn areas, and one at each corner of the map near the Bounce Pads. Work with teammates to identify which capture point is active and consider pausing for a few moments when it is the central point. This tight space is perfect for racking up multiple kills. Let the other team gather at the point, then attack from both ends with Pipe Bombs, the RPG, or even the Freeze Ray. Take over the point and pile on the points while the other team regroups.

Use the Jetpack and Devastator to provide aerial support when the capture point is near the tentacles.

The team spawn areas are one of those rare capture point locations where it's possible to keep all of the action in front of your team. Work with teammates to watch the various approaches, place Trip Mines in the tunnels and be ready with the Ripper and Shotgun to defend the point. A coordinated team can hold these points for an extended time, especially if one player is across the hole (near the Statue or Steroids pick-up) and catching enemies from behind as they attack.

Lastly, the Jetpack is very helpful when attacking an enemy-controlled capture point near the Bounce Pads. Grab the Devastator from the secret area and land atop the tentacle nearest the contested point and open fire. Let your teammates capture the point while you fly off to slaughter the enemy as they try to race across the map after re-spawning.

Bounce Pad

Bounce Pad

SECRET AREA

x2

Bounce Pad

x2

Bounce Pad

Bounce Pad

Bounce Pad

Bounce Pad

Bounce Pad

x2

x2

Bounce Pad

HOLLYWOOD
A MAP FROM THE ORIGINAL DUKE NUKEM 3D.

The walls won't be stained only with paint by the time the fighting is done here! This sprawling, multi-story paintball arena blends close-quarters weapons combat with a heavy dose of Jetpack antics and rocket-propelled explosions for an entirely unique combat experience. This map truly requires players to shift between two dramatically different tactics when moving from outdoors to indoors. The theater, interior bathrooms and concession area are tight, twisty, and lead to numerous surprise encounters at very close range. The exterior street is quite expansive, yet lacks much in the way of cover. It's a virtual death trap for anyone without a Jetpack.

In a completely unique twist, one of the primary spawn points takes place high atop a fenced-in roof. The only way down is by plummeting numerous stories via garbage chute. And speaking of heights, one of the two secret areas is located behind a pass-through wall exceedingly high above the street. If you were looking for a truly hard-to-find secret area, then this is the right map.

DUKE AND TEAM DUKE MATCH

Explosive Barrel
Light Switch
Light Switch
Light Switch
Shrink Pad
SECRET AREA
Elevator
SECRET AREA

AVAILABLE GAME MODES

Duke Match

Hail to the King

Team Duke Match

WEAPONS & POWER-UPS

Shotguns are the name of the game on the Hollywood map, as no fewer than 10 are available in each mode. The Ripper and Pipe Bombs weigh in with the second largest representation. Although you may want something a bit more powerful, players who avoid using the Jetpack should gather these more modest weapons, string together the Statue power-ups, and have at it!

The twisting halls in the paintball theater are no place for the Devastator and RPG—save them for the exterior! Steroids and Whiskey also play a big role on this map, in addition to the Jetpack. Much of the exterior street area, including all the pick-ups, are accessible on foot but taking this approach is very dangerous.

There are three Jetpacks, two RPGs and two Devastators on this map. Moving around on the street without a Jetpack, or while under the influence of Whiskey, is a fool's endeavor. Do so at your own risk, or unless you know everyone else is inside.

WEAPONS/POWER-UPS MATRIX

NAME		DM	TDM	CTB	HTTK
	Shotgun	10	10	-	10
	Ripper	4	4	-	4
	Railgun	-	-	-	-
	AT Laser	-	-	-	-
	Freeze Ray	2	2	-	2
	Shrink Ray	-	-	-	-
	Enforcer	-	-	-	-
	Devastator	2	2	-	2
	RPG	2	2	-	2
	Pipe Bomb	6	6	-	6
	Trip Mine	2	2	-	2
	Steroids	3	3	-	3
	Holoduke	1	1	-	1
	Jetpack	3	3	-	3
	Beer	-	-	-	6
	Statue	3	3	-	3
	Whiskey	2	2	-	2

GENERAL TACTICS

DUKE ON A HOT WOODEN ROOF

Players frequently respawn on the upper rooftop in the northwest corner of the map, a potentially scary and confusing experience the first time it happens. First, the fall may be quite lengthy, but it won't prove fatal! That is, unless there's someone lying in wait on the street below. Consider tossing a Pipe Bomb down the chute before making the drop just in case another player is waiting on the ground. Similarly, if you just killed an enemy, he may very well spawn on the roof. Don't be afraid to camp the bottom of the chute (not within Pipe Bomb range), or perhaps even fire up the chute.

Never let down your guard when descending through the trash chute; someone may be waiting for you to respawn.

This is also a prime place to gain some extra kills, particularly if you possess the Jetpack. Fly up to the rooftop spawn area using the Jetpack and fire through the fence at enemies after they spawn. This is particularly effective with the RPG and Devastator. Watch out, as players can shoot through the fence, too!

FLYING OUT OF THEIR SEATS

Another common spawn point is inside the cinema. Quickly leap onto the stage, grab the Statue to the left, then move behind the curtain to get the Jetpack and Ripper. Exit to the street and fly to the alcove directly above to find the Devastator. Now you're set to make a move on the streets! Grab the Whiskey in the corner and start patrolling from the air looking for players spawning on the rooftop or exiting the concession area. Remember that when the Jetpack is in use, consider setting down on a ledge now and then since players can hear it. This will conserve fuel and increase your element of surprise.

Don't hesitate to fly higher than you might deem necessary, especially if you have the Devastator!

The corner building opposite the theater marquee has another Jetpack, plus there's an RPG on the billboard at the end of the street. All of this is accessible on foot, but it's much simpler to reach them while flying. It's also easier to access the secret near the marquee with a Jetpack, although this is doable on foot. Enter the secret area to replenish your Devastator ammo, switch weapons, or grab some Pipe Bombs.

A WORD ON SECRET AREAS

Both secret areas on this map are hidden behind pass-through walls. This won't likely be an issue for the one located high on the wall in the south end of the map, but bullets (and rockets!) can also pass through these false walls. Throw a Pipe Bomb or fire the RPG into the secret area near the marquee before going inside. Once inside, exit quickly to avoid suffering the same fate, or take advantage of your ability to see through the wall to launch stealth attacks on passersby!

FOOT PATROL

Don't think for a second that you need the Jetpack to reach the pick-ups in the street. Players often spawn below the billboard, providing easy access to the RPG. Carefully hop up the padded barriers to the ledge and leap and grab the RPG underneath the billboard. You'll be a sitting duck out in the open, so make a quick run along ledge to the corner room where the Jetpack and Steroids are situated. Many enemies will enter this area to get the Jetpack, but few look for the Steroids. Consider hiding out in the alcove with the Steroids to surprise players as they enter through the window.

Run along the southern ledge to reach the Whiskey, then turn north and sprint for the Jetpack and RPG further up the road.

It's also possible to reach the Whiskey, the Devastator, and even the secret area all on foot. This is important for those spawning in an area away from the Jetpacks. Enter the cinema room and proceed up the sloped walkway to the right of the screen. This loops around to the bridge-like platform that leads to the Devastator. Use one of the narrow ledges that ring both sides of the street area to access the Whiskey, the room on the corner, the RPG, or even the secret area. Leap onto the corrugated metal near the marquee to reach the secret area.

DUMPSTER DIVING TO SAFETY

It's a lonely feeling, being caught out in the open when there are one or two Jetpacking playing patrolling the sky. Unless you're armed with the RPG, it's best to just run, leap and zigzag back inside. However, there is an alternative if you don't get spotted by the fliers. Climb into the small dumpster on the south end of the street and crouch down. It's very easy to overlook a stationary target inside a known obstacle when flying around, thus giving the player on the street a clean shot. Use the Pistol or Ripper to target the Jetpack for a very gratifying kill!

SWAT TACTICS AT THE THEATER

The interior section of Hollywood is very different from the outside street and it rewards players who adapt their playing style accordingly. The Shotgun is king here, as is the ability to move quickly, check the corners, and swiftly sweep through a room. Statues are in abundance throughout the theater and it pays to grab them whenever possible, even if only to make another player wait for it to respawn. Make frequent trips through the concession area and projection room to claim the Whiskey in each area; jump atop the garbage can near the concession counter to reach the Whiskey on the ledge in that room.

Jump from the garbage can to the top edge of the corrugated metal to reach the Whiskey in this upper alcove.

Unlike other maps, there are only two Trip Mines on the entire map, one in the game room and the other in the bathroom. Place one of the Trip Mines near the elevator to catch players blinded by the disco lights as they go for the Holoduke pick-up. Place the other one inside the nearby spiraling stairway or inside the projection room (behind the crates) near the RPG.

The element of surprise can be a big advantage in the theater. There are numerous spots where players can launch an attack by firing at enemies from an elevated perch. This is possible near the concession counter (near the Whiskey) and by the elevator (close to the Pipe Bombs). Firing down at enemies from the projection room is also an option. Give yourself another advantage by turning off the lights in the concession area (look for the switch next to the cash register). Although this will result in a small change, it can help a player wearing a dark colored shirt blend into the background a bit better. There's a second light switch near the entrance by the Shotguns.

HOT ROUTE

It's best to run back and forth along this route rather than in a loop to get the Jetpacks, Whiskey bottles, and RPGs. Note that the following description assumes a spawn location near the concession counter.

Sprint up the spiraling staircase to reach the projection room and grab the RPG and Whiskey for invincibility. Fire at any opponents in the theater below, then leap through the open window and go behind the curtain to get the Jetpack. Fly out to the street to pick up the Whiskey. Fight off any enemies here en route to the RPG near the billboard and the Jetpack inside the corner room. Return the way you came, but cut the route off at the theater. Rather than return to the projection room, simply grab the Jetpack behind the curtain and swap weapons for the Devastator near the bridge.

SECRET AREA

Duke likes it when you leave the lights on.

STEEL COFFIN

The elevator can quickly bring players from the game room to the upstairs concession area, but at what cost? Anyone in either room will hear the elevator coming and it's just too easy to get trapped inside as it comes to a stop. In fact, one of the easiest ways to get a kill on this map is to drop a Pipe Bomb on the floor near the elevator and remotely detonate it when the enemy steps out.

Take some time to learn how to use the security monitors scattered throughout the map. There's no time to sit and stare at the tube for too long, but a quick glance may reveal where a firefight is taking place, or even where another player is camped out. The monitors automatically cycle from one room to the next every few seconds, so check them out.

HAIL TO THE KING

Hail to the King matches on the Hollywood map will test players unlike on any map thanks to the map's complexity and varying size of the space in which the capture points are placed. Whereas some of the capture points are inside the theater (near the game room, by the concession), others are in the street. The susceptibility to overhead fire of nearly every capture location makes it necessary to keep an eye to the sky when defending; always be on the lookout for a Jetpack or balcony when on the offensive.

Resist the urge to run into an uncontested capture point in the street—it likely means there's a Jetpacking opponent with an RPG nearby.

The capture points in the street are near each of the secret areas, making it possible to gain quick access to some very useful power-ups and weapons. Coordinate with teammates and determine who will get them so that half the team doesn't move away from the capture point. This goes for the capture point inside the theater as well: make sure one player heads to the projection room to claim the Whiskey and RPG before the enemy.

The other capture points are in rather tight spaces, so it can be tricky to coordinate a defense. Sometimes, though, the best defense is a good offense. Try to have as many players armed with the Shotgun or Ripper as possible and make sure your teammates take full advantage of the available Whiskey, Statues, and Beer.

SECRET AREA #1: DEVASTATOR, FREEZE RAY, RIPPER, 2X PIPE BOMBS

The first secret area is located along the main road to the right of the cinema. There's a large room hidden behind the pass-through wall directly above the corrugated metal to the right of the marquee. It's easiest to simply fly through the wall using the Jetpack, but

it is possible to enter on foot. To do so, follow the narrow ledge around the corner from the south, then leap onto the metal and into the secret area.

This area contains a wealth of weapons and Pipe Bombs and a Shrink Pad. Keep the secret area's location a mystery by using the Shrink Pad to escape to the game room. Approach the tiny hole in the wall near the floor, then crouch to enter it in Duke's shrunken state (yes, it's really so small that you need to crouch even while shrunk). Duke will drop to the floor in a relatively safe corner of the game room.

SECRET AREA #2: RIPPER, STEROIDS, JETPACK

Acquire the Jetpack from behind the stage in the theater and exit to the street. Face west in the small area where the platforms extend like a partial bridge. Take to the skies to the right of the doorway and count seven of the alternating dark bands of metal. There is a small secret area behind the wall panel high on the right-hand side of this towering structure. Push against the wall surface to reveal it. The wall will disappear briefly, making it possible to see the opening when backing up. Fly through the wall to access the weapons stash. Be sure to grab the Jetpack to refuel.

Explosive Barrel

Light Switch

Light Switch

x2

Light Switch

Shrink Pad

SECRET AREA

Elevator

SECRET AREA

x2

x2

x2

x2

HOOVER DAMNED

THE DAM WITH AN INTERESTING VISITOR.

DUKE AND TEAM DUKE MATCH

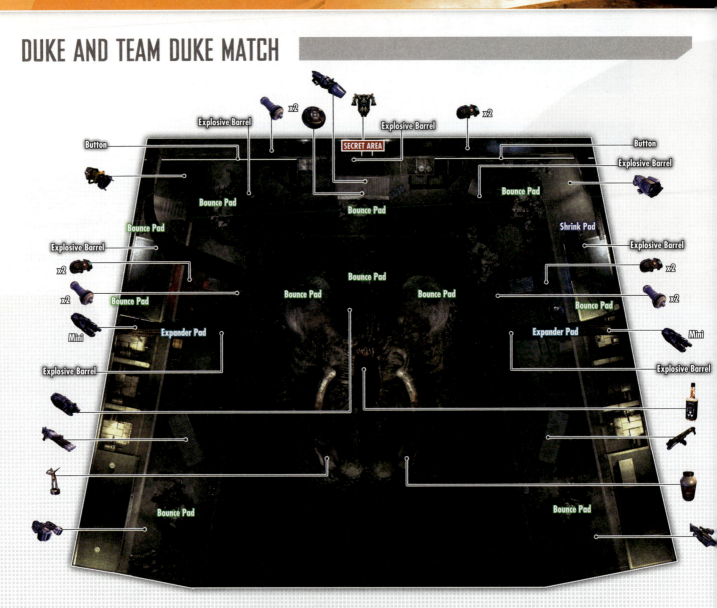

Duke isn't one to pass up an invitation to go skinny dipping with the ladies, but he insists they at least be human. That can't be said for the massive amalgamation of alien lady-parts floating in the electrified water of Hoover Damned. Although players will always spawn along the grounded concrete walkway surrounding the water-filled tank on three sides, the action gets hot and heavy atop—and inside—the alien form in the middle. Use the Bounce Pads to leap over the high-voltage waters, or else risk the most shocking of discoveries. Run along the ridges to reach the Statue, or dive into the central crevice to find the Whiskey.

The narrow walkway along the perimeter of the map encourages close-quarters combat set around a handful of shipping containers and electrical

generators. The elevated ledge set high on the northern wall provides refuge for those who prefer to keep their enemies at a distance. Similarly, both the west and east sides of the map contain a small side room where players may try to escape the main lines of fire. Use the Shrink Pads to access a small drainage channel underneath the floor that leads to a miniature Enforcer. Exit the channel, step on the Particle Expander Pad, and put the new weapon to use before getting trampled.

AVAILABLE GAME MODES

Duke Match	Capture the Bab
Team Duke Match	Hail to the King

IT'S ELECTRIC!

The electricity charging through the metal container on the northern side of the map is deadly to the touch, but it can be turned off. Use either of the buttons flanking the container along the northern wall to cut the power for roughly 15 seconds. Sprint to the container and grab the Holoduke from within. Deploy the Holoduke to gain invisibility, then use the ramp on either side to leap onto the container to pick up the RPG before the electricity returns. This is a great way to gain two of the most valuable items without drinking the Whiskey.

GENERAL TACTICS

DRUNKEN DEVASTATION

There are a number of successful first moves to take at Hoover Damned, depending on your preferred style of play and initial spawn location. Those starting on the western (red) side of the map should grab the Devastator and briefly pause before using the Bounce Pad to leap onto the alien. Any opponent who attempts to obtain the Whiskey from the other side of the map will be a sitting duck! Additionally, if a teammate grabs the Devastator first, head straight to the Bounce Pad, grab the Whiskey, and use the Bounce Pad inside the alien tunnel to reach the RPG atop the electrified shipping container.

Grab the Devastator, pause for a moment, then use the Bounce Pad to reach the alien and blow up anyone going for the Whiskey. There's always one...

RAILGUN SNIPING

If you're starting from the eastern (blue) side of the map, grab the Railgun and use the Bounce Pad to reach the alien in the middle. Go for the Whiskey if you want, however, it's probably more advantageous to sneak around the outer edge of the alien to lay claim to the Steroids or Statue. Either side serves as a useful vantage point from which to snipe.

The Railgun is a one-shot kill even without the Statue, but the double-damage bonus helps if you need to make a quick escape.

WEAPONS & POWER-UPS

The entire assortment of weapons and power-ups are in play during DM, TDM, and CTB matches and only the Freeze Ray is absent during HTTK matches. Perhaps the most significant difference between each mode is the presence of a lone Devastator in the southwest corner during DM and TDM matches, thus giving players who spawn in that area an early advantage, while those on the other side of the map have access to a Railgun.

Note that the Jetpack is not in play during CTB matches, as the secret area becomes home to the Steroids. Similarly, the Holoduke inside the electrified container is not available during HTTK matches. The power-ups located atop the alien in the center require some careful balance; take it slow to avoid falling off the narrow ridge.

WEAPONS/POWER-UPS MATRIX

ITEM	DM	TDM	CTB	HTTK
Shotgun	1	1	2	2
Ripper	1	1	2	2
Railgun	1	1	1	1
AT Laser	1	1	1	1
Freeze Ray	1	1	2	-
Shrink Ray	1	1	2	2
Enforcer	2	2	2	2
Devastator	1	1	2	2
RPG	1	1	1	1
Pipe Bomb	6	6	6	6
Trip Mine	6	6	6	6
Steroids	1	1	1	1
Holoduke	1	1	1	-
Jetpack	1	1	-	1
Beer	-	-	-	9
Statue	1	1	2	1
Whiskey	1	1	1	1

The ridges atop the alien aren't the only spot to use the Railgun. Grab the Railgun at the start of the round, sprint for the Trip Mines and then use the Bounce Pad on the right to reach the roof of the control room. Run along the pipe to the ledge on the northern side of the map. Gather more Trip Mines and throw them in the recesses so they can't be shot (the black body of the Trip Mine is often more revealing than the laser). Crouch and back into a recess to snipe opponents from atop the alien. This is an excellent vantage point, as it overlooks multiple capture points in HTTK matches and also provides a view onto the two ridges where the Steroids and Statue are located.

Lay some Trip Mines down on either side, then use the Railgun to snipe enemies atop the alien and near the containers below.

TRIPMINING AWAY

The relatively narrow width of the concrete walkway surrounding the perimeter of the map makes for some deadly Trip Mine usage! Although Trip Mines tend to be easily detectable on this map when set against the gray background of the concrete, you can counter this by placing them in duplicate so that the player leaps over one and lands on the other.

Enemies might avoid the first Trip Mine, but they won't get so lucky with the second. Placing them near explosive barrels will result in multi-kills.

Toss Trip Mines inside the electrified container, low on the side wall, so the laser extends across the container near the Holoduke power-up. Players are often so amped to rush in and grab the Holoduke before the electricity returns that they will fail to spot the laser from the Trip Mine. It's also completely worthwhile to place Trip Mines along the upper northern ledge, even if you don't have the Railgun to do any sniping.

SHRUNKEN MASTER

There are two Enforcers on this map (one on each side), but you must be small to reach them. Locate the Shrink Pad in the control room on either side of the map and shoot the grate in the wall to access the hole in the floor. Drop into the hole to get whisked along with the water current to the Enforcer. Quickly grab the weapon and sprint to the right to exit the tunnel before the effects of the Shrink Pad where off. The Enforcer's homing ability is an excellent counter to enemies wielding the Devastator or AT Laser.

It's not the size of the Enforcer, it's what you do with it that counts.

HOT ROUTE

Start this route at the Devastator pick-up. Grab the weapon near the spawn point, then use the Bounce Pad to reach the Whiskey. Use the Bounce Pad while invincible to reach to the RPG (or to the walkway if the Whiskey hasn't re-spawned yet), then drop off the side of the container and grab the Holoduke from inside it. Instantly deploy the Holoduke and use the weapons and Pipe Bombs to blast a path of destruction back to the Devastator. Pause for a moment if the coast is clear and use the RPG's lock-on ability to gain a target or two before repeating the route.

CAPTURE THE BABE

Each team's Babe is positioned in the southwest and southeast corners of the map, respectively, and both teams have access to a nearby Devastator so expect plenty of firepower. At least one player should grab the Devastator and head directly for the Whiskey inside the alien, which makes reaching the enemy babe much easier!

It's possible to cross the map rather quickly by using a Bounce Pad to reach the alien, and then running and leaping onto the tentacle that extends outward to the enemy's side. This is definitely recommended, especially if your team has two other members drawing attention along the standard path. The path you should take with the babe depends on your teammates' positions and those of your opponents. By all means, take the safe route around the perimeter if you have an escort. But, when flying solo, take to the Bounce Pads to bypass the northern portion of the map where an adversary may be lying in wait.

No reason to fear the enemy's shotgun when you're invincible. The Whiskey will never let you down!

SECRET AREA: JETPACK

Circle around the watery tank via the main walkway to the electrified silver container on the north side of the area. Locate the grate on the wall directly behind this container. Crouch down and walk straight through the grate—it's magic!—to lay claim to the power-up. This secret area contains

a Jetpack during Duke Match and Hail to the King matches and Steroids during Capture the Babe matches. Players should expect to encounter elevated fire coming from the north; use the Jetpack to fly above the water and take them out from the south!

HAIL TO THE KING

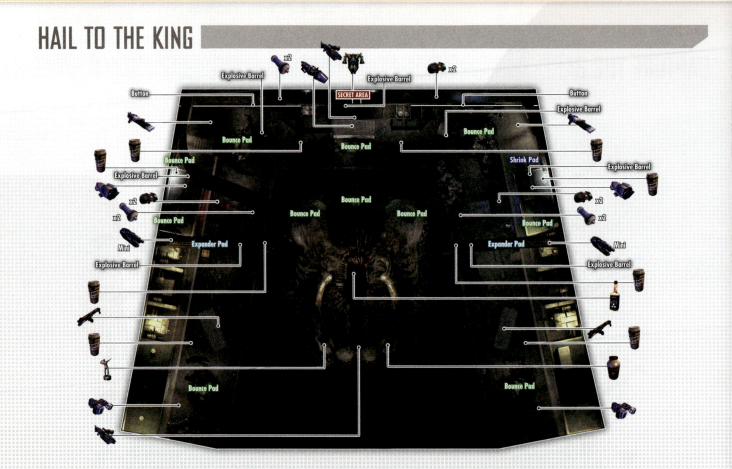

There are a large number of capture points for HTTK matches at Hoover Damned, but only one is located atop the alien. This makes it possible to employ similar tactics for each capture point. For starters, make sure to detonate any and all explosive barrels that are near the capture point before entering. It's way too easy for someone to shoot a barrel and kill half your team when you're being careless. Second, split up! Too many teams will try to place three or even four members into the capture circle. This is fine on larger maps when it may take longer for your rivals to reach the capture point after re-spawning, but it's dangerous on this map. It's better to have one or two enemies outside the circle, providing cover fire. This way, even if those in the circle are killed, the others can rush to contend the point until their teammates re-spawn.

The pick-ups certainly play a big role in HTTK matches, particularly the Pipe Bombs, Steroids, and Statue. Remember that most enemies will be drinking Beer to gain some enhanced damage protection, so use the Steroids and Statue for an attack power boost. Lastly, having a player completely sacrifice his own personal point-scoring ability to provided elevated support can go a long way. Take the Railgun and some Pipe Bombs and head up the northern walkway. Snipe anyone running alone, then toss down some Pipe Bombs for those approaching in groups.

Two in the circle, one watching atop the alien, and another providing elevated support to the north. Game. Set. Match!

MORNINGWOOD

A GHOST TOWN IN THE NEVADA DESERT.

DUKE AND TEAM DUKE MATCH

Grab your cowboy hat and spurs, because it's time to bring the fight to the old west! The long-abandoned town of Morningwood is about to see its first shoot-out in decades and the action is as hot as the Nevada sand. This symmetrical map packs every weapon and power-up in the game, along with more than a half-dozen explosive barrels. Much of the fighting will take place on the southern half of the map in the vicinity of the RPG. The interiors of the three central structures will also get their fair share of gunfights.

The RPG is a hotly-contested weapon on this map, more so than any other, but there are plenty of other options. For starters, there are six spots on the map that are only accessible while in a shrunken state. Use the power of the Shrink Pads to claim the Enforcer and load up on Trip Mines and Pipe Bombs too. The Devastator is often overlooked amongst the rocks north of the mine cart tracks and makes a healthy alternative to the RPG. And for those who prefer to combine the Shotgun or Shrink Ray with the power of the Holoduke and Whiskey, check out the tactics for this map's hot route.

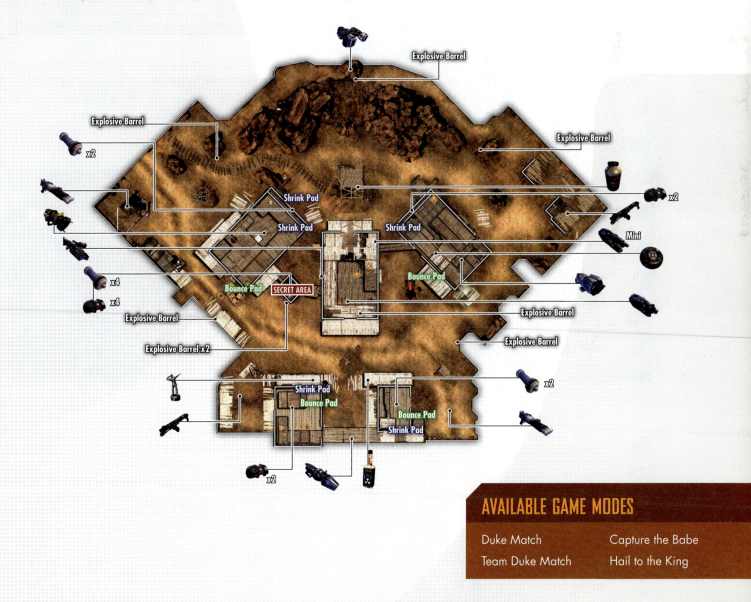

Explosive Barrel	Explosive Barrel	Explosive Barrel
Explosive Barrel x2	Shrink Pad	Shrink Pad
Shrink Pad	Shrink Pad	Mini
Bounce Pad	SECRET AREA	Bounce Pad
Explosive Barrel	Explosive Barrel	Explosive Barrel
Shrink Pad	Bounce Pad	Bounce Pad
Bounce Pad	Shrink Pad	

AVAILABLE GAME MODES

| Duke Match | Capture the Babe |
| Team Duke Match | Hail to the King |

WEAPONS & POWER-UPS

The weapon selection doesn't change much between game modes, but the location of the weapons do. There are more Freeze and Shrink Rays during Capture the Babe games. The key difference in the objective-based modes is that there is a greater concentration of weapons around the center of the map, as the Ripper and Shotgun (which are typically in the southern corners of the map) are closer to the team spawn areas.

Power-ups are largely unchanged across the different modes, although the Statue and Whiskey power-ups are much easier to reach during Capture the Babe games. The net result is that it draws less attention to the RPG during objective-based modes, making it potentially easier for someone to sneak off and get it, much like the Devastator to the north. On the other hand, players moving through the buildings in the center of the map must be extra careful, as a player in that area will likely have a deadly weapon in hand.

WEAPONS/POWER-UPS MATRIX

ITEM		DM	TDM	CTB	HTTK
	Shotgun	2	2	2	2
	Ripper	2	2	2	2
	Railgun	1	1	1	1
	AT Laser	1	1	1	1
	Freeze Ray	1	1	2	1
	Shrink Ray	1	1	2	1
	Enforcer	1	1	1	1
	Devastator	1	1	1	1
	RPG	1	1	1	1
	Pipe Bomb	8	8	8	8
	Trip Mine	8	8	8	8
	Steroids	1	1	1	1
	Holoduke	1	1	-	1
	Jetpack	-	-	-	-
	Beer	-	-	-	10
	Statue	1	1	1	1
	Whiskey	1	1	1	1

GENERAL TACTICS

THE PATHS LESS TRAVELLED

There's just something about the RPG at Morningwood that draws a crowd. Let the horde head south while you branch off to the north to get the Devastator. Follow the rocky path uphill from the mine cart tracks until you reach the Devastator in the center. Do yourself a favor and shoot the explosive barrel before getting too close, just in case there's someone waiting to spring a trap from the other side.

Always shoot the explosive barrel before making a move on the Devastator, just in case there's an adversary looking to blast you with lead.

Those looking for another heavy weapon on the sly can find it tucked away within the stack of hay bales inside the barn. Use the Shrink Pad behind the Parched Gully Saloon and sprint to the back of the barn (center building) and go inside. Use Duke's shrunken size to slip through the gap in the stack of hay bales to find a miniaturized Enforcer. Quickly exit before the effects of the Shrink Pad wear off, though!

Although that stack of hay looks innocuous, it contains one of the most deadly weapons Duke can possess.

TRIP MINES & TINY MEN

There are a large number of Pipe Bombs and Trip Mines on this map, but the majority are accessible only while in a shrunken state. Use the Shrink Pads inside the Blacklung Supply building and Saloon to gather the Trip Mines and Pipe Bombs within the rear walls of those buildings. Look for the hole in the side of the wall and run between the beams to gather the explosives. There is also a huge cache of Pipe Bombs and Trip Mines inside the secret area.

HOT ROUTE

Run along the cliffs toward the Devastator, grab the heavy weapon and drop down for the Steroids. Sprint straight across the Steroids power-up and enter the central building. Ascend to the second floor, exit on the right atop the stairs, and cross over to the Blacklung Supply building where the Holoduke is located. Deploy the Holoduke and immediately exit onto the balcony to the left and hit the Bounce Pad to leap across to the Whiskey power-up. Drop down off the left-hand side and use the invisibility and invincibility to annihilate those going for the RPG before looping through the building with the Pipe Bombs and back towards the start of this route.

There are an abundance of places to use Trip Mines. Start by placing them on the stairs and walkway leading to the RPG and near the balcony Bounce Pads. Also, consider dropping them near the Whiskey and Statue. Planting Trip Mines inside the doorways leading into the barn, saloon, and supply building works well too, as the laser is often difficult to spot against the brightly-lit exterior of Morningwood.

If these walls could talk... they'd yell BOOM!

TINY BOMBS

Make sure that you are full size before placing the Trip Mine, or else they'll remain in a permanently small state and only inflict minor damage when triggered. Remember that only the items in Duke's inventory return to normal size when he does, while dropped weapons, Trip Mines and Pipe Bombs will simply remain small.

BALCONY BUSTIN'

There are multiple ways to obtain the Whiskey and Statue on the balconies outside the hotel and the adjacent building to the south. The most direct way is to use the Shrink Pad and tiny Bounce Pad in the corner of each building to access the rafters. From there, a shrunken Duke can slip through the missing window pane to the balcony outside and grab the item after returning to full size. Another way is to get the RPG, drop to the ground, and then rocket jump onto the balcony with the Whiskey. From there, turn, run, and rocket jump across the gap to the balcony with the Statue. Always get the Whiskey first, then use double damage to deal devastating splash damage with the RPG—even at close range!

Shrink yourself down in size, then hit the Bounce Pad to reach the rafters.

It's possible to reach each balcony via the Bounce Pads on the balconies outside the saloon and Blacklung Supply building. Head upstairs inside each building (or the barn) and proceed to the balcony nearer the center of the map. The Bounce Pad will send Duke flying to the southern building nearest him, whether it be for the Whiskey or the Statue.

Grab the rocket, drop down, then perform a rocket jump to reach the Whiskey. It sure beats taking the long way around to the Bounce Pad.

SHOTGUN SURPRISE

There are a number of spots (both inside and out) to launch surprise attacks, whether you're using the Shotgun, Ripper, or the Freeze Ray. Try using the wagons and crates on the outskirts of the map for cover and catch unsuspecting enemies as they run past. Another good spot is behind the bar in the saloon, although this approach will probably only trick players once or twice. Similarly, you can duck into the chimney inside the center of the Blacklung Supply building and startle someone as he enters and exits the building.

The Shotgun is useful when making a move for the RPG. Watch for Trip Mines on the stairs and be ready to toss a Pipe Bomb or two to trigger the blast. Open fire with the Shotgun on anyone on the walkway near the RPG spawn, then switch to the Pistol and swap it for the RPG if it hasn't already been taken.

Always check your blindside when moving around the map—this poor guy forgot to.

SECRET AREA: 4X PIPE BOMBS, 4X TRIP MINES

This secret area is within the small, locked shack near the center of the map. Accessing it requires a daring run out in the open while shrunk, so it's not for the faint of heart! Limit the risk by first shooting the explosive barrel inside the shack—take aim through one of the cracks in the wall to hit it. Enter the westernmost building, wait until the coast is clear, then step onto the Shrink Pad and make a run for the shack. Hop onto the helmet, then the bucket, and quickly leap through the hole in the shack before Duke returns to normal size. Pull the lever to the right of the door to exit once you've collected the plethora of explosives. Those who don't like suffering from another case of shrinkage can use the lever in the main barn to open the door to this supply shed. But keep in mind, a full-grown Duke is a lot easier to spot—and trap—inside the shed than a shrunken Duke.

CAPTURE THE BABE

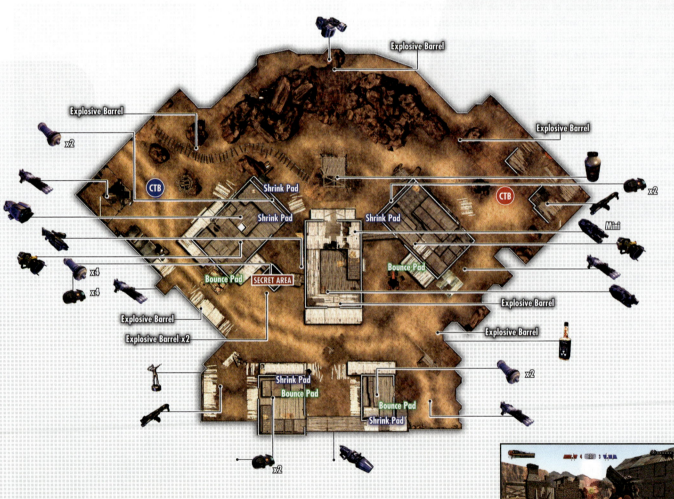

The babes are located in the eastern and western ends of the map, granting players three primary paths to use. Since nearly all of the weapons are clustered within and around the three buildings in the center of the map, it leaves the routes past the Devastator and RPG less trafficked. These routes are preferred to use when carrying the babe, particularly the one leading past the Devastator.

Be sure to butt spank the babe whenever she starts to block your vision, or else you may not see who to shoot with the Garter Pistol.

There's little reason to use the Bounce Pads atop the balconies during Capture the Babe matches unless you need to escape an attack. Utilize the building interiors and the bridges connecting each balcony to advance across the map toward your enemies' base rather than the northern and southern routes so they don't catch on to your escape plans. Always have a defender positioned behind the crumbling structure near each base.

SECRET LEAD

It's a little risky if your team is trailing, but a great way to hold on to a lead is to have one player pilfer the secret area for Pipe Bombs and Trip Mines. Then position Trip Mines throughout the area surrounding the enemy's base to catch them when they return with the babe. Hide near your base to protect the babe should the enemy move in as a group.

HAIL TO THE KING

The capture points at Morningwood are scattered around the periphery of the map. Nearly every capture point can be viewed from a nearby balcony, providing a coordinated team an opportunity to position someone up high, helping to defend those scoring the points.

Few players will take the time to secure one of the main weapons, never mind the Trip Mines and Pipe Bombs. Steroids, the Whiskey, and Statue (along with an ample supply of Beer) all yield quite a large benefit, thus making it possible to conduct much of the fight with Shotguns and Pistols, but it still pays to seek out the heavier weaponry.

When the capture point is about to switch positions, go ahead and forfeit the final few seconds in order to gather up explosives and a stronger weapon before moving to the next capture point. Lining capture points with Trip Mines, Pipe Bombs, or just lurking abo

Attaching Trip Mines on the mine shaft and hanging out on the barn balcony with the RPG is a great way to rack up kills and make sure your team doesn't lose the point.

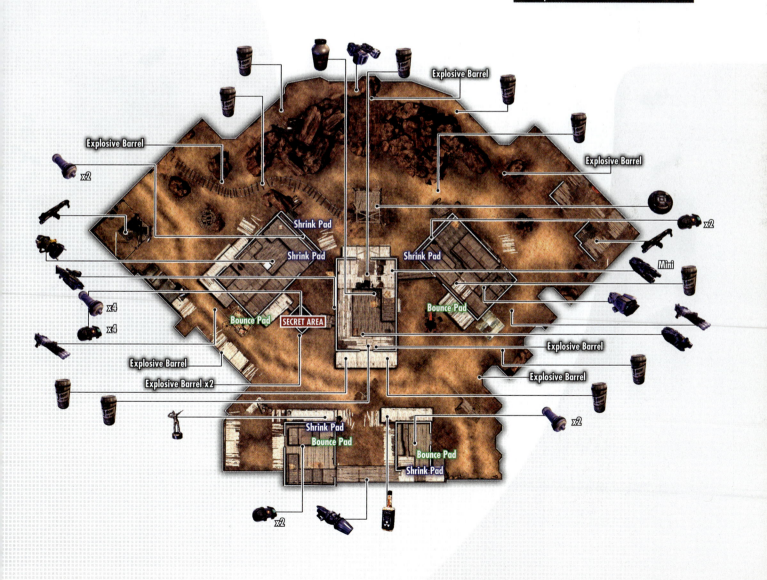

Explosive Barrel

Explosive Barrel

Explosive Barrel

x2

Explosive Barrel

Shrink Pad

Shrink Pad

Shrink Pad

Shrink Pad

Mini

x2

Bounce Pad

Bounce Pad

Bounce Pad

x4

SECRET AREA

Explosive Barrel

Explosive Barrel

Explosive Barrel

Explosive Barrel x2

x2

Shrink Pad

Bounce Pad

Bounce Pad

Shrink Pad

x2

SAUSAGE FACTORY

AN INDUSTRIAL COMPLEX BUILT IN 1997.

DUKE AND TEAM DUKE MATCH

Nobody quite knows what nefarious discoveries will be uncovered at Sausage Factory, nor what possible need the workers could have for installing a toxic pool of shrink-inducing goo, but Duke isn't one to ask questions. For that matter, why are there random, man-sized tunnels leading throughout the facility? Why are there secret alcoves beneath the floor? All Duke cares about is kicking ass. He'll let the eggheads try to sort the rest out.

The Sausage Factory industrial facility isn't nearly as confusing as it may seem at first. You'll soon realize that the pipes leading to and from the spawn area are straight, the map is entirely symmetrical (though the sides are flipped), and the complex isn't as tall or as large as it feels. These features give Sausage Factory a welcome old-school vibe that pits players against one another in a tug-of-war for powerful weapons and command of the best vantage points. What truly makes Sausage Factory unique is the toxic liquid lurking beneath the metal screen in the center. Press a button to raise the liquid and instantly shrink all players standing above it.

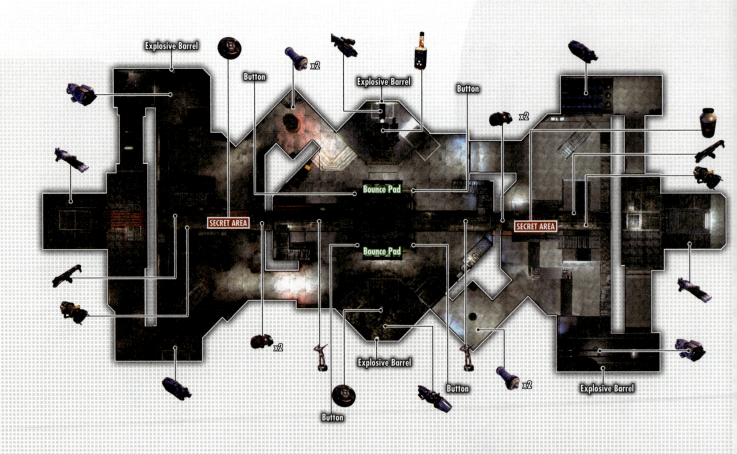

AVAILABLE GAME MODES

Duke Match

Team Duke Match

Capture the Babe

Hail to the King

SHRINK-ON-DEMAND

The center room in Sausage Factory contains a mysterious green substance just below a metal grate. The liquid won't cause any problems, however, until someone presses one of the four nearby buttons. When pushed, each button will cause the toxic sludge to rise to the level of the grate and shrink anyone caught standing atop it. Use this to snare opponents and quickly trample them, or purposely shrink yourself to make use of the Bounce Pads set within the columns to reach power-ups that can't be obtained while full size.

GENERAL TACTICS

SECRET MOVES

Forgo the pipe at your team's spawn point and run to the AT Laser and grab it instead. Immediately enter the secret area on your side of the map, grab the Holoduke or Steroids, exit in the center of the map, skim around the side to the other secret area vent and enter it to get the other item. This should give you a nice leg up on the competition, especially in Team Duke Matches or objective-based modes as this route may allow you to sneak behind enemy lines.

Shoot the grate off the wall below the pipe, then crawl inside to grab the power-up on your side of the map.

WHAT'S YOUR SIGN?

The pipes leading up to the center of the map (where the Statues are located in Duke Match) offer an excellent vantage point from which to shoot opponents especially if you have an RPG, AT Laser, or Railgun. Leap onto the pipe via the forklift and platforms to the right of the red pipe, or the valves and pipes to the right of the blue one. It's possible to reach the pipe from the left-hand side, but it's a bit trickier and it's easier to get spotted by enemies exiting the other pipe.

WEAPONS & POWER-UPS

There are no Enforcers on this map and the Devastator is only available during objective-based matches. The low ceilings also preclude the use of the Jetpack. That said, each side of the map contains the basic assortment of mid-level weapons and the center is home to a Railgun and RPG.

Aside from the rush for the RPG during Duke Matches, the big draws here are the powerful weapons and the uniqueness of their whereabouts. Players can climb onto the large pipes in the center to claim a Statue, they can raid the secret areas to claim the Steroids or Holoduke, or they can shrink themselves and follow a rather obscure path to the Whiskey or Holoduke at the risk of suicide-by-enlargement.

WEAPONS/POWER-UPS MATRIX

ITEM		DM	TDM	CTB	HTTK
	Shotgun	2	2	2	2
	Ripper	2	2	2	2
	Railgun	1	1	2	1
	AT Laser	2	2	2	2
	Freeze Ray	2	2	1	2
	Shrink Ray	2	2	1	2
	Enforcer	-	-	-	-
	Devastator	-	-	2	2
	RPG	1	1	2	1
	Pipe Bomb	4	4	4	4
	Trip Mine	4	4	4	4
	Steroids	1	1	1	1
	Holoduke	2	2	1	1
	Jetpack	-	-	-	-
	Beer	-	-	-	12
	Statue	2	2	1	1
	Whiskey	1	1	1	1

Grab the RPG and climb onto the pipe where the Statue is located before anyone sees you.

The holes on the floor near the sides of the central room are there to allow a shrunken player to escape without being trampled.

Once on the pipe, move toward the center of the map to hide deeper in the shadows and gain a view of the two approaches coming from the spawn area. Disregard the no camping sign, as the most fervent players will do so.

SHRINK ONE FOR THE TEAM

Not every shot fired from atop the pipes has to deal a mortal blow. Don't be afraid to head up onto the pipe with just a Shrink Ray, provided you have teammates nearby. Communicate with them during Team Duke Matches so they know when you've shrunk an enemy.

SHRINK JUICE RISING

You may think that intentionally shrinking yourself is a bad idea, but not so at Sausage Factory! Press any of the four buttons on the central pillars to raise the level of the radioactive goop beneath the screen and step into it to shrink Duke. Quickly get onto one of the miniature Bounce Pads inside each column to be vaulted onto a narrow ledge on the north or south side of the central platform. Quickly run along the edge to the Bounce Pad in the middle to send Duke flying through the air intake chute on either side of the map. Grab the power-up on the respective side and drop down before Duke returns to normal size.

Each column has a button and a miniature Bounce Pad inside it. Press the button to shrink anyone standing atop the screen.

There are also two miniature escape holes near the RPG and Railgun pick-ups that Duke can use if he gets hit with the Shrink Ray. Don't hesitate to drop through the hole in the floor near these weapons if this occurs. The draft will carry mini-Duke out the front of the structure's base (this is a one-way path). Hide underneath the small overhang for a few seconds to avoid being trampled, then step out from under cover before Duke returns to normal size.

TRICK 'EM NUKEM

The incoming firepower, the toxic pool of unmentionable origin, and the various pipes and secret paths all combine to give crafty players the advantage of surprise. There are numerous ways to catch distracted foes off guard. For starters, nobody expects to encounter other players inside the pipe leading away from their spawn area. Consider grabbing the Ripper and hanging out near the Shotgun spawn area just beyond the sloped portion of the pipe. Place a Trip Mine behind you to protect against a sneak attack. Thanks to the downward slope of the ramp leading to the pipe, there's a moment where you can see the enemy coming before he can see you. Open fire!

Few players expect to encounter another enemy near an available weapon pick-up. They'll see the Shotgun followed by a muzzle flash!

Place a Trip Mine on the wall directly above the pipe you leap onto to access the Statue. It's likely to go undetected by players attempting to get up there, as they'll be more focused on making the jumps and climbing the ledges. Place it low enough so you can set it behind you, then camp the upper bend in the pipe.

Place the Trip Mine low enough so you don't set the laser off while sniping on the upper bend in the pipe.

Also, grab the Freeze Ray underneath the large pipe and then circle around and climb on top of it. Crouch down, approach the edge, and watch for enemies entering the pipe near the Trip Mine pick-ups. Freeze 'em solid, then leap down and execute them! You'll be open to surprise attacks from behind while attempting this maneuver, so don't camp this area for too long. Be careful around the explosive barrels near the RPG and Railgun, as they can be very dangerous. There are others on the map and it's a fine idea to place hidden Trip Mines near these barrels.

HOT ROUTE

The design of Sausage Factory isn't conducive for having a preset route given the spacious central room that tends to pull players in different directions. Nevertheless, it's possible to get to the red team's side, grab the Shotgun in the pipe, and slip through the secret area to snag the Holoduke. Exit the secret area inside the center room and make a move for the RPG while invisible. Fire at the players fighting it out near the center of the map and circle back around to the Pipe Bombs.

Explosive Barrel

x2

SECRET AREA

Explosive Barrel

CAPTURE THE BABE

There's no other way to put it: teams are going to clash in the center of the map when playing Capture the Babe here. Whether they slip through the large pipes, crawl through the secret area, or take the north or south route, all roads lead to the center. You may get lucky and slip around the side where the Freeze Ray and Shrink Ray are located, but don't count on it.

Explosive Barrel

Button

x2

Explosive Barrel

Button

x2

CTB

SECRET AREA

Bounce Pad

Bounce Pad

SECRET AREA

CTB

x2

Explosive Barrel

Button

Button

x2

Explosive Barrel

When all else fails, grab the most powerful weapon possible and rush to the enemy's base before they can return with your babe.

CHALLENGES

EARN BONUS XP AND UNLOCK CLOTHES FOR YOUR VERY OWN DUKE DOLL!

A long time ago, with a videogame far, far from forgotten, players competed for the thrill, for the good of the team, and for bragging rights. A map, some rockets, and a mighty boot was all they needed to get their kicks. The only fluff being handed out was going on backstage in Duke's dressing room. But players these days have gone limp—and this makes Duke sad. It seems today's players get upset if their television isn't constantly chiming in to tell them how special they are. It used to be that players would happily wield any weapon capable of painting the walls with their opponent's guts. Nowadays, they'll kill their own teammates in order to steal the weapon that earns them 20 space-points and a trophy for their dollhouse. Sigh…

Alas, even Duke's creators admit you can't stop change. If players need a steady stream of rewards and milestones to keep them glued to the couch, then that's what they're going to get! *Duke Nukem Forever* packs no fewer than 315 various Challenges into the multiplayer portion of the game. These Challenges weren't added just to stroke fragile egos. Hell no! Completing Challenges also earns bonus XP and item and title unlocks. The bonus XP adds to the player's personal multiplayer career total and helps them level up faster—and the faster you level up, the faster you unlock that sweet golden babe statue for your digs! The item and title unlocks add ways to customize your multiplayer character with new shirts, glasses, hats, and titles in the Changeroom.

CHALLENGE LISTS

The following six tables contain a complete listing of all 315 Challenges crammed into the multiplayer mode. Many of them come in four progressively difficult flavors, designed to reward your continued dedication to a specific method of inflicting pain and humiliation on your opponents. Other Challenges are designed to reward a singular action of badness or lack thereof (see also: suicide, you). There are more than enough Challenges to provide plenty of incentive and encouragement to all players, regardless of style of play, skill level, or preferred game mode or weapon.

Turn on your microphone and tell the other players that you unlocked a new Challenge. Your opponents will be happy for you, we promise.

The Challenges screen illustrates where to focus your efforts in order to get that next XP bonus, a far more worthwhile endeavor than assisting with the team objective.

A FEW NOTES ABOUT CHALLENGES

Challenge rewards can only be earned once. For example, you will only earn 500 XP and the Limbo King title the first time you crouch underneath a Trip Mine laser. Performing this action multiple times does not unlock multiple Limbo Challenge bonuses.

There are 39 different shirts to unlock along with 21 styles of glasses and 31 types of hats. Item unlocks that specify a logo design refer to a style of shirt with a small graphic in the center. For example, there are both United States Flag Logo and American Flag Shirt unlocks. The former has a small flag on the chest, whereas the latter design extends across the entire shirt.

Use the Challenges and Player Statistics options on the Multiplayer Menu to track your progress. The Challenges option provides a whole-numbers breakdown along with a progress meter to show your advancement across every Challenge, along with the reward for unlocking them. The Player Statistics screen reveals a wealth of data on player performance, but also several "Entertainment Statistics" that provide exact distances ran (and fallen) for the Marathon and Free Fallin' Challenges, among many others.

WEAPON CHALLENGES

The Challenges in this group will likely be among the first you unlock in your multiplayer career. There are 16 groups of challenges—one for each type of weapon and attack—with four levels of each Challenge. The item and title unlocks aren't earned until the third and fourth levels are completed, respectively.

Patience, Grasshopper: There are enough Challenges here to keep you busy for a long time, so don't get too wrapped up in trying to complete specific Challenges right away. Just play the game, let the bodies land where they may, and enjoy the small XP boosts you get from unlocking the first one or two levels of each weapon's Challenge.

More Bang = More Corpses: Once you've unlocked a few of these Challenges and are ready to start earning the higher level rewards, turn your attention to the weapons with splash damage. Trip Mines, Pipe Bombs, the Rocket Launcher, Devastator, and Enforcer are all capable of dealing fatal splash damage to multiple enemies. Some of these weapons are harder to come by than others, but each one (and explosive barrels) provide the opportunity to get a multi-kill. This not only helps you complete the corresponding weapon Challenge faster, but other Challenges as well.

Become a Specialist...: Those who aim to complete every Challenge will ultimately need to focus their efforts on just one or two specialty weapons. Nobody likes a weapon hog, but it doesn't hurt to let your teammates know that you're trying to complete a specific weapon Challenge. They may, if you ask nicely, provide some cover fire while you run for a weapon pick-up.

...But Stay Flexible: Your opponents are probably smarter than you think, so don't become so devoted to using a single weapon that you become predictable. Players who constantly go for the same weapon pick-up ultimately find themselves stepping right into another player's crosshairs. It's not uncommon for players to camp the weapon spawns, so be careful and remember to mix things up, Challenge be damned!

WEAPON-SPECIFIC CHALLENGES

NAME	DESCRIPTION	XP	ITEM	TITLE
Watch Your Step I	Get 10 kills with Trip Mines.	100	None	None
Watch Your Step II	Get 25 kills with Trip Mines.	250	None	None
Watch Your Step III	Get 75 kills with Trip Mines.	750	Jester Hat	None
Watch Your Step IV	Get 200 kills with Trip Mines.	2000	None	Laser Cat
Splatter King I	Get 10 kills with Pipe Bombs.	100	None	None
Splatter King II	Get 25 kills with Pipe Bombs.	250	None	None
Splatter King III	Get 75 kills with Pipe Bombs.	750	Baseball Cap	None
Splatter King IV	Get 200 kills with Pipe Bombs.	2000	None	Splatter King
Punchy McPuncher I	Get 10 melee kills.	100	None	None
Punchy McPuncher II	Get 25 melee kills.	250	None	None
Punchy McPuncher III	Get 75 melee kills.	750	Hoplite Helmet	None
Punchy McPuncher IV	Get 200 melee kills.	2000	None	Primitive Screwhead
Roid Rage I	Get 10 kills with Steroids.	100	None	None
Roid Rage II	Get 25 kills with Steroids.	250	None	None
Roid Rage III	Get 75 kills with Steroids.	750	Wolf Logo	None
Roid Rage IV	Get 200 kills with Steroids.	2000	None	Furious George
Size Doesn't Matter I	Get 25 kills with the Pistol.	250	None	None
Size Doesn't Matter II	Get 100 kills with the Pistol.	1000	None	None
Size Doesn't Matter III	Get 250 kills with the Pistol.	2500	Military Hat	None
Size Doesn't Matter IV	Get 1000 kills with the Pistol.	10000	None	Gunslinger
Burger Face I	Get 25 kills with the Shotgun.	250	None	None
Burger Face II	Get 100 kills with the Shotgun.	1000	None	None
Burger Face III	Get 250 kills with the Shotgun.	2500	Backwards Baseball Cap	None
Burger Face IV	Get 1000 kills with the Shotgun.	10000	None	Boom Sticker
Swiss Cheese I	Get 25 kills with the Ripper.	250	None	None
Swiss Cheese II	Get 100 kills with the Ripper.	1000	None	None
Swiss Cheese III	Get 250 kills with the Ripper.	2500	Cheese Hat	None
Swiss Cheese IV	Get 1000 kills with the Ripper.	10000	None	Triple Threat
Boom Goes the Weasel I	Get 25 kills with the Rocket Launcher.	250	None	None
Boom Goes the Weasel II	Get 100 kills with the Rocket Launcher.	1000	None	None
Boom Goes the Weasel III	Get 250 kills with the Rocket Launcher.	2500	Detonator Logo	None
Boom Goes the Weasel IV	Get 1000 kills with the Rocket Launcher.	10000	None	Master Blaster
Laser-Seeking Missiles I	Get 25 kills with the Enforcer.	250	None	None
Laser-Seeking Missiles II	Get 100 kills with the Enforcer.	1000	None	None
Laser-Seeking Missiles III	Get 250 kills with the Enforcer.	2500	Brain Sucker	None
Laser-Seeking Missiles IV	Get 1000 kills with the Enforcer.	10000	None	The Enforcer

NAME	DESCRIPTION	XP	ITEM	TITLE
Meat Grinder I	Get 25 kills with the Devastator.	250	None	None
Meat Grinder II	Get 100 kills with the Devastator.	1000	None	None
Meat Grinder III	Get 250 kills with the Devastator.	2500	Retro Duke Logo	None
Meat Grinder IV	Get 1000 kills with the Devastator.	10000	None	Carpet Bomber
Medium Rare I	Get 25 kills with the AT Laser.	250	None	None
Medium Rare II	Get 100 kills with the AT Laser.	1000	None	None
Medium Rare III	Get 250 kills with the AT Laser.	2500	Tie-Dye Shirt	None
Medium Rare IV	Get 1000 kills with the AT Laser.	10000	None	Assault Trooper
Right In the Eye I	Get 25 kills with the Railgun.	250	None	None
Right In the Eye II	Get 100 kills with the Railgun.	1000	None	None
Right In the Eye III	Get 250 kills with the Railgun.	2500	I Shot Stupid Logo	None
Right In the Eye IV	Get 1000 kills with the Railgun.	10000	None	Straight Shooter
Ice to See You I	Execute a frozen player 10 times.	100	None	None
Ice to See You II	Execute a frozen player 25 times.	250	None	None
Ice to See You III	Execute a frozen player 75 times.	750	Ski Goggles	None
Ice to See You IV	Execute a frozen player 200 times.	2000	None	Iceman
Pee Wee Vermin I	Stomp on 10 enemies.	100	None	None
Pee Wee Vermin II	Stomp on 25 enemies.	250	None	None
Pee Wee Vermin III	Stomp on 75 enemies.	750	Uncle Sam Hat	None
Pee Wee Vermin IV	Stomp on 200 enemies.	2000	None	Exterminator
Smile You Son of a Bitch I	Get 10 kills with exploding barrels.	100	None	None
Smile You Son of a Bitch II	Get 25 kills with exploding barrels.	250	None	None
Smile You Son of a Bitch III	Get 75 kills with exploding barrels.	750	WTF Logo	None
Smile You Son of a Bitch IV	Get 200 kills with exploding barrels.	2000	None	Waste Manager
Tiny But Deadly I	Get 10 kills with the Garter Pistol.	100	None	None
Tiny But Deadly II	Get 25 kills with the Garter Pistol.	250	None	None
Tiny But Deadly III	Get 75 kills with the Garter Pistol.	750	Canadian Flag Logo	None
Tiny But Deadly IV	Get 200 kills with the Garter Pistol.	2000	None	Jealous Type

MOBILITY & PICK-UP

The seven groups of Challenges in this category will simply be earned over time—and some not for a long time. These Challenges reward players who get the most out of Duke's chemically-enhanced physique and high-tech toys. As with the weapon-based Challenges, the item and title rewards are unlocked upon completing the third and fourth tier of each Challenge type.

Laziness Is for Losers: Don't walk when you can run and don't jump when you can rocket jump (just watch where you point that thing). You'll never earn the Marathon and Explosive Gas Challenges if you don't put some effort into your movements. So bear down and push that Sprint button to move with some urgency. The same goes for rocket jumping; don't be afraid to expend a rocket or two using the RPG to launch Duke onto a higher ledge.

Moderation Is Unhealthy: Pay no attention to the advice of your physician; there's no better way to complete more Challenges and unlock bonus XP than by hitting the bottle. Hard. Using Steroids, drinking Beers, and deploying Holodukes are all going to naturally occur over time, but you can earn those level IV Challenges faster by making a point of gathering up and using as many pick-ups as possible.

ABILITY CHALLENGES

NAME	DESCRIPTION	XP	ITEM	TITLE
Mile High Club I	Fly for 10 minutes.	500	None	None
Mile High Club II	Fly for 30 minutes.	1500	None	None
Mile High Club III	Fly for 60 minutes.	3000	Bird S*!t Logo	None
Mile High Club IV	Fly for 90 minutes.	4500	None	High Flier
Free Fallin' I	Fall 250 feet in total.	100	None	None
Free Fallin' II	Fall 750 feet in total.	1000	None	None
Free Fallin' III	Fall 1500 feet in total.	2500	Balls Logo	None
Free Fallin' IV	Fall 2500 feet in total.	10000	None	Drop Out
Marathon I	Run 5 miles.	125	None	None
Marathon II	Run 10 miles.	250	None	None
Marathon III	Run 50 miles.	1250	Sport Shades	None
Marathon IV	Run 150 miles.	3750	None	Forrest
That Wasn't Me I	Use a Holoduke 10 times.	250	None	None
That Wasn't Me II	Use a Holoduke 25 times.	625	None	None
That Wasn't Me III	Use a Holoduke 75 times.	1875	3D Glasses	None
That Wasn't Me IV	Use a Holoduke 200 times.	5000	None	Predator
Prescription Only I	Use 10 Steroids.	250	None	None
Prescription Only II	Use 25 Steroids.	625	None	None
Prescription Only III	Use 75 Steroids.	1875	Radioactive Logo	None
Prescription Only IV	Use 200 Steroids.	5000	None	Pill Popper
Really Thirsty I	Drink 10 beers.	250	None	None
Really Thirsty II	Drink 25 beers.	625	None	None
Really Thirsty III	Drink 75 beers.	1875	Beer Hat	None
Really Thirsty IV	Drink 200 beers.	5000	None	Frat Boy
Explosive Gas I	Rocket jump 10 times.	100	None	None
Explosive Gas II	Rocket jump 25 times.	250	None	None
Explosive Gas III	Rocket jump 75 times.	750	Balls of Steel Logo	None
Explosive Gas IV	Rocket jump 200 times.	2000	None	Rocketman

PERFORMANCE CHALLENGES

The bulk of the Challenges award your commitment to each of the various game modes and also the skill you exhibit while playing. The majority of these Challenges will simply come over time as you continue to play the game, experiment with Duke's abilities, and get better at the team objective matches. Continue to play, cross your fingers that you land on a good team, and rack up the victories and the kills to unlock these Challenges.

Study the List: While some of these Challenges are exactly what you may expect from a system such as this, there are quite a few that require some unorthodox techniques. For example, the "Stuck on You" Challenges require that you directly stick enemies with Trip Mines. "Breaking the Mold" requires that you melee kill an enemy after freezing him. Another Challenge called "Going on Safari" requires you to string together a very specific kill streak with a set list of weapons. Consult the list (both in the book and within the game) to see which Challenges you're close to completing.

Team Player: The loading screen tip that speaks of the importance of the team objective being greater than your kill-to-death ratio isn't a joke, it's a reminder that is all-too needed for many players. Players who focus on the team objective, or even a certain role within the team's overall strategy, are greatly rewarded with bonus XP, new items, and titles. Be a team player, focus on the team objective when playing Capture the Babe and Hail to the King and reap the rewards.

It'll Destroy Your Mouth: You scratch their itch, they scratch yours. We don't condone it and every one of these Challenges is certainly attainable if you play long enough, but it's not against the rules to get together with other players and help one another unlock some of these Challenges. There are a few that will go a lot faster if you coordinate with the enemy and none more than "Hot Pockets." Trapping two enemies in the microwave just doesn't happen that often by chance, let alone 50 times. And that 25,000 bonus XP is just too tempting to pass up!

PERFORMANCE CHALLENGES

NAME	DESCRIPTION	XP	ITEM	TITLE
Duke Match Veteran	Play two hours of Duke Matches.	500	Tropical Shirt	None
Team Duke Match Veteran	Play two hours of Team Duke Matches.	500	Double Rainbow Logo	None
Capture the Babe Veteran	Play two hours of Capture the Babe matches.	500	Heart Glasses	None
Hail to the King Veteran	Play two hours of Hail to the King matches.	500	Pickelhaube	None
S*!t Talker	Taunt once in any multiplayer mode.	50	None	None
Super Ninja	Kill a player while you are using the Holo Duke	150	Groucho Glasses	None
I See You	Kill a player while they are using the Holo Duke	250	Samurai Helmet	None
Double Your Fun	Kill a player while using double damage.	100	None	None
Nothing Can Stop Me	Kill a player while invincible.	100	Wraparound Shades	None
Just Chillin'	Freeze an enemy.	50	None	None
All About Perspective	Shrink an enemy.	50	None	None
So Hot	Survive being frozen.	100	Inuit Goggles	None
The Water Was Cold	Survive being shrunk.	100	Tea Shades	None
Crusader I	Win a Duke Match.	100	None	None
Crusader II	Win 25 Duke Matches.	2500	None	None
Crusader III	Win 75 Duke Matches.	7500	United States Flag Logo	None
Crusader IV	Win 200 Duke Matches.	20000	None	Lone Wolf
All About Me I	Get 10 kills in Duke Match.	100	None	None
All About Me II	Get 50 kills in Duke Match.	500	None	None
All About Me III	Get 200 kills in Duke Match.	2000	American Flag Shirt	None
All About Me IV	Get 500 kills in Duke Match.	5000	None	Grim Reaper
My Brother's Keeper I	Win a Team Duke Match.	100	None	None
My Brother's Keeper II	Win 25 Team Duke Matches.	2500	None	None
My Brother's Keeper III	Win 75 Team Duke Matches.	7500	Ducks Shirt	None
My Brother's Keeper IV	Win 200 Team Duke Matches.	20000	None	Sarge
Get Off My Coattails I	Get 10 kills in Team Duke Matches.	100	None	None
Get Off My Coattails II	Get 50 kills in Team Duke Matches.	500	None	None
Get Off My Coattails III	Get 200 kills in Team Duke Matches.	2000	Christmas Shirt	None
Get Off My Coattails IV	Get 500 kills in Team Duke Matches.	5000	None	Teamster
Face Rolled I	Get the most kills in a Team Duke Match.	100	None	None
Face Rolled II	Get the most kills in 10 Team Duke Matches.	2500	None	None
Face Rolled III	Get the most kills in 50 Team Duke Matches.	7500	Star Glasses	None
Face Rolled IV	Get the most kills in 100 Team Duke Matches.	20000	None	MVP
I'm Gonna Let You Finish I	Get 10 assists in Team Duke Matches.	100	None	None
I'm Gonna Let You Finish II	Get 50 assists in Team Duke Matches.	500	None	None
I'm Gonna Let You Finish III	Get 125 assists in Team Duke Matches.	1250	Shutter Shades	None
I'm Gonna Let You Finish IV	Get 250 assists in Team Duke Matches.	2500	None	Wingman
Ladies Man I	Win a Capture the Babe game.	100	None	None
Ladies Man II	Win 25 Capture the Babe games.	2500	None	None
Ladies Man III	Win 75 Capture the Babe games.	7500	Groping Hands Logo	None
Ladies Man IV	Win 200 Capture the Babe games.	20000	None	Ladies Man
You're Married? I	Get the most Babes in a Capture the Babe game.	10	None	None
You're Married? II	Get the most Babes in 10 Capture the Babe games.	100	None	None
You're Married? III	Get the most Babes in 50 Capture the Babe games.	500	Tux Logo	None
You're Married? IV	Get the most Babes in 150 Capture the Babe games.	1500	None	Sexy Beast
Womanizer I	Capture the Babe in Capture the Babe mode.	25	None	None
Womanizer II	Capture 20 Babes in Capture the Babe mode.	500	None	None
Womanizer III	Capture 69 Babes in Capture the Babe mode.	1725	Boobs Logo	None
Womanizer IV	Capture 150 Babes in Capture the Babe mode.	3750	None	Chick Magnet
Lady Savior I	Return your Babe to your base.	50	None	None

NAME	DESCRIPTION	XP	ITEM	TITLE
Lady Savior II	Return your Babe to your base 10 times.	500	None	None
Lady Savior III	Return your Babe to your base 50 times.	2500	Cherry Logo	None
Lady Savior IV	Return your Babe to your base 150 times.	7500	None	Pick Up Artist
C%(k Blocker I	Kill an enemy Babe carrier.	50	None	None
C%(k Blocker II	Kill 10 enemy Babe carriers.	500	None	None
C%(k Blocker III	Kill 50 enemy Babe carriers.	2500	Pimp Hat	None
C%(k Blocker IV	Kill 150 enemy Babe carriers.	7500	None	C%(k Blocker
Kingmaker I	Win a Hail to the King game.	100	None	None
Kingmaker II	Win 25 Hail to the King games.	2500	None	None
Kingmaker III	Win 75 Hail to the King games.	7500	Coat of Arms Logo	None
Kingmaker IV	Win 200 Hail to the King games.	20000	None	Royalty
Grubby Mitts I	Earn 50 points for your team in Hail to the King mode.	200	None	None
Grubby Mitts II	Earn 200 points for your team in Hail to the King mode.	800	None	None
Grubby Mitts III	Earn 500 points for your team in Hail to the King mode.	2000	Seal of Approval Logo	None
Grubby Mitts IV	Earn 1000 points for your team in Hail to the King mode.	4000	None	Point Whore
Our House I	Take the control point back from the enemy team.	100	None	None
Our House II	Take the control point back from the enemy team 10 times.	2500	None	None
Our House III	Take the control point back from the enemy team 50 times.	7500	Radioactive Fist Logo	None
Our House IV	Take the control point back from the enemy team 150 times.	20000	None	Control Freak
Hail Mary I	Kill 10 enemies while they're in the control point.	100	None	None
Hail Mary II	Kill 25 enemies while they're in the control point.	250	None	None
Hail Mary III	Kill 75 enemies while they're in the control point.	750	Leeroy Logo	None
Hail Mary IV	Kill 200 enemies while they're in the control point.	2000	None	Party Pooper
Follow My Lead I	Get the highest score in 5 Team Duke Matches	250	None	None
Follow My Lead II	Get the highest score in 10 Team Duke Matches	500	None	None
Follow My Lead III	Get the highest score in 25 Team Duke Matches	1250	Traffic Cone	None
Follow My Lead IV	Get the highest score in 75 Team Duke Matches	3750	None	Squad Leader
Battle for the Circle I	Get the highest score in 5 Hail to The King matches.	250	None	None
Battle for the Circle II	Get the highest score in 10 Hail to The King matches.	500	None	None
Battle for the Circle III	Get the highest score in 25 Hail to The King matches.	1250	Crown	None
Battle for the Circle IV	Get the highest score in 75 Hail to The King matches.	3750	None	The King
Propane Accessories	Kill 4 enemies inside the control point at the same time.	500	Classic Glasses	None
Scraping Bottom	Finish last in a Duke Match.	10	None	None
I Tried My Best	Get the highest score on the losing team in a Team Duke Match.	125	None	None
I'm Here for the Food	Get the lowest score on the losing team in a Team Duke Match.	10	None	None
We Tried	Get the highest score on the losing team in a Hail to The King match.	125	None	None
My Team Sucked	Get the lowest score on the losing team in a Hail to The King Match.	10	None	None
Major Shrinkage	Get shrunk while carrying the Babe in Capture the Babe.	10	None	None
Spring Loaded	Kill a player while you are in flight from a Jump Pad.	2500	None	Bouncer

NAME	DESCRIPTION	XP	ITEM	TITLE
Ralph	Drink 20 beers in a single HTTK match.	2000	Video Glasses	None
Dirty Rats	Kill a shrunk player while shrunk.	500	Bugeye Glasses	None
Leap Frog	Jump over a RPG round.	500	None	Hurdler
Limbo	Crouch under a trip mine laser.	500	None	Limbo King
She Was Frigid	Get frozen while carrying the Babe in Capture The Babe.	10	Middle Finger Logo	None
Top Gun I	Kill 10 players after locking on to them.	250	None	None
Top Gun II	Kill 25 players after locking on to them.	625	None	None
Top Gun III	Kill 75 players after locking on to them.	1875	Aviator Sunglasses	None
Top Gun IV	Kill 200 players after locking on to them.	5000	None	Ace
Flak You I	Kill 10 enemies by exploding their Jetpacks.	100	None	None
Flak You II	Kill 25 enemies by exploding their Jetpacks.	250	None	None
Flak You III	Kill 75 enemies by exploding their Jetpacks.	750	Hunting Logo	None
Flak You IV	Kill 200 enemies by exploding their Jetpacks.	2000	None	Duck Hunter
Bouncing Betty I	Jump on 50 jump pads.	500	None	None
Bouncing Betty II	Jump on 150 jump pads.	1500	None	None
Bouncing Betty III	Jump on 500 jump pads.	5000	Horn-Rimmed Glasses	None
Bouncing Betty IV	Jump on 1000 jump pads.	10000	None	Spring Chicken
Hot Pockets I	Kill 2 or more players at once with the microwave in Duke Burger.	500	None	None
Hot Pockets II	Kill 2 or more players at once with the microwave in Duke Burger 5 times.	2500	None	None
Hot Pockets III	Kill 2 or more players at once with the microwave in Duke Burger 10 times.	5000	Ballissimo Logo	None
Hot Pockets IV	Kill 2 or more players at once with the microwave in Duke Burger 50 times.	25000	None	Radioactive
Squeaky Clean I	Get 5 kills with the dishwasher in Duke Burger.	500	None	None
Squeaky Clean II	Get 10 kills with the dishwasher in Duke Burger.	1000	None	None
Squeaky Clean III	Get 50 kills with the dishwasher in Duke Burger.	5000	Scuba Mask	None
Squeaky Clean IV	Get 150 kills with the dishwasher in Duke Burger.	15000	None	The Cleaner
Fire and Ice	Use a barrel to kill a frozen player.	1000	None	Elemental Wizard
Ménage à Death	Outmaneuver a trio of Enforcer missiles that have locked onto you.	1000	None	Slick Willy
Kangaroo Jack	Kill 10 players while not on the ground.	1000	Propeller Beanie	None
Pigeon Precision	Kill 10 players while flying with a Jetpack.	1000	Feathered Headdress	None
Pull!	Use the Shotgun to kill a player in flight from a Jump Pad.	1000	None	Skeeter
Drinking Makes You Tougher	Survive a melee attack by having drunk a beer first.	1000	None	None
Freezing Rain	Freeze an enemy who is in midair.	150	None	None
Falling Down Shrunk	Shrink an enemy who is in midair.	150	None	None
Midair Collision	Use the Railgun to kill an enemy while you're being launched by a Jump Pad.	2500	Hypno-Goggles	None
Perfect Aim	Use the Railgun to kill a shrunk enemy.	1000	Tattoo Shirt	None
The Sheriff	Get 10 kills using the Pistol in Morningwood during a single match.	1000	None	Sheriff
Your Shirt's Da Bomb	Equip the F-Bomb shirt logo and win a DM match.	500	None	None

NAME	DESCRIPTION	XP	ITEM	TITLE
MADF	Fly a Jetpack while drunk.	250	None	Plastered Pilot
Old School	Get 30 kills in a single match in Hollywood.	1000	None	Hollywood Star
Special Sauce	Destroy 1 of each type of condiment during a single match in Duke Burger.	500	Hot Dog Logo	None
One Man Army I	Kill an entire 4 man team within 5 seconds of each other.	500	None	None
One Man Army II	Kill an entire 4 man team within 5 seconds of each other 5 times.	2500	None	None
One Man Army III	Kill an entire 4 man team within 5 seconds of each other 10 times.	5000	Cone Head	None
One Man Army IV	Kill an entire 4 man team within 5 seconds of each other 50 times.	25000	None	One Man Army
Scalp Collector I	Kill all enemies at least once in a single match 5 times.	500	None	None
Scalp Collector II	Kill all enemies at least once in a single match 10 times.	1000	None	None
Scalp Collector III	Kill all enemies at least once in a single match 50 times.	5000	iPwned Logo	None
Scalp Collector IV	Kill all enemies at least once in a single match 150 times.	15000	None	Scalp Collector
Payback I	Get a payback kill.	25	None	None
Payback II	Get 10 payback kills.	250	None	None
Payback III	Get 50 payback kills.	1250	Trick Arrow	None
Payback IV	Get 150 payback kills.	3750	None	Bronson
That Last Step I	Kill 5 players in a single match with Trip Mines.	100	None	None
That Last Step II	Kill 5 players in a single match with Trip Mines 10 times.	1000	None	None
That Last Step III	Kill 5 players in a single match with Trip Mines 50 times.	5000	Foot Logo	None
That Last Step IV	Kill 5 players in a single match with Trip Mines 150 times.	15000	None	Major Miner
Lemmings... All of Them I	Get 5 multi-kills with Trip Mines.	250	None	None
Lemmings... All of Them II	Get 10 multi-kills with Trip Mines.	500	None	None
Lemmings... All of Them III	Get 50 multi-kills with Trip Mines.	2500	Piranha Logo	None
Lemmings... All of Them IV	Get 150 multi-kills with Trip Mines.	7500	None	Master Baiter
Stuck On You I	Kill 5 players by sticking Trip Mines to them.	500	None	None
Stuck On You II	Kill 10 players by sticking Trip Mines to them.	1000	None	None
Stuck On You III	Kill 50 players by sticking Trip Mines to them.	5000	Miner Helmet	None
Stuck On You IV	Kill 150 players by sticking Trip Mines to them.	15000	None	Sticky Fingers
That's Chunky I	Kill 5 players in a single match with Pipe Bombs.	100	None	None
That's Chunky II	Kill 5 players in a single match with Pipe Bombs 10 times.	1000	None	None
That's Chunky III	Kill 5 players in a single match with Pipe Bombs 50 times.	5000	Hoodie Logo	None
That's Chunky IV	Kill 5 players in a single match with Pipe Bombs 150 times.	15000	None	Chili Maker
Curiosity Killed the Cat I	Get 5 multi-kills with Pipe Bombs.	250	None	None
Curiosity Killed the Cat II	Get 10 multi-kills with Pipe Bombs.	500	None	None
Curiosity Killed the Cat III	Get 50 multi-kills with Pipe Bombs.	2500	F-Bomb Logo	None
Curiosity Killed the Cat IV	Get 150 multi-kills with Pipe Bombs.	7500	None	Crowd Killer
El Toro I	Kill 5 players in a single match with melee attacks.	250	None	None
El Toro II	Kill 5 players in a single match with melee attacks 5 times.	1250	None	None
El Toro III	Kill 5 players in a single match with melee attacks 10 times.	2500	Skulls Logo	None

NAME	DESCRIPTION	XP	ITEM	TITLE
El Toro IV	Kill 5 players in a single match with melee attacks 50 times.	12500	None	Pugilist
K.O. King I	Kill 5 players in a single match while using Steroids.	250	None	None
K.O. King II	Kill 5 players in a single match while using Steroids 5 times.	1250	None	None
K.O. King III	Kill 5 players in a single match while using Steroids 10 times.	2500	Flexing Arm Logo	None
K.O. King IV	Kill 5 players in a single match while using Steroids 50 times.	12500	None	The Incredible Bulk
Blast Radius I	Kill 4 or more players at once with the RPG.	500	None	None
Blast Radius II	Kill 4 or more players at once with the RPG 5 times.	2500	None	None
Blast Radius III	Kill 4 or more players at once with the RPG 10 times.	5000	Chicken Hat	None
Blast Radius IV	Kill 4 or more players at once with the RPG 50 times.	25000	None	Big Shot
Running Man	Trigger 4 Trip Mines by running through them and not dying.	1000	None	Running Man
Remote Bomber	Get a kill by detonating a Pipe Bomb while more than 200 feet away.	1000	None	Mad Bomber
Bar Fight	Punch-kill a player while you are drunk and on Steroids.	1000	None	Bar Brawler
Inhuman	Be under the effects of Double Damage and Invincibility at the same time.	1000	None	Inhuman
We're Going Streaking! I	Get 5 kills in a row without dying.	250	None	None
We're Going Streaking! II	Get 5 kills in a row without dying 5 times.	1250	None	None
We're Going Streaking! III	Get 5 kills in a row without dying 10 times.	2500	Skull and Balls Logo	None
We're Going Streaking! IV	Get 5 kills in a row without dying 25 times.	6250	None	Spree Killer
Untouchable I	Play an entire match without getting killed.	1000	Prisoner Mask	None
Untouchable II	Play 5 matches without getting killed.	5000	None	None
Untouchable III	Play 20 matches without getting killed.	20000	None	None
Untouchable IV	Play 50 matches without getting killed.	50000	None	Untouchable
Going on Safari	Kill a player with each of the following: Pistol, Ripper, Shotgun, and Steroids one after the other, without dying.	2500	Grand Pooh-Bah Hat	None
Nuke 'Em I	Get 5 kills with the microwave in Duke Burger.	500	None	None
Nuke 'Em II	Get 10 kills with the microwave in Duke Burger.	1000	None	None
Nuke 'Em III	Get 50 kills with the microwave in Duke Burger.	5000	Chef's Hat	None
Nuke 'Em IV	Get 150 kills with the microwave in Duke Burger.	15000	None	Duke Nuker
Overkill	Use an explosive weapon to kill a frozen, shrunk player.	2500	Texas Flag Logo	None
Breaking the Mold	Freeze a player, allow them to thaw and finish him off with a melee attack.	2500	Goggles	None
Dance Party	Have all 4 team members squat and stand 3 times on a single capture point in a HTTK match.	5000	Headphones	None
Hot Potato	Have all 4 team members get a kill with a Pipe Bomb in a single TDM match.	5000	Football Helmet	None
Ogre Rush	Kill everyone on a capture point while on Steroids.	2500	Viking Helmet	None
Joust	Melee kill a player while flying with the Jetpack.	2500	Plague Doctor Mask	None
One Shot One Kill	Fire 3 RPG shots in a row that each kill at least one enemy.	5000	Alien Cockpit	None
From Beyond the Grave	Kill a player after you are already dead.	2500	Pumpkin Hat	None
Giant Killer	Kill a player that shrunk you before you grow big or die.	2500	Fez	None

SUICIDE CHALLENGES

There's more than one way to die in *Duke Nukem Forever* and it's often your own fault. Not every weapon you wield can prove suicidal, but each of the explosive ones can. Just fire the weapon (or detonate a Pipe Bomb) on the ground directly below you to die in the blast. It's also possible to fire an RPG or other explosive weapon into a nearby wall to score the suicide.

So Big!: Duke is killed when he returns to normal size if he's not in a large enough space to accommodate his height. Get the "No Head Room" suicide by using a Shrink Pad and waiting inside a shrunken mini-route for Duke to return to full size again.

Hydro Power: The best place to perform a suicide by electricity is on the Hoover Damned map. Run into the electrified shipping container or leap into the water near the alien to unlock the "Shocking, Huh?" Challenge.

SUICIDE CHALLENGES

NAME	DESCRIPTION	XP	ITEM	TITLE
My Emo Life	Complete all other suicide challenges.	20	Banzai Headband	None
Watch Where You're Going	Suicide by Trip Mines.	10	None	None
Acme Inc.	Suicide by RPG.	10	None	None
O.M.G.	Suicide by Pipe Bomb.	10	None	None
I'll Never Learn	Suicide by Devastator.	10	None	None
Stupid Seeking Missiles	Suicide by Enforcer.	10	None	None
Never Taken Alive	Suicide by falling.	10	None	None
Don't Touch	Suicide by exploding barrel.	10	None	None
No Head Room	Suicide when you unshrink.	10	None	None
Where's My Parachute?	Suicide by falling to your death after running out of Jetpack fuel.	10	None	None
Shocking, Huh?	Suicide by electricity.	10	None	None
Forgot to Flip	Suicide by the stove in Duke Burger.	10	None	None

SECRET AREA CHALLENGES

Each of the multiplayer maps has what is known as a "secret area." Some of them can be found by using a strategically placed Bounce Pad (Duke Burger) or Shrink Pad (Highway Noon), while others require far more searching on your part. Several of the secret areas are even hidden behind pass-through walls (Hollywood has two of these). Consult our coverage for each of the maps to get the lowdown on how to access each map's secret area. Some maps have multiple secret areas, but you only need to access one to get credit for the Challenge. Secret Areas typically conceal a really powerful weapon or power-up, so don't just find them for the Challenge—make them part of your standard strategy!

SECRET AREA CHALLENGES

NAME	DESCRIPTION	XP	ITEM	TITLE
Secret Snoop	Find all secret areas.	1500	Pith Helmet	None
Secret Area: Duke Burger	Find the secret area in Duke Burger.	100	None	None
Secret Area: Hoover Damned	Find the secret area in Hoover Damned.	100	None	None
Secret Area: Hive	Find the secret area in Hive.	100	None	None
Secret Area: Morningwood	Find the secret area in Morningwood.	100	None	None
Secret Area: Vegas Ruins	Find the secret area in Vegas Ruins.	100	None	None
Secret Area: Industrial	Find the secret area in Industrial.	100	None	None
Secret Area: Casino	Find the secret area in Casino.	100	None	None
Secret Area: Highway Noon	Find the secret area in Highway Noon.	100	None	None
Secret Area: Construction	Find the secret area in Construction.	100	None	None
Secret Area: Hollywood	Find the secret area in Hollywood.	100	None	None

ULTIMATE CHALLENGE

Behold, the 315th Challenge. Complete all 314 Challenges listed in the previous tables to earn the right to be called The True Duke.

ULTIMATE CHALLENGE

NAME	DESCRIPTION	XP	ITEM	TITLE
Perfectionist	Complete every challenge.	100000	None	The True Duke

CHANGE ROOM

Access the Change Room from the Multiplayer menu to alter your Duke character's appearance in multiplayer mode. Select any of the titles you've unlocked by completing Challenges and pick out new combinations of hat, face, and shirt for Duke to wear. You can even change the color of the t-shirt when wearing one of the logo style shirts. The following pages showcase every item available for the Change Room. Consult the previous tables to see which Challenges need to be completed to unlock them!

Remember to keep it high and tight when picking out a hat—leave the bulky Traffic Cone and Hoplite Hat for those who like getting sniped!

HATS

ITEM	DESCRIPTION
No Hat—Default	No hat.
Jester Hat	Camouflage for fighting the clowns you're up against.
Baseball Cap	Cover up bed head with this simple baseball cap.
Hoplite Helmet	March into battle looking like a giant rooster.
Military Cap	Proud member of the Duke Nukem army of one.
Backwards Baseball Cap	Keepin' it real.
Cheese Hat	Includes pre-made holes to confuse your enemies.
Brain Sucker	Must… destroy… mankind.
Uncle Sam Hat	The greatness of America, distilled into hat form.
Beer Helmet	A drunk scout is always prepared.
Pickelhaube	Great Grandfather Otto Heinrich Franz Werner Herzog von Nukem's spiky helmet.
Samurai Helmet	He was wearing a samurai helmet! No officer, I'm not on drugs.
Pimp Hat	Fraggin' ain't easy.
Traffic Cone	Be sure to parallel park a rocket into your enemy's face.
Crown	His Royal Highness, King Duke, declares that it's time to kick ass.
Banzai Headband	Let your adversary know that neither of you are coming back from this fight.

ITEM	DESCRIPTION
Propeller Beanie	Don't go thinking that the propeller will let you fly if you go leaping off of any buildings.
Feathered Headdress	It looks so good that all the ladies will want to see your totem pole.
Cone Head	Prepare to consume great amounts of awesomeness.
Trick Arrow	Well excuuuse me for being a wild and insane guy.
Chicken Hat	Hey, that chicken's got a Duke stuck on its ass.
Grand Pooh-Bah Hat	Only Duke knows what sort of animal this hat was made from.
Chef's Hat	Chef Duke is cooking up a seven-layer casserole of pain.
Headphones	These babies pick up both AM and FM stations!
Football Helmet	4th and inches to kicking some ass.
Viking Helmet	Send your enemies to the halls of Valhalla.
Alien Cockpit	Who's really in charge here?
Pumpkin Hat	Great pumpkin? No, the greatest pumpkin.
Fez	Be a member of the Ancient Order of Ass Kicking.
Miner Helmet	It not only protects your skull from falling debris, but that light is great for reading in bed.
Pith Helmet	It's not war, it's an adventure!

FACE

ITEM	DESCRIPTION
Default Sunglasses	These are Duke's default sunglasses.
Ski Goggles	Hit the slopes or shoot an enemy and look cool doing it.
Sport Shades	Whoever said that killing your enemies wasn't a sport?
3D Glasses	It's like those bullets are coming right at you!
Heart Glasses	Show your love to your enemies.
Groucho Glasses	No one will be able to guess your true identity in these.
Wraparound Shades	Not to be confused with reach-around.
Inuit Goggles	Low-tech shades that look like a sci-fi visor.
Teashades	Woah… trippy man.
Star Glasses	Get your glam on while destroying your enemies.
Shutter Glasses	The view through your blinds everywhere you go.

ITEM	DESCRIPTION
Classic Glasses	Frag your foes while looking like your dad.
Video Glasses	I only have eyes for brew.
Bugeye Glasses	Looking cool and bug free.
Aviator Sunglasses	The classic big D sunglasses.
Horn-Rimmed Glasses	Aunt Nukem's reading glasses.
Scuba Mask	You never know when there's going to be a flood.
Hypno-Goggles	Daze your opponents while you mess with their hands.
Prisoner Mask	Frag your enemies all you want, just don't eat them afterwards. That's gross.
Goggles	Protects your eyes and helps you focus on kicking ass.
Plague Doctor Mask	Protect yourself from their filthy germs.

SHIRT

ITEM	DESCRIPTION
Plain Shirt	Duke's regular shirt.
Wolf Logo	Pure, unbridled fury.
Retro Duke Logo	Old school action.
I Shot Stupid Logo	Make sure that someone's standing to your left, otherwise it just looks silly.

ITEM	DESCRIPTION
WTF Logo	OMG WTF BBQ!
Canadian Flag Logo	Take off to the Great White North.
Hunting Logo	Real men hunt with their bare hands.
Bird Sh*# Logo	Let your opponents know that you're ready to crap on their lives.

ITEM		DESCRIPTION
	Balls Logo	Let the world know that you're proud of your balls.
	Radioactive Logo	More than just a symbol… it's a way of life.
	Double Rainbow	For when you want to go all the way.
	United States Flag Logo	America, f*!@ yeah!
	Groping Hands Logo	They can't keep their hands off you.
	Tux Logo	For those times that require a touch of class.
	Boobs Logo	It's not like cross-dressing, you just really like looking at boobs.
	Cherry Logo	There's something about this shirt that just sort of pops.
	Coat of Arms Logo	The Nukem family crest, dating back generations.
	Seal of Approval Logo	You've been fully certified and approved by the Duke himself.
	Radioactive Fist Logo	Duke power!
	Leeroy Logo	Let your teammates know that you're ready to charge into battle.
	Middle Finger Logo	For those times when you're too lazy for words.
	Balls of Steel Logo	You want to know what it takes to win games? It takes steel balls to win games.
	Ballissimo Logo	The perfect recipe… for carnage!
	Detonator's Logo	Delivering the long bombs.

ITEM		DESCRIPTION
	Piranha Logo	Unleash your bloodlust and start a feeding frenzy.
	F-Bomb Logo	Somebody set you up the f-bomb.
	Hot Dog Logo	Suggestive? Maybe. Delicious? Definitely.
	iPwnd Logo	iCame. iSaw. iPwnd.
	Foot Logo	Don't be so sentimental. Things explode every day.
	Hoodie Logo	You're so good that you've made everyone's most wanted list.
	Skulls Logo	Just like the skulls of your enemies, piled at your feet.
	Flexing Arm Logo	Steroids aren't cheating, and I'll punch out anyone who says otherwise.
	Skull and Balls Logo	If they make a joke about you having balls for eyes, frag 'em.
	Texas Flag Logo	Don't let them mess with you while you're wearing this shirt.
	Tie-Dye Shirt	There's only one word to describe this shirt: groovy.
	Tropical Shirt	Nothing says, "Party time!" quite like a Hawaiian shirt.
	American Flag Shirt	The Red, White and Blue is ready to pwn you.
	Ducks Shirt	Be sure to keep your ducks in a row, it makes them easier to kill.
	Christmas Shirt	This year, give the gift of pain.
	Tattoo Shirt	It's like body art for those who are too scared to get permanently inked.

MY DIGS

THE ULTIMATE MAN CAVE, MINUS THE CAVE... AND THE STENCH

Take a break from those marathon sessions of Duke Matches every now and then to stretch out in Duke's Digs. Duke's apartment is nothing less than a penthouse suite loaded with more than 60 pieces of art, statues, interactive games, and a half-dozen babes craving a little Duke. This bitchin' bachelor pad doesn't come fully-stocked though; you need to turn this penthouse into a Holsom home.

DUKE'S PENTHOUSE: THE FLOOR PLAN

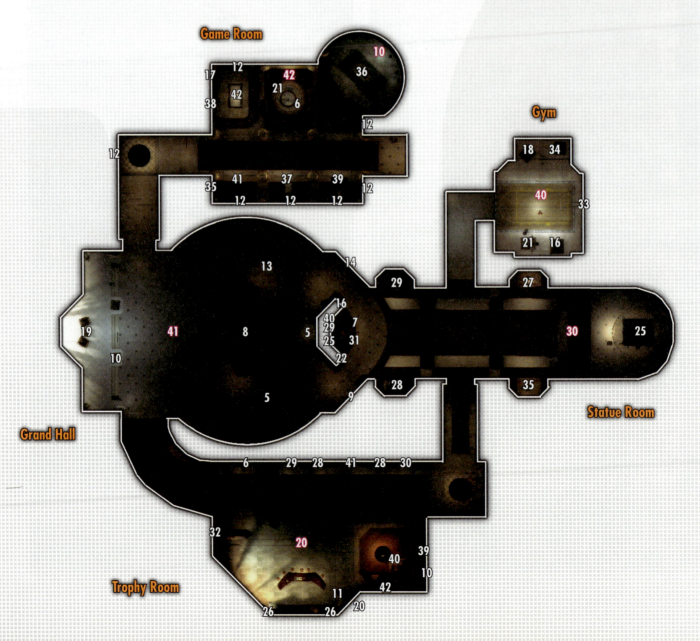

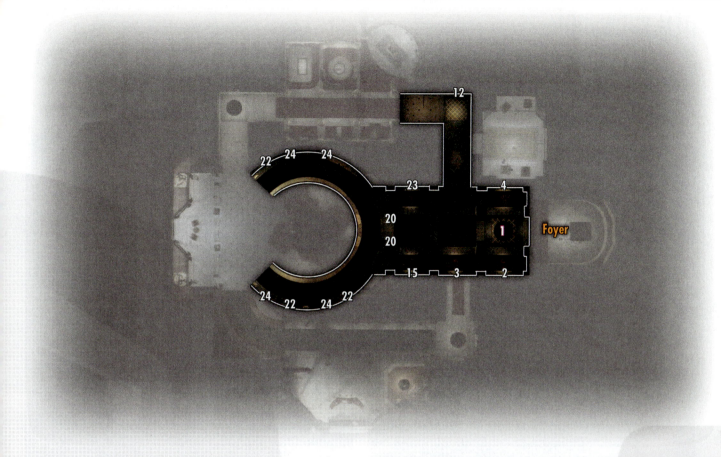

Foyer

Select the "My Digs" option via the Multiplayer menu to visit the place Duke goes when he needs a break from kicking alien you-know-what. The penthouse is somewhat bare at first, containing little more than the scantily-clad Kitty Pousoix and her feather-duster. Although having a French maid all to yourself may sound like more than enough, there's plenty more where she came from. Continue playing the multiplayer mode (and completing Challenges) to earn XP, level up and unlock more items for your digs. Access the customization screen to toggle on/off the various items you've unlocked. This is important, as the items you unlock in multiplayer won't appear in My Digs until you activate them from within this menu.

The accompanying floor plans contain numbered callouts that correspond to the location of the items you unlock at each experience level. The number indicates the player's experience level needed to access the item that goes in its location within the penthouse. Pink numbers correspond to Babes. Note that some levels unlock multiple items, hence some duplicate numbers. Explore the digs, interact with the games, ogle the babes, and kick back and bask in the warm digital glow of a life you'll never know!

PLEASE TOUCH THE EXHIBITS!

You can interact with many of the items in the penthouse to some extent (please no flash photography near the artwork). Whether it's simply ogling one of the babes, shooting basketballs, smoking a cigar, or playing pinball, approach each item to see what it can do, as experimenting with new awards is half the fun of the My Digs mode!

Visit the game room and chat with Miso Ho'ney when you've got a hankerin' for an Asian kitten. Although the maid continuously wanders the penthouse, the other babes hang out in a single room.

Who let the dude in? Well, at least Duke's got someone to play air hockey with...

ITEM SHOWROOM

ITEM		DESCRIPTION
	#1: Babe: Kitty Pousoix	The maid of the house and always ooo la la!
	#2: Champion Duke Photo	Undefeated in the cage.
	#3: Duke Portrait Photo	The man himself.
	#4: Duke Shark Photo	Duke proving that he's king of the oceans as well.
	#5: Mountain Climbing Photo	Duke at the summit of Everest for the 10th time.
	#5: Cigar Duke Photo	Duke enjoying a hand-rolled cigar.
	#6: Enforcer Plaque	Duke used most of its hide to create a pair of boots and a matching handbag for one of his babes.
	#6: Donuts	Yes… donuts… got a problem with that?
	#7: Duke Cardboard Cutout	A bigger-than-life cardboard cutout of Duke Nukem.
	#8: Duke Globe	Duke lifting the weight of the world.
	#9: Awards Duke Photo	A photo of Duke receiving his Golden Statue awards.
	#10: Babe: Miso Ho'ney	A sexy Asian bombshell complete with cat ears.
	#10: Battlelord Plaque	Duke showed him who's the true battle lord.
	#10: Bronze Babe 1	Capturing the essence of beauty and success.
	#11: Cigarette Machine	Can't smoke 'em, but fun to throw around.
	#12: Retro Paintings	Relive Duke's history through this series of pixelated paintings.
	#13: Astronaut Duke Photo	Duke during his space exploration period.

ITEM		DESCRIPTION
	#14: Duke Football Photo	After receiving every major football award in the league.
	#15: Poker Duke Photo	What else? It's Duke playing poker.
	#16: Duke Action Figure	Tiny plastic form.
	#16: Punching Bag	A little stress relief after talking with the President.
	#17: Snack Machine	Goodies wrapped in tinfoil.
	#18: Free Weights	A new definition for pipe bombs.
	#19: Cigar	These are hand-rolled beauties from Cu… America.
	#20: Babe: Funky Nefertiti	A lot of attitude and sass but damn hot.
	#20: Cycloid Emperor Plaque	Fact: The Emperor's eye was replaced with Duke's championship bowling ball.
	#20: Bronze Babe 2	Shiny… sexy… hot!
	#21: Steroids	Nutritional supplements to help gain strength… riiight.
	#21: Weight Bench	Gotta keep in shape for the ladies.
	#22: Classic Paintings	The finest art around, made better by the inclusion of Duke.
	#22: Action Figure Accessories	Collect them all! $19.95 each!
	#23: Helmeted Pigcop Plaque	Scientists are still trying to figure out why something with such a thick skull needs a helmet.
	#23: Military Duke Photo	After operation Desert Cold Front.

ITEM		DESCRIPTION
	#24: Modern Paintings	Four works of art on loan from prestigious museums around the world.
	#25: Action Figure Playsets	Just remember, the moment you take them out of their boxes, they become worthless.
	#25: Animatronic Duke	A huge animatronic Duke Nukem.
	#26: Neon Signs	Nothing sets the mood like crackling tubes of inert gasses.
	#27: Cycloid Eye	After kicking a field goal with the eye, Duke used it to play basketball, dodgeball, and volleyball.
	#28: Small Octabrain Plaque	It had eight legs, three eyes, and no chance.
	#28: Octabrain	The remains of an Ocatabrain from the last encounter.
	#29: Pigcop Action Figure	Now with ragin' bacon action!
	#29: Pigcop Plaque	The rest of his body was roasted up for the victory party.
	#29: Pigcop	Part pig... part cop... it's a Pigcop!
	#30: Babe: Sgt. Peppa	Personal security never looked this good.
	#30: Octababy Plaque	Duke doesn't normally kill alien babies, but he made an exception for hideous alien freaks.
	#30: Bronze Babe 3	The maid has asked that you quit leaving fingerprints on this one.
	#31: Throne	This seat is reserved.
	#32: Energy Leech Plaque	This leech sucks, big time.
	#33: Basketball Hoop	Basketball... the champion's choice of training grenade throws.
	#34: Speed Bag	Timing... pacing... neither will help you with this.

ITEM		DESCRIPTION
	#35: Devastator	Take a deadly weapon, bronze it, and you've got the most awesome paperweight ever made.
	#35: Video Poker	Play poker without having to wait for the asshat with sunglasses to make his move.
	#36: Pool Table	9-ball bar table.
	#37: Pinball Machine	Balls of steel, baby!
	#38: Slot Machine	A more entertaining way of getting rid of your money than flushing it down the toilet.
	#39: Large Octabrain Plaque	Just because he was bigger doesn't mean this 'brain was any tougher.
	#39: Arcade Hoops	Arcade basketball at its finest.
	#40: Babe: Trudy Uprights	A personal trainer with a great... personality.
	#40: Babe Action Figures	They're here to provide your Duke figure with some action.
	#40: Pigcop Rug	The perfect touch to set the mood in front of a roaring fire.
	#40: Bronze Babe 4	The last piece for your collection.
	#41: Babe: Chastity	An exchange student you never want to go back.
	#41: Bug Ball Plaque	Sure, it was harmless, but Duke needed to complete his collection.
	#41: Alien Abortion	A test of reflexes and timing... how high can you score?
	#42: Babe: Holsom Twins	2 Girls, 1 Duke.
	#42: Alien Queen Plaque	This is the only way anyone should ever mount this bitch.
	#42: Air Hockey	The famous knuckle-buster gameroom classic.

AWARDS & EGO BOOSTS

"I AM THE DUKE. I AM A-NUMBER-ONE."

TROPHIES & ACHIEVEMENTS

Trophies, Achievements, and Ego boosts are earned for all sorts of activities.

BOOM! Headshot!

Compete a chapter, then choose the Chapter Select Menu to revisit it. This makes it easy to go back and search for things you may have missed.

Like all modern games, *Duke Nukem Forever* is full of unlockable items to keep you content while blasting through the alien infestation. Achievements and Trophies are centered entirely around the single-player campaign—multiplayer modes are served by a different progression scheme.

Playing all the way through the campaign on "Let's Rock" difficulty (think "normal" difficulty), you can expect to earn at least 550 Gamerscore without breaking a sweat. This does not include the points that you can tally by completing the game again on "Damn, I'm Good" difficulty, nor the points earned by the completist-type challenges (such as killing every catfish) or more obscure kill requirements (such as killing 15 frozen aliens).

The rest of the points come from just these types of challenges: completing the game on harder difficulties, performing a specific task a certain number of times, finding a particular object, and so on. All Trophies and Achievements are listed in this section. Some are self-explanatory, but a few aren't. If you require clarification on one and it isn't listed here, then consult the appropriate walkthrough chapter for further details or a more specific location—chapter numbers are provided where appropriate!

TROPHY/ACHIEVEMENT SUMMARY

CATEGORY	# OF UNLOCKS	GAMERSCORE
Kills	17	350
Odds & Ends	6	45

CATEGORY	# OF UNLOCKS	GAMERSCORE
Equipment	4	25
Gaming	4	90

CATEGORY	# OF UNLOCKS	GAMERSCORE
Completion	8	185
Victory	11	305

KILLING IS MY BUSINESS...AND BUSINESS IS GOOD!
GAMERSCORE: 350

Many Trophies and Achievements are unlocked simply by passing certain murderous milestones. Most of these will occur as a matter of course while playing through the single-player campaign. If you miss one, just travel to an area where it's easy to stockpile the type of kill in question.

INDULGE IN EQUIPMENT!

There's an Achievement/Trophy for scoring numerous kills with just about anything, whether it's stuff Duke carries with him or something environmental. Plenty of Trip Mines, explosive barrels, regular barrels, and Steroids are spread throughout the game, so don't stockpile supplies thinking you'll need them right around the next corner. Also, even if you're not fond of using the Freeze Ray, make a point to use it until you get the Achievement during the times the weapon is available. In short, don't save stuff for a rainy day!

The forklift is only drivable during a brief section of "The Forkstop, Part 2." Use it to get some fork-skewer kills!

Steroids are fantastic to use against large groups of lesser foes.

Five gunships or dropships may sound like a lot, but you'll have enough encounters to reach this total during a single campaign playthrough.

ICON / NAME	DESCRIPTION	GAMERSCORE	TROPHY TYPE	CHAPTERS OF NOTE
Extermination	Kill 50 aliens.	25	Bronze	-
Annihilation	Kill 100 aliens.	40	Bronze	-
Nuclear Devastation	Kill 250 aliens.	50	Bronze	-
Hippy Stomper	Foot stomp 12 aliens.	20	Bronze	-
Judge Jury Executioner	Execute 20 aliens.	20	Bronze	-
Trapper	Kill 10 aliens with Trip Mines.	20	Bronze	5, 8
Freeze Well	Kill 15 frozen aliens.	20	Bronze	16, 19
Road Rage	Kill 15 aliens with the monster truck.	20	Bronze	12, 13, 14
Fork the Pork	Kill 6 aliens with the forklift.	10	Bronze	17
Dead Useful	Kill 10 aliens with environmental explosives.	15	Bronze	-
Tosser in the Literal Sense ("Downtown Barrel Beatdown" on Xbox 360)	Kill 10 aliens with tossed objects.	15	Bronze	-
Duke Angry Duke Smash	Kill 15 aliens with melee attacks while on Steroids.	20	Bronze	-
Natural Disaster 3x	Kill 3 aliens at once.	10	Bronze	-
Baron von Nukem	Shoot down 20 alien fighters.	20	Bronze	3, 10
Sticky Bomb Like You	Put a Trip Mine on a live alien.	10	Bronze	-
Big Guns Big Ships	Blow up 5 enemy gunships or dropships.	10	Bronze	3, 6, 10, 14
On the Noggin	Kill 30 aliens with headshots.	25	Bronze	-

ODDS & ENDS
GAMERSCORE: 45

None of these tasks are difficult by themselves, but it is easy to overlook one. The first four listed below are all easy to access right away in the first two chapters of the game. "I Need a Date" and "Companion Barrel" are both found much later during Chapter 17, "The Forkstop."

ICON / NAME	DESCRIPTION	GAMERSCORE	TROPHY TYPE	CHAPTER FOUND
Turd Burglar	Find and steal a piece of poo.	10	Bronze	Prologue, 11
Drawrings	Doodle something on the whiteboard in single player.	10	Bronze	Prologue, 9, 19, 20
Sunday Black Sunday	Shoot down the blimp above the stadium.	5	Bronze	Prologue
Nobody Likes a Whiner	Knock out the talent at the talk show.	5	Bronze	1
I Need a Date	Look at every page of a calendar in single player.	5	Bronze	16, 17
Companion Barrel	Unlock the secret closet at the end of The Forkstop.	10	Bronze	17

EQUIPMENT USE
GAMERSCORE: 25

Beer heavily reduces damage taken (while also impairing vision, but hey, what are you gonna do?), while Steroids grant tremendous strength to punches. Additionally, the Holoduke provides a foolproof decoy. Using equipment properly can easily mean the difference between victory and defeat, especially on the harder difficulty modes.

ICON / NAME	DESCRIPTION	GAMERSCORE	TROPHY TYPE
Flagon of Chuckles	Drink a Beer in single player.	5	Bronze
Juiced	Take Steroids in single player.	5	Bronze
He's Got a Hologram	Use a Holoduke in single player.	5	Bronze
Substance Abuser	Drink Beer while on Steroids or vice-versa in single player.	10	Bronze

DUKE THE PLAYER
GAMERSCORE: 90

All work and no play makes Duke a dull boy. These diversions all take place in Duke's own strip club. He also has a pinball machine in the Duke Cave. If you're having trouble finding all the Beer in the strip club, consult the map found in Chapter 9 of the campaign walkthrough. Remember that one of the Beers is located in the Champagne Room, which you can only enter after bringing all the quest items to the waiting stripper.

The air hockey goal is just a matter of plugging along. Alien Abortion, another strip club game, is like that too.

The key to shutting out the other dude at air hockey is to stay calm. He won't get fancy or hurried, so don't try too hard, lest you end up scoring against yourself!

ICON / NAME	DESCRIPTION	GAMERSCORE	TROPHY TYPE	CHAPTER FOUND
Air Duke	Win air hockey with a score of 7-0 in the strip club.	30	Silver	9
Balls of Steel	Earn a 1,000,000 pinball score in single player.	25	Silver	2, 9
Lots of Whacking	Win a game of Alien Abortion in the strip club.	25	Bronze	9
Party Animal	Drink all of the Beers in the strip club.	10	Bronze	9

BALLS OF STEEL

MULTIPLAYER LANES

MULTIPLIER INDICATOR

Pinball is a little more complicated. The key to getting high scores is to earn the x2, x4, and x6 score multipliers. This is accomplished by lighting up all three lanes at once at the top of the board (see screenshot). A lane is turned on or off when the pinball passes through it. Light all three lanes at once and you'll level up to the next multiplier. Use deft flipper movement and tilt control to coax the ball to the top of the board, so you can work on earning a x6 multiplier. Be advised that flipper activation rearranges the "lit" lanes (without changing how many lanes are lit), so beware accidentally flipping a "lit" lane on into the path of the pinball, as the pinball will then shut it off!

Use tilt conservatively to avoid tilting the machine, thereby automatically losing a ball in the process. Instead, use tilt to avoid losing the ball down the Babe Kick Back holes after the babe bumpers disappear (you'll have one or two grace saves by these bumpers for each ball before they disappear). Also, use tilt to get the ball where you want it at the bumpers and lanes on top of the board. The pinball can be tilted left, right, or up.

COMPLETION
GAMERSCORE: 185

These Achievements and Trophies all require that you persevere toward a specific goal. Some of them are easy and quick (you can clear "Noms" at the first vending machine in the game during chapter 1), while others are much more involved.

CHECKING PHONES, COUNTING HEADS, KILLING CATFISH

A few more unusual collectibles are spread throughout certain chapters. There are voicemails on phones; three helmets that should look strangely familiar; and a school of catfish begging to be fried up. For the specific locations all this content, consult the appropriate chapter in the walkthrough.

As you might imagine, the messages left in the last day or so range from amusing, to strange, and back again.

One of the bucket heads is impossible to miss, but the other two are fairly well hidden.

Killing catfish. Why not? Check the map in Chapter 21 of the walkthrough for locations and images of the hidden catfish.

GUNSLINGER

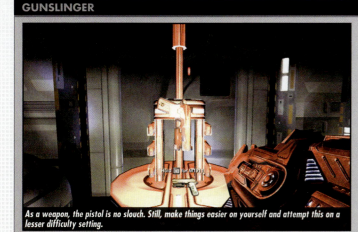

As a weapon, the pistol is no slouch. Still, make things easier on yourself and attempt this on a lesser difficulty setting.

One of the game's most involving Achievements/Trophies requires that you complete each chapter while carrying Duke's golden M1911. The first two chapters don't count, of course, since you don't have access to the weapon. Starting with "The Duke Cave," though, you must complete each chapter with the golden gun in hand.

It's okay to set down the golden pistol and use a different weapon, but don't forget to pick it back up before moving on. Be particularly careful about accidentally moving too far in certain chapters, triggering the loading screen for the next section. Although these chapter breaks aren't frequent, if you happen to cross the threshold without the gun, it is lost.

NAME		DESCRIPTION	GAMERSCORE	TROPHY TYPE	CHAPTER FOUND
	Noms	Eat 10 pieces of food during the single-player campaign.	10	Bronze	Numerous
	Full Body Tourettes ("FBT" on Xbox 360)	Get knocked down 10 times.	10	Bronze	Numerous
	I Need a Towel	Get hit by 10 Pregnator bombs.	10	Bronze	7, 8, 19, 20
	Call Waiting	Listen to all phone messages (12 total).	25	Silver	Prologue (x1), 6 (x1), 9 (x3), 11 (x1), 12 (x1), 16 (x1), 18 (x1), 20 (x3)
	Bucket Head	Find all 3 helmets in the single-player campaign.	30	Bronze	5, 7, 21
	Pescaphobe	Kill all the catfish in the underwater level.	10	Bronze	21
	I Am All That Is Man	Discover all Ego cap awards.	40	Silver	Numerous (see the end of this chapter)
	Gunslinger	Carry the gold pistol through the whole single-player campaign.	50	Silver	All except Prologue and 1

BOSSES & VICTORY
GAMERSCORE: 305

A large number of accomplishments are saved for downing most of the bosses and completing the game on each difficulty. Refer to the walkthrough and enemies chapters for strategies and tips on defeating the bosses. As for those associated with difficulty settings, they are cascading—that is, if you finish the game on "Come Get Some", you'll unlock the Achievements/Trophies for "Let's Rock" and "Piece of Cake". Note that the hardest difficulty, "Damn, I'm Good," is not available until you've completed the game at least once on any other setting.

Defeating every boss doesn't always result in a reward, but there are two feats associated with the Battlelord!

DAMN, I'M GOOD

Get used to this.

The most intensive reward comes from finishing the game on the "Damn, I'm Good" difficulty. Think of this difficulty as the "Insane" or "Veteran" setting common with other shooters. The long and short of it is that Duke deals half the normal damage to enemies, while enemies inflict twice as much damage to Duke.

Now, maybe that doesn't sound like a huge deal, but the weaponry in *Duke Nukem Forever* is carefully balanced so that weapons can be relied upon for certain things even on "Come Get Some," the second-highest difficulty, but not on "Damn, I'm Good." It's a slippery slope. Although Duke deals 75% of his normal damage in the "Come Get Some" difficulty, that still doesn't mean that a square shotgun blast or Railgun round won't finish off most targets. The amount of ammo required for a good marksman isn't necessarily different in many cases, compared to "Let's Rock." A shotgun blast to the head for a kill is still a shotgun blast to the head for a kill, penalty or no penalty.

But bump it up to "Damn, I'm Good" and suddenly a point-blank shotgun blast or dead-on Railgun shot won't even drop a Pigcop anymore. A premium, not present on lower difficulties, is suddenly put on ammo, meaning you'll find yourself looting the battlefield for any kind of ammo. Meanwhile, Duke is only ever two or three solid shots in a row from defeat. It's important to always manage weapons, ammo, equipment, and Ego in order to survive.

ICON / NAME		DESCRIPTION	GAMERSCORE	TROPHY TYPE
	One Eyed Freak	Defeat the Cycloid.	10	Bronze
	Pit Champion	Defeat the Battlelord in Las Vegas.	25	Bronze
	Not Bad for a Human	Defeat the Alien Queen.	40	Silver
	A Good Dam Fight	Defeat the Battlelord on the Hoover Dam.	25	Silver
	Octacide	Defeat the Octaking.	25	Silver
	Beating the One Eyed Worm	Defeat the Energy Leech.	35	Silver
	Piece of Cake	Complete the single-player campaign on Easy Difficulty.	20	Bronze
	Let's Rock	Complete the single-player campaign on Normal Difficulty.	30	Silver
	Come Get Some	Complete the single-player campaign on Hard Difficulty.	40	Gold
	Damn, I'm Good	Complete the single-player campaign on Insane Difficulty.	50	Gold
	Special Thanks	Watch the credits all the way through.	5	Bronze

EGO BOOSTS

In addition to Trophies and Achievements, there are also Ego boosts to find throughout the campaign. As long as you don't start a new campaign over completely, which resets all your progress, any Ego boosts you find will have a permanent effect on the size of Duke's Ego.

It starts at 40 but can eventually be increased to 100 by finding all 60 points of Ego boosts. Finding every unique Ego boost also unlocks a Trophy/Achievement. Building a significant Ego goes a long way toward surviving the tougher stretches of the game, especially on harder difficulty settings. For more specific locations for each Ego boost, refer to the relevant chapters of the campaign walkthrough.

Clearing the pool table can actually prove to be very difficult. Contrary to the rules of pool, you can hit the cue ball while it is in motion, so keep that in mind if you're about to scratch.

Duke's club is positively packed with Ego-boosting opportunities.

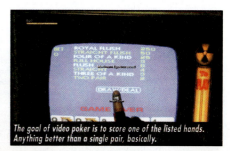

The goal of video poker is to score one of the listed hands. Anything better than a single pair, basically.

REQUIREMENT	TOTAL EGO BOOST	CHAPTER AVAILABLE
Admire self in mirror.	+1	Numerous
Urinate.	+1	Numerous
Clear pool table without scratching.	+2	Prologue, 9
Microwave popcorn, or a rat. (Rats cannot be microwaved in the European PlayStation 3 versions)	+2	1, 9, 13
Autograph "Why I'm So Great."	+2	1
Curl dumbbell.	+2	2, 8
Bench press at least 600 pounds.	+3	2, 8
Punch speedbag.	+1	2
Punch punching bag.	+1	2, 8
Shoot basketball through hoop (or leap through hoop as shrunken Duke).	+1	2, 9, 11
Beat pinball high score.	+3	2 (280,897), 9 (137,900)
Win slot machine.	+2	4, 9
Kill Las Vegas Battlelord.	+3	5
Make a scanned copy of Duke's butt.	+1	6, 9
Slap wall boobs.	+1	7, 8, 19
Kill Alien Queen.	+4	8

REQUIREMENT	TOTAL EGO BOOST	CHAPTER AVAILABLE
Win all five rounds of Alien Abortion.	+1	9
Request special dance from stripper.	+1	9
Win video poker.	+1	9
Use hole in bathroom.	+2	9
Watch "Pooty Party."	+2	9
Win air hockey.	+3	9
Throw developer frisbee.	+1	10, 12
Read Slutbutts magazine.	+1	11, 20
Smoke cigar.	+1	11, 20
Look at computer porn.	+1	12, 19
Use observation binoculars.	+1	12
Read Funbags magazine.	+1	13, 19
Throw paper airplane.	+1	15, 16, 19, 21
Kill Hoover Dam Battlelord.	+4	15
Look at wall calendar.	+1	16, 17
Read 69MM magazine.	+1	17, 21
Kill Octaking.	+3	18
Kill the Energy Leech	+4	21

OFFICIAL STRATEGY GUIDE

By Joe Epstein & Doug Walsh

DK/BradyGames, a division of Penguin Group (USA) Inc.
800 East 96th Street, 3rd Floor
Indianapolis, IN 46240

This game is published and distributed by 2K Games, a subsidiary of Take-Two Interactive Software, Inc. 2K Games, Take-Two Interactive Software and their respective logos are trademarks of Take-Two Interactive Software, Inc. All other marks are property of their respective owners.

The ratings icon is a registered trademark of the Entertainment Software Association. All other trademarks and trade names are properties of their respective owners.

Please be advised that the ESRB ratings icons, "EC", "E", "E10+", "T", "M", "AO", and "RP" are trademarks owned by the Entertainment Software Association, and may only be used with their permission and authority. For information regarding whether a product has been rated by the ESRB, please visit www.esrb.org.

For permission to use the ratings icons, please contact the ESA at esrblicenseinfo@theesa.com.

ISBN: 978-0-7440-1297-2

Printing Code: The rightmost double-digit number is the year of the book's printing; the rightmost single-digit number is the number of the book's printing. For example, 11-1 shows that the first printing of the book occurred in 2011.

14 13 12 11   4 3 2 1

Printed in the USA.

BRADYGAMES STAFF

Publisher
Mike Degler

Editor-In-Chief
H. Leigh Davis

Licensing Manager
Christian Sumner

Digital and Trade Publisher
Brian Saliba

Operations Manager
Stacey Beheler

CREDITS

Title Manager
Tim Cox

Lead Designer
Dan Caparo

Designers
Keith Lowe
Ashley Hardy

Art Book Designer
Brent Gann

Production Designers
Areva
Julie Clark

ACKNOWLEDGEMENTS

Special thanks to: Josh Morton, Michael Kelly, Kelly Miller, and Melissa Miller of 2K Games for their hospitality and assistance during our California stay; David Riegel of Triptych Games and Brian Burleson of Gearbox Software for their indispensable data, maps, and information; my co-author Doug and the usual suspects at BradyGAMES for helping put the book together; and finally Leigh Davis and Stacey Beheler for graciously flying my girlfriend Mia out for a bit, and Blake Cormier, Dan Tran, and Anthony Ramirez for showing us a good time in the Bay Area.—**Joe Epstein**

The multiplayer portion of this guide couldn't have been possible without the on-site support of Josh Morton and Melissa Miller of 2K Games and their ability to provide a steady stream of targets, err, players to compete and develop strategies against. Huge thanks to Andrew Dutra, Erica Denning, Chris Solis, Chris Maas, Jennie Sue, Garrett Bittner, Drew Smith, Evan Rice, Ben Chang, Jennifer Heinser, Scott James, and Charlie Sinhaseni for their assistance. Huge thanks to Brian Burleson and Mike Wardwell of Gearbox, David Riegel of Triptych Games, and Geoff Gordon of Piranha Games for all your support. You guys are truly a pleasure to work with! Lastly, I want to thank the BradyGames team for continuing to raise the bar and giving authors like Joe Epstein and myself everything we need to help create a guide that lives up to the game.—**Doug Walsh**

DEVELOPER ACKNOWLEDGEMENTS

The entire staff at BradyGames wishes to thank all the talented and dedicated folks at Gearbox Software, Piranha Games and Triptych Games. Without their support, this strategy guide would not have been possible. Thank you!

GEARBOX SOFTWARE

PRODUCTION MANAGERS
Brian Burleson
Adam Fletcher

FACT CHECKERS
James Lopez
Chris Brock
Tommy Eubanks

PIRANHA GAMES

Geoff Gordon
Paul Inouye
Thad Jantzi
Kevin Meek
Ryan Van Vliet

TRIPTYCH GAMES

CHARACTER & WEAPON SCREENSHOTS
Chris DeSimone
Andrew Kerschner

DATA GATHERING & FACT CHECKING
David Riegel